TITLE 3—THE PRESIDENT

This title was enacted by act June 25, 1948, ch. 644, §1, 62 Stat. 672

AMENDMENTS

1996—Pub. L. 104–331, §2(c), Oct. 26, 1996, 110 Stat. 4068, added item for chapter 5.

1951—Act Oct. 31, 1951, ch. 655, §4, 65 Stat. 711, added item for chapter 4.

POSITIVE LAW; CITATION

This title has been made positive law by section 1 of act June 25, 1948, ch. 644, 62 Stat. 672, which provided in part that: "Title 3 of the United States Code, entitled 'The President', is codified and enacted into positive law and may be cited as '3 U. S. C., §—.'"

SAVINGS CLAUSE

Section 2 of act June 25, 1948, provided that: "The provisions of title 3, 'The President', set out in section 1 of this Act, shall be construed as a continuation of existing law and no loss of rights, interruption of jurisdiction, nor prejudice to matters pending on the effective date of this Act shall result from its enactment."

REPEALS

Section 3 of act June 25, 1948, provided that the sections or parts thereof of the Statutes at Large or the Revised Statutes covering provisions codified in this Act are repealed insofar as the provisions appeared in former Title 3, and provided that any rights or liabilities now existing under the repealed sections or parts thereof shall not be affected by the repeal.

PRIOR REPEALS

Former sections 21 and 22 relating to performance of presidential duties in absence of both the President and Vice President were repealed by act July 18, 1947, ch. 264, §1(g), 61 Stat. 381.

TABLE SHOWING DISPOSITION OF ALL SECTIONS OF FORMER TITLE 3

Title 3 Former Sections	Revised Statutes Statutes at Large	Title 3 New Sections
1	R.S. §131	1
2	R.S. §132	3
3	R.S. §133	4
4	R.S. §134	2
5	Feb. 3, 1887, ch. 90, §1, 24 Stat. 373	7
5a	May 29, 1928, ch. 859, §1, 45 Stat. 945	7
	June 5, 1934, ch. 390, §6(a), 48 Stat. 879.	

TABLE SHOWING DISPOSITION OF ALL SECTIONS OF FORMER TITLE 3—Continued

Title 3 Former Sections	Revised Statutes Statutes at Large	Title 3 New Sections
6	Feb. 3, 1887, ch. 90, §2, 24 Stat. 373	5
7	Feb. 3, 1887, ch. 90, §3, 24 Stat. 373	6
7a	May 29, 1928, ch. 859, §2, 45 Stat. 946	6
8	R.S. §137	8
9	R.S. §138	9
9a	May 29, 1928, ch. 859, §3, 45 Stat. 946	9
10	R.S. §139	10
11	R.S. §140	11
	Oct. 19, 1888, ch. 1216, §1, 25 Stat. 613.	
11a	May 29, 1928, ch. 859, §4, 45 Stat. 946	11
11b	May 29, 1928, ch. 859, §5, 45 Stat. 946	12
	June 5, 1934, ch. 390, §6(b), 48 Stat. 879..	
11c	May 29, 1928, ch. 859, §6, 45 Stat. 946	13
	June 5, 1934, ch. 390, §6(c), 48 Stat. 879.	
12	Oct. 19, 1888, ch. 1216, §1, 25 Stat. 613	11, 12
13	R.S. §141	13
	Oct. 19, 1888, ch. 1216, §2, 25 Stat. 613.	
14	R.S. §143	11
15	R.S. §144	11
16	R.S. §145	14
17	Feb. 3, 1887, ch. 90, §4, 24 Stat. 373	15
	June 5, 1934, ch. 390, §7, 48 Stat. 879.	
18	Feb. 3, 1887, ch. 90, §5, 24 Stat. 374	18
19	Feb. 3, 1887, ch. 90, §6, 24 Stat. 375	17
20	Feb. 3, 1887, ch. 90, §7, 24 Stat. 375	16
21	Jan. 19, 1886, ch. 4, §1, 24 Stat. 1	19
22	Jan. 19, 1886, ch. 4, §2, 24 Stat. 1	19
23	R.S. §151	20
24	July 18, 1947, ch. 264, §1(a-f), 61 Stat. 380, 381.	19
	July 26, 1947, ch. 343, §311, 61 Stat. 509..	
41	R.S. §152	101
	June 5, 1934, ch. 390, §1, 48 Stat. 879.	
42	R.S. §153	102
	Mar. 4, 1909, ch. 297, §1, 35 Stat. 859.	
43	June 23, 1906, ch. 3523, 34 Stat. 454	103
	Aug. 2, 1946, ch. 744, §17(c), 60 Stat. 811.	
44	R.S. §154	104
	Feb. 26, 1907, ch. 1635, §4, 34 Stat. 993.	
	Mar. 4, 1925, ch. 549, §4, 43 Stat. 1301.	
	Aug. 2, 1946, ch. 753, §601(a), 60 Stat. 850.	
45	Apr. 22, 1926, ch. 171, §1, 44 Stat. 305	105
45a	Apr. 3, 1939, ch. 36, §301, 53 Stat. 565	106
46	June 12, 1922, ch. 218, 42 Stat. 636	107
	Feb. 13, 1923, ch. 72, 42 Stat. 1227.	
	June 7, 1924, ch. 292, §1, 43 Stat. 521.	
	Mar. 3, 1925, ch. 468, §1, 43 Stat. 1198, 1199.	
	Apr. 22, 1926, ch. 171, §1, 44 Stat. 305.	
	Feb. 11, 1927, ch. 104, §1, 44 Stat. 1069.	
	May 16, 1928, ch. 580, §1, 45 Stat. 573.	
	Feb. 20, 1929, ch. 270, §1, 45 Stat. 1230.	
	Apr. 19, 1930, ch. 201, §1, 46 Stat. 229.	
	Feb. 23, 1931, ch. 281, §1, 46 Stat. 1355.	
	June 30, 1932, ch. 330, §1, 47 Stat. 452.	
	June 16, 1933, ch. 101, §1, 48 Stat. 284.	
	Mar. 28, 1934, ch. 102, §1, 48 Stat. 509.	
	Feb. 2, 1935, ch. 3, §1, 49 Stat. 6.	
	Mar. 19, 1936, ch. 156, §1, 49 Stat. 1148.	
	June 28, 1937, ch. 396, §1, 50 Stat. 350.	
	May 23, 1938, ch. 259, §1, 52 Stat. 411.	
	Mar. 16, 1939, ch. 11, §1, 53 Stat 524.	
	Apr. 8, 1940, ch. 107, §1, 54 Stat. 112.	
	Apr. 5, 1941, ch. 40, §1, 55 Stat. 93.	
	June 27, 1942, ch. 450, §1, 56 Stat. 392.	
	June 26, 1943, ch. 145, §101, 57 Stat. 169.	
	June 27, 1944, ch. 286, §101, 58 Stat. 361.	
	May 3, 1945, ch. 106, §101, 59 Stat. 106.	
	Mar. 28, 1946, ch. 113, §101, 60 Stat. 61.	
47	Mar. 4, 1911, ch. 285, §1, 36 Stat. 1404	108
48	June 25, 1910, ch. 384, §9, 36 Stat. 773	109
49	R.S. §1829	110
	Feb. 26, 1925, ch. 377, §§1, 2, 43 Stat. 1091.	
50	R.S. §1832	109
51	R.S. §1833	109
52	R.S. §1834	109
53	June 23, 1913, ch. 3, §1, 38 Stat. 23	201
54	June 9, 1941, ch. 189, 55 Stat. 247	Elim.
61	Sept. 14, 1922, ch. 308, §1, 42 Stat. 841	202

---

[1] Chapter repealed by Pub. L. 109–177 without a corresponding amendment of chapter analysis.

TABLE SHOWING DISPOSITION OF ALL SECTIONS OF
FORMER TITLE 3—Continued

Title 3 Former Sections	Revised Statutes Statutes at Large	Title 3 New Sections
62	May 14, 1930, ch. 277, §1, 46 Stat. 328. Sept. 14, 1922, ch. 308, §2, 42 Stat. 841 .... May 14, 1930, ch. 277, §2, 46 Stat. 328. May 28, 1935, ch. 154, 49 Stat. 304. Apr. 22, 1940, ch. 133, 54 Stat. 156. June 9, 1947, ch. 102, 61 Stat. 132.	203
62a	Oct. 9, 1942, ch. 582, §1, 56 Stat. 778	205
62b	Oct. 9, 1942, ch. 582, §2, 56 Stat. 778	206
63	Sept. 14, 1922, ch. 308, §3, 42 Stat. 842 .... May 14, 1930, ch. 277, §3, 46 Stat. 328.	204
64	Sept. 14, 1922, ch. 308, §4, 42 Stat. 842	207
65	Sept. 14, 1922, ch. 308, §5, 42 Stat. 842	Rep.
66	Sept. 14, 1922, ch. 308, §6, 42 Stat. 842	Rep.
67	Sept. 14, 1922, ch. 308, §7, 42 Stat. 843 .... May 14, 1930, ch. 277, §4, 46 Stat. 329.	208

CHAPTER 1—PRESIDENTIAL ELECTIONS AND VACANCIES

Sec.
1. Time of appointing electors.
2. Failure to make choice on prescribed day.
3. Number of electors.
4. Vacancies in electoral college.
5. Determination of controversy as to appointment of electors.
6. Credentials of electors; transmission to Archivist of the United States and to Congress; public inspection.
7. Meeting and vote of electors.
8. Manner of voting.
9. Certificates of votes for President and Vice President.
10. Sealing and endorsing certificates.
11. Disposition of certificates.
12. Failure of certificates of electors to reach President of Senate or Archivist of the United States; demand on State for certificate.[1]
13. Same; demand on district judge for certificate.
14. Forfeiture for messenger's neglect of duty.
15. Counting electoral votes in Congress.
16. Same; seats for officers and Members of two Houses in joint meeting.
17. Same; limit of debate in each House.
18. Same; parliamentary procedure at joint meeting.
19. Vacancy in offices of both President and Vice President; officers eligible to act.
20. Resignation or refusal of office.
21. Definitions.

AMENDMENTS

1984—Pub. L. 98–497, title I, §107(e)(3), Oct. 19, 1984, 98 Stat. 2292, substituted "Archivist of the United States" for "Administrator of General Services" in items 6 and 12.

1961—Pub. L. 87–389, §2(b), Oct. 4, 1961, 75 Stat. 820, added item 21.

1951—Act Oct. 31, 1951, ch. 655, §5, 65 Stat. 711, substituted "Administrator of General Services" for "Secretary of State" in items 6 and 12.

§ 1. Time of appointing electors

The electors of President and Vice President shall be appointed, in each State, on the Tuesday next after the first Monday in November, in every fourth year succeeding every election of a President and Vice President.

(June 25, 1948, ch. 644, 62 Stat. 672.)

SHORT TITLE OF 2010 AMENDMENT

Pub. L. 111–283, §1, Oct. 15, 2010, 124 Stat. 3045, provided that: "This Act [enacting provisions set out as a

---

[1] So in original. Does not conform to section catchline.

note under section 102 of this title and amending provisions set out as notes under section 102 of this title, section 1101 of Title 5, Government Organization and Employees, and section 435b of Title 50, War and National Defense] may be cited as the 'Pre-Election Presidential Transition Act of 2010'."

SHORT TITLE OF 1996 AMENDMENT

Pub. L. 104–331, §1(a), Oct. 26, 1996, 110 Stat. 4053, provided that: "This Act [enacting sections 401, 402, 411 to 417, 421, 425, 431, 435, 451 to 456, and 471 of this title and sections 1296, 1413, and 3901 to 3908 of Title 28, Judiciary and Judicial Procedure, amending sections 1346 and 2402 of Title 28, repealing section 1219 of Title 2, The Congress, and enacting provisions set out as notes under section 401 of this title, section 1219 of Title 2, and section 1296 of Title 28] may be cited as the 'Presidential and Executive Office Accountability Act'."

SHORT TITLE OF 1988 AMENDMENT

Pub. L. 100–398, §1, Aug. 17, 1988, 102 Stat. 985, provided that: "This Act [amending sections 3345, 3348, and 5723 of Title 5, Government Organization and Employees, and enacting and amending provisions set out as notes under section 102 of this title] may be cited as the 'Presidential Transitions Effectiveness Act'."

CONSTITUTIONAL PROVISIONS

Time of choosing electors, see Const. Art. 2, §1, cl. 3.

§ 2. Failure to make choice on prescribed day

Whenever any State has held an election for the purpose of choosing electors, and has failed to make a choice on the day prescribed by law, the electors may be appointed on a subsequent day in such a manner as the legislature of such State may direct.

(June 25, 1948, ch. 644, 62 Stat. 672.)

§ 3. Number of electors

The number of electors shall be equal to the number of Senators and Representatives to which the several States are by law entitled at the time when the President and Vice President to be chosen come into office; except, that where no apportionment of Representatives has been made after any enumeration, at the time of choosing electors, the number of electors shall be according to the then existing apportionment of Senators and Representatives.

(June 25, 1948, ch. 644, 62 Stat. 672.)

§ 4. Vacancies in electoral college

Each State may, by law, provide for the filling of any vacancies which may occur in its college of electors when such college meets to give its electoral vote.

(June 25, 1948, ch. 644, 62 Stat. 673.)

§ 5. Determination of controversy as to appointment of electors

If any State shall have provided, by laws enacted prior to the day fixed for the appointment of the electors, for its final determination of any controversy or contest concerning the appointment of all or any of the electors of such State, by judicial or other methods or procedures, and such determination shall have been made at least six days before the time fixed for the meeting of the electors, such determination made pursuant to such law so existing on said day, and made at least six days prior to said time of meeting of the electors, shall be conclusive, and shall govern in the counting of the electoral votes as provided in the Constitution, and as hereinafter regulated, so far as the ascertainment of the electors appointed by such State is concerned.

(June 25, 1948, ch. 644, 62 Stat. 673.)

§ 6. Credentials of electors; transmission to Archivist of the United States and to Congress; public inspection

It shall be the duty of the executive of each State, as soon as practicable after the conclusion of the appointment of the electors in such State by the final ascertainment, under and in pursuance of the laws of such State providing for such ascertainment, to communicate by registered mail under the seal of the State to the Archivist of the United States a certificate of such ascertainment of the electors appointed, setting forth the names of such electors and the canvass or other ascertainment under the laws of such State of the number of votes given or cast for each person for whose appointment any and all votes have been given or cast; and it shall also thereupon be the duty of the executive of each State to deliver to the electors of such State, on or before the day on which they are required by section 7 of this title to meet, six duplicate-originals of the same certificate under the seal of the State; and if there shall have been any final determination in a State in the manner provided for by law of a controversy or contest concerning the appointment of all or any of the electors of such State, it shall be the duty of the executive of such State, as soon as practicable after such determination, to communicate under the seal of the State to the Archivist of the United States a certificate of such determination in form and manner as the same shall have been made; and the certificate or certificates so received by the Archivist of the United States shall be preserved by him for one year and shall be a part of the public records of his office and shall be open to public inspection; and the Archivist of the United States at the first meeting of Congress thereafter shall transmit to the two Houses of Congress copies in full of each and every such certificate so received at the National Archives and Records Administration.

(June 25, 1948, ch. 644, 62 Stat. 673; Oct. 31, 1951, ch. 655, § 6, 65 Stat. 711; Pub. L. 98–497, title I, § 107(e)(1), (2)(A), Oct. 19, 1984, 98 Stat. 2291.)

Amendments

1984—Pub. L. 98–497 substituted "Archivist of the United States" for "Administrator of General Services" in section catchline and wherever appearing in text and "National Archives and Records Administration" for "General Services Administration".

1951—Act Oct. 31, 1951, substituted "Administrator of General Services" for "Secretary of State" in section catchline and several places in text, and for "Secretary of State of the United States" in one place, and "General Services Administration" for "State Department".

Effective Date of 1984 Amendment

Amendment by Pub. L. 98–497 effective Apr. 1, 1985, see section 301 of Pub. L. 98–497, set out as a note under section 2102 of Title 44, Public Printing and Documents.

Termination of Reporting Requirements

For termination, effective May 15, 2000, of provisions of law requiring submittal to Congress of any annual, semiannual, or other regular periodic report listed in House Document No. 103–7 (in which the requirement under this section that the Archivist transmit to Congress copies of certificates of ascertainment is listed as a report on page 179), see section 3003 of Pub. L. 104–66, as amended, set out as a note under section 1113 of Title 31, Money and Finance.

§ 7. Meeting and vote of electors

The electors of President and Vice President of each State shall meet and give their votes on the first Monday after the second Wednesday in December next following their appointment at such place in each State as the legislature of such State shall direct.

(June 25, 1948, ch. 644, 62 Stat. 673.)

Constitutional Provisions

Day of voting by electors, see Const. Art. II, § 1, cl. 3. Voting by electors, see Const. Amend. XII.

§ 8. Manner of voting

The electors shall vote for President and Vice President, respectively, in the manner directed by the Constitution.

(June 25, 1948, ch. 644, 62 Stat. 674.)

§ 9. Certificates of votes for President and Vice President

The electors shall make and sign six certificates of all the votes given by them, each of which certificates shall contain two distinct lists, one of the votes for President and the other of the votes for Vice President, and shall annex to each of the certificates one of the lists of the electors which shall have been furnished to them by direction of the executive of the State.

(June 25, 1948, ch. 644, 62 Stat. 674.)

§ 10. Sealing and endorsing certificates

The electors shall seal up the certificates so made by them, and certify upon each that the lists of all the votes of such State given for President, and of all the votes given for Vice President, are contained therein.

(June 25, 1948, ch. 644, 62 Stat. 674.)

§ 11. Disposition of certificates

The electors shall dispose of the certificates so made by them and the lists attached thereto in the following manner:

First. They shall forthwith forward by registered mail one of the same to the President of the Senate at the seat of government.

Second. Two of the same shall be delivered to the secretary of state of the State, one of which shall be held subject to the order of the President of the Senate, the other to be preserved by him for one year and shall be a part of the public records of his office and shall be open to public inspection.

Third. On the day thereafter they shall forward by registered mail two of such certificates and lists to the Archivist of the United States at the seat of government, one of which shall be held subject to the order of the President of the Senate. The other shall be preserved by the Archivist of the United States for one year and shall be a part of the public records of his office and shall be open to public inspection.

Fourth. They shall forthwith cause the other of the certificates and lists to be delivered to the judge of the district in which the electors shall have assembled.

(June 25, 1948, ch. 644, 62 Stat. 674; Oct. 31, 1951, ch. 655, § 7, 65 Stat. 712; Pub. L. 98–497, title I, § 107(e)(1), Oct. 19, 1984, 98 Stat. 2291.)

AMENDMENTS

1984—Pub. L. 98–497 substituted "Archivist of the United States" for "Administrator of General Services" two places in par. "Third".

1951—Act Oct. 31, 1951, substituted "Administrator of General Services" for "Secretary of State" two places in par. "Third".

EFFECTIVE DATE OF 1984 AMENDMENT

Amendment by Pub. L. 98–497 effective Apr. 1, 1985, see section 301 of Pub. L. 98–497, set out as a note under section 2102 of Title 44, Public Printing and Documents.

§ 12. Failure of certificates of electors to reach President of the Senate or Archivist of the United States; demand on State for certificate

When no certificate of vote and list mentioned in sections 9 and 11 of this title from any State shall have been received by the President of the Senate or by the Archivist of the United States by the fourth Wednesday in December, after the meeting of the electors shall have been held, the President of the Senate or, if he be absent from the seat of government, the Archivist of the United States shall request, by the most expeditious method available, the secretary of state of the State to send up the certificate and list lodged with him by the electors of such State; and it shall be his duty upon receipt of such request immediately to transmit same by registered mail to the President of the Senate at the seat of government.

(June 25, 1948, ch. 644, 62 Stat. 674; Oct. 31, 1951, ch. 655, § 8, 65 Stat. 712; Pub. L. 98–497, title I, § 107(e)(1), (2)(B), Oct. 19, 1984, 98 Stat. 2291.)

AMENDMENTS

1984—Pub. L. 98–497 substituted "Archivist of the United States" for "Administrator of General Services" in section catchline and two places in text.

1951—Act Oct. 31, 1951, substituted "Administrator of General Services" for "Secretary of State" in section catchline and two places in text.

EFFECTIVE DATE OF 1984 AMENDMENT

Amendment by Pub. L. 98–497 effective Apr. 1, 1985, see section 301 of Pub. L. 98–497, set out as a note under section 2102 of Title 44, Public Printing and Documents.

§ 13. Same; demand on district judge for certificate

When no certificates of votes from any State shall have been received at the seat of government on the fourth Wednesday in December, after the meeting of the electors shall have been held, the President of the Senate or, if he be ab-

sent from the seat of government, the Archivist of the United States shall send a special messenger to the district judge in whose custody one certificate of votes from that State has been lodged, and such judge shall forthwith transmit that list by the hand of such messenger to the seat of government.

(June 25, 1948, ch. 644, 62 Stat. 674; Oct. 31, 1951, ch. 655, § 9, 65 Stat. 712; Pub. L. 98–497, title I, § 107(e)(1), Oct. 19, 1984, 98 Stat. 2291.)

AMENDMENTS

1984—Pub. L. 98–497 substituted "Archivist of the United States" for "Administrator of General Services".

1951—Act Oct. 31, 1951, substituted "Administrator of General Services" for "Secretary of State".

EFFECTIVE DATE OF 1984 AMENDMENT

Amendment by Pub. L. 98–497 effective Apr. 1, 1985, see section 301 of Pub. L. 98–497, set out as a note under section 2102 of Title 44, Public Printing and Documents.

§ 14. Forfeiture for messenger's neglect of duty

Every person who, having been appointed, pursuant to section 13 of this title, to deliver the certificates of the votes of the electors to the President of the Senate, and having accepted such appointment, shall neglect to perform the services required from him, shall forfeit the sum of $1,000.

(June 25, 1948, ch. 644, 62 Stat. 675.)

§ 15. Counting electoral votes in Congress

Congress shall be in session on the sixth day of January succeeding every meeting of the electors. The Senate and House of Representatives shall meet in the Hall of the House of Representatives at the hour of 1 o'clock in the afternoon on that day, and the President of the Senate shall be their presiding officer. Two tellers shall be previously appointed on the part of the Senate and two on the part of the House of Representatives, to whom shall be handed, as they are opened by the President of the Senate, all the certificates and papers purporting to be certificates of the electoral votes, which certificates and papers shall be opened, presented, and acted upon in the alphabetical order of the States, beginning with the letter A; and said tellers, having then read the same in the presence and hearing of the two Houses, shall make a list of the votes as they shall appear from the said certificates; and the votes having been ascertained and counted according to the rules in this subchapter provided, the result of the same shall be delivered to the President of the Senate, who shall thereupon announce the state of the vote, which announcement shall be deemed a sufficient declaration of the persons, if any, elected President and Vice President of the United States, and, together with a list of the votes, be entered on the Journals of the two Houses. Upon such reading of any such certificate or paper, the President of the Senate shall call for objections, if any. Every objection shall be made in writing, and shall state clearly and concisely, and without argument, the ground thereof, and shall be signed by at least one Senator and one Member of the House of Representatives before the same shall be received. When all objections so made to any vote or paper from a State shall have been received and read, the Senate shall thereupon withdraw, and such objections shall be submitted to the Senate for its decision; and the Speaker of the House of Representatives shall, in like manner, submit such objections to the House of Representatives for its decision; and no electoral vote or votes from any State which shall have been regularly given by electors whose appointment has been lawfully certified to according to section 6 of this title from which but one return has been received shall be rejected, but the two Houses concurrently may reject the vote or votes when they agree that such vote or votes have not been so regularly given by electors whose appointment has been so certified. If more than one return or paper purporting to be a return from a State shall have been received by the President of the Senate, those votes, and those only, shall be counted which shall have been regularly given by the electors who are shown by the determination mentioned in section 5 of this title to have been appointed, if the determination in said section provided for shall have been made, or by such successors or substitutes, in case of a vacancy in the board of electors so ascertained, as have been appointed to fill such vacancy in the mode provided by the laws of the State; but in case there shall arise the question which of two or more of such State authorities determining what electors have been appointed, as mentioned in section 5 of this title, is the lawful tribunal of such State, the votes regularly given of those electors, and those only, of such State shall be counted whose title as electors the two Houses, acting separately, shall concurrently decide is supported by the decision of such State so authorized by its law; and in such case of more than one return or paper purporting to be a return from a State, if there shall have been no such determination of the question in the State aforesaid, then those votes, and those only, shall be counted which the two Houses shall concurrently decide were cast by lawful electors appointed in accordance with the laws of the State, unless the two Houses, acting separately, shall concurrently decide such votes not to be the lawful votes of the legally appointed electors of such State. But if the two Houses shall disagree in respect of the counting of such votes, then, and in that case, the votes of the electors whose appointment shall have been certified by the executive of the State, under the seal thereof, shall be counted. When the two Houses have voted, they shall immediately again meet, and the presiding officer shall then announce the decision of the questions submitted. No votes or papers from any other State shall be acted upon until the objections previously made to the votes or papers from any State shall have been finally disposed of.

(June 25, 1948, ch. 644, 62 Stat. 675.)

COUNTING OF ELECTORAL VOTES

2009—Pub. L. 110–430, § 2, Oct. 15, 2008, 122 Stat. 4846, provided that: "The meeting of the Senate and House of Representatives to be held in January 2009 pursuant to section 15 of title 3, United States Code, to count the electoral votes for President and Vice President cast by the electors in December 2008 shall be held on January 8, 2009 (rather than on the date specified in the first sentence of that section)."

1997—Pub. L. 104–296, § 2, Oct. 11, 1996, 110 Stat. 3558, provided that: "The meeting of the Senate and House of Representatives to be held in January 1997 pursuant to section 15 of title 3, United States Code, to count the electoral votes for President and Vice President cast by the electors in December 1996 shall be held on January 9, 1997 (rather than on the date specified in the first sentence of that section)."

1989—Pub. L. 100–646, Nov. 9, 1988, 102 Stat. 3341, provided: "That in carrying out the procedure set forth in section 15 of title, 3, United States Code, for 1989, 'the fourth day of January' shall be substituted for 'the sixth day of January' in the first sentence of such section."

1985—Pub. L. 98–456, Oct. 9, 1984, 98 Stat. 1748, provided: "That, in carrying out the procedure set forth in section 15 of title 3, United States Code, for 1985, 'the seventh day of January' shall be substituted for 'the sixth day of January' in the first sentence of such section."

§ 16. Same; seats for officers and Members of two Houses in joint meeting

At such joint meeting of the two Houses seats shall be provided as follows: For the President of the Senate, the Speaker's chair; for the Speaker, immediately upon his left; the Senators, in the body of the Hall upon the right of the presiding officer; for the Representatives, in the body of the Hall not provided for the Senators; for the tellers, Secretary of the Senate, and Clerk of the House of Representatives, at the Clerk's desk; for the other officers of the two Houses, in front of the Clerk's desk and upon each side of the Speaker's platform. Such joint meeting shall not be dissolved until the count of electoral votes shall be completed and the result declared; and no recess shall be taken unless a question shall have arisen in regard to counting any such votes, or otherwise under this subchapter, in which case it shall be competent for either House, acting separately, in the manner hereinbefore provided, to direct a recess of such House not beyond the next calendar day, Sunday excepted, at the hour of 10 o'clock in the forenoon. But if the counting of the electoral votes and the declaration of the result shall not have been completed before the fifth calendar day next after such first meeting of the two Houses, no further or other recess shall be taken by either House.

(June 25, 1948, ch. 644, 62 Stat. 676.)

§ 17. Same; limit of debate in each House

When the two Houses separate to decide upon an objection that may have been made to the counting of any electoral vote or votes from any State, or other question arising in the matter, each Senator and Representative may speak to such objection or question five minutes, and not more than once; but after such debate shall have lasted two hours it shall be the duty of the presiding officer of each House to put the main question without further debate.

(June 25, 1948, ch. 644, 62 Stat. 676.)

§ 18. Same; parliamentary procedure at joint meeting

While the two Houses shall be in meeting as provided in this chapter, the President of the Senate shall have power to preserve order; and no debate shall be allowed and no question shall be put by the presiding officer except to either House on a motion to withdraw.

(June 25, 1948, ch. 644, 62 Stat. 676; Sept. 3, 1954, ch. 1263, § 3, 68 Stat. 1227.)

Amendments

1954—Act Sept. 3, 1954, substituted "chapter" for "subchapter".

§ 19. Vacancy in offices of both President and Vice President; officers eligible to act

(a)(1) If, by reason of death, resignation, removal from office, inability, or failure to qualify, there is neither a President nor Vice President to discharge the powers and duties of the office of President, then the Speaker of the House of Representatives shall, upon his resignation as Speaker and as Representative in Congress, act as President.

(2) The same rule shall apply in the case of the death, resignation, removal from office, or inability of an individual acting as President under this subsection.

(b) If, at the time when under subsection (a) of this section a Speaker is to begin the discharge of the powers and duties of the office of President, there is no Speaker, or the Speaker fails to qualify as Acting President, then the President pro tempore of the Senate shall, upon his resignation as President pro tempore and as Senator, act as President.

(c) An individual acting as President under subsection (a) or subsection (b) of this section shall continue to act until the expiration of the then current Presidential term, except that—

(1) if his discharge of the powers and duties of the office is founded in whole or in part on the failure of both the President-elect and the Vice-President-elect to qualify, then he shall act only until a President or Vice President qualifies; and

(2) if his discharge of the powers and duties of the office is founded in whole or in part on the inability of the President or Vice President, then he shall act only until the removal of the disability of one of such individuals.

(d)(1) If, by reason of death, resignation, removal from office, inability, or failure to qualify, there is no President pro tempore to act as President under subsection (b) of this section, then the officer of the United States who is highest on the following list, and who is not under disability to discharge the powers and duties of the office of President shall act as President: Secretary of State, Secretary of the Treasury, Secretary of Defense, Attorney General, Secretary of the Interior, Secretary of Agriculture, Secretary of Commerce, Secretary of Labor, Secretary of Health and Human Services, Secretary of Housing and Urban Development, Secretary of Transportation, Secretary of Energy, Secretary of Education, Secretary of Veterans Affairs, Secretary of Homeland Security.

(2) An individual acting as President under this subsection shall continue so to do until the expiration of the then current Presidential term, but not after a qualified and prior-entitled individual is able to act, except that the removal of the disability of an individual higher on the list contained in paragraph (1) of this subsection or the ability to qualify on the part of an individual higher on such list shall not terminate his service.

(3) The taking of the oath of office by an individual specified in the list in paragraph (1) of this subsection shall be held to constitute his resignation from the office by virtue of the holding of which he qualifies to act as President.

(e) Subsections (a), (b), and (d) of this section shall apply only to such officers as are eligible to the office of President under the Constitution. Subsection (d) of this section shall apply only to officers appointed, by and with the advice and consent of the Senate, prior to the time of the death, resignation, removal from office, inability, or failure to qualify, of the President pro tempore, and only to officers not under impeachment by the House of Representatives at the time the powers and duties of the office of President devolve upon them.

(f) During the period that any individual acts as President under this section, his compensation shall be at the rate then provided by law in the case of the President.

(June 25, 1948, ch. 644, 62 Stat. 677; Pub. L. 89–174, § 6(a), Sept. 9, 1965, 79 Stat. 669; Pub. L. 89–670, § 10(a), Oct. 15, 1966, 80 Stat. 948; Pub. L. 91–375, § 6(b), Aug. 12, 1970, 84 Stat. 775; Pub. L. 95–91, title VII, § 709(g), Aug. 4, 1977, 91 Stat. 609; Pub. L. 96–88, title V, § 508(a), Oct. 17, 1979, 93 Stat. 692; Pub. L. 100–527, § 13(a), Oct. 25, 1988, 102 Stat. 2643; Pub. L. 109–177, title V, § 503, Mar. 9, 2006, 120 Stat. 247.)

Amendments

2006—Subsec. (d)(1). Pub. L. 109–177 inserted ", Secretary of Homeland Security" after "Secretary of Veterans Affairs".

1988—Subsec. (d)(1). Pub. L. 100–527 inserted reference to Secretary of Veterans Affairs.

1979—Subsec. (d)(1). Pub. L. 96–88 substituted "Secretary of Health and Human Services" for "Secretary of Health, Education, and Welfare" and inserted reference to Secretary of Education.

1977—Subsec. (d)(1). Pub. L. 95–91 inserted reference to Secretary of Energy.

1970—Subsec. (d)(1). Pub. L. 91–375 struck out "Postmaster General," after "Attorney General,".

1966—Subsec. (d)(1). Pub. L. 89–670 inserted reference to Secretary of Transportation.

1965—Subsec. (d)(1). Pub. L. 89–174 inserted reference to Secretary of Health, Education, and Welfare and Secretary of Housing and Urban Development.

Effective Date of 1988 Amendment

Amendment by Pub. L. 100–527 effective Mar. 15, 1989, see section 18(a) of Pub. L. 100–527, set out as a Department of Veterans Affairs Act note under section 301 of Title 38, Veterans' Benefits.

Effective Date of 1979 Amendment

Amendment by Pub. L. 96–88 effective May 4, 1980, with specified exceptions, see section 601 of Pub. L. 96–88, set out as an Effective Date note under section 3401 of Title 20, Education.

Effective Date of 1970 Amendment

Amendment by Pub. L. 91–375 effective within 1 year after Aug. 12, 1970, on date established therefor by

Board of Governors of United States Postal Service and published by it in Federal Register, see section 16(a), formerly section 15(a) of Pub. L. 91–375, set out as an Effective Date note preceding section 101 of Title 39, Postal Service.

EFFECTIVE DATE OF 1966 AMENDMENT

Amendment by Pub. L. 89–670 effective Apr. 1, 1967, as prescribed by President and published in Federal Register, see section 16(a), formerly § 15(a), of Pub. L. 89–670, and Ex. Ord. No. 11340, Mar. 30, 1967, 32 F.R. 5453.

EFFECTIVE DATE OF 1965 AMENDMENT

Amendment by Pub. L. 89–174 effective upon expiration of first period of sixty calendar days following Sept. 9, 1965 or on earlier date specified by Executive order, see section 11(a) of Pub. L. 89–174 set out as an Effective Date note under section 3531 of Title 42, The Public Health and Welfare.

§ 20. Resignation or refusal of office

The only evidence of a refusal to accept, or of a resignation of the office of President or Vice President, shall be an instrument in writing, declaring the same, and subscribed by the person refusing to accept or resigning, as the case may be, and delivered into the office of the Secretary of State.

(June 25, 1948, ch. 644, 62 Stat. 678.)

PRESIDENTIAL RECORDINGS AND MATERIALS PRESERVATION ACT

For protection and preservation of tape recordings of conversations involving former President Richard M. Nixon, see sections 101 to 106 of Pub. L. 93–526, set out as a note under section 2107 of Title 44, Public Printing and Documents.

§ 21. Definitions

As used in this chapter the term—
(a) "State" includes the District of Columbia.
(b) "executives of each State" includes the Board of Commissioners of the District of Columbia.

(Added Pub. L. 87–389, § 2(a), Oct. 4, 1961, 75 Stat. 820.)

TRANSFER OF FUNCTIONS

Except as otherwise provided in Reorg. Plan No. 3 of 1967, eff. Aug. 11, 1967 (in part), 32 F.R. 11669, 81 Stat. 948, functions of Board of Commissioners of District of Columbia transferred to Commissioner of District of Columbia by section 401 of Reorg. Plan No. 3 of 1967. Office of Commissioner of District of Columbia, as established by Reorg. Plan No. 3 of 1967, abolished as of noon Jan. 2, 1975, by Pub. L. 93–198, title VII, § 711, Dec. 24, 1973, 87 Stat. 818, and replaced by office of Mayor of District of Columbia by section 421 of Pub. L. 93–198.

CHAPTER 2—OFFICE AND COMPENSATION OF PRESIDENT

AMENDMENTS

1998—Pub. L. 105–339, § 4(b)(2), Oct. 31, 1998, 112 Stat. 3185, added item 115.
1978—Pub. L. 95–570, §§ 1(b), 2(b), 3(b), 5(b)(2), (c)(2), Nov. 2, 1978, 92 Stat. 2447, 2449, 2450, 2451, substituted in item 105 "Assistance and services for the President" for "Compensation of secretaries and executive, administrative, and staff assistants to President"; in item 106 "Assistance and services for the Vice President" for "Administrative assistants"; in item 107 "Domestic Policy Staff and Office of Administration; personnel" for "Detail of employees of executive departments to office of President"; in item 108 "Assistance to the President for unanticipated needs" for "Accommodations for vehicles"; and in item 109 "the Executive Residence at the White House" for "Executive Mansion"; inserted in item 110 "the Executive Residence at the" before "White House"; and added items 112, 113 and 114.

EXECUTIVE OFFICE PERSONNEL BACKGROUND INVESTIGATIONS; LEAVES OF ABSENCE

Pub. L. 103–329, title VI, § 632, Sept. 30, 1994, 108 Stat. 2425, provided that:
"(a) IN GENERAL.—Hereafter, the employment of any individual within the Executive Office of the President shall be placed on leave without pay status if the individual—
"(1) has not, within 30 days of commencing such employment or by October 31, 1994 (whichever occurs later), submitted a completed questionnaire for sensitive positions (SF–86) or equivalent form; or
"(2) has not, within 6 months of commencing such employment or by October 31, 1994 (whichever occurs later), had his or her background investigation, if completed, forwarded by the counsel to the President to the United States Secret Service for issuance of the appropriate access pass.
"(b) EXEMPTION.—Subsection (a) shall not apply to any individual specifically exempted from such subsection by the President or his designee."
[For transfer of the functions, personnel, assets, and obligations of the United States Secret Service, including the functions of the Secretary of the Treasury relating thereto, to the Secretary of Homeland Security, and for treatment of related references, see sections 381, 551(d), 552(d), and 557 of Title 6, Domestic Security, and the Department of Homeland Security Reorganization Plan of November 25, 2002, as modified, set out as a note under section 542 of Title 6.]

REORGANIZATION PLAN NO. 1 OF 1977

42 F.R. 56101, 91 Stat. 1633, as amended by Pub. L. 97–195, § 1(c)(5), June 16, 1982, 96 Stat. 115

Prepared by the President and transmitted to the Senate and the House of Representatives in Congress assembled, July 15, 1977,[1] pursuant to the provisions of Chapter 9 of Title 5 of the United States Code.

EXECUTIVE OFFICE OF THE PRESIDENT

SECTION 1. REDESIGNATION OF DOMESTIC COUNCIL STAFF

The Domestic Council staff is hereby designated the Domestic Policy Staff and shall consist of such staff personnel as are determined by the President to be nec-

---

[1] As amended Sept. 15, 1977.

essary to assure that the needs of the President for prompt and comprehensive advice are met with respect to matters of economic and domestic policy. The staff shall continue to be headed by an Executive Director who shall be an Assistant to the President, designated by the President, as provided in Section 203 of Reorganization Plan No. 2 of 1970 [set out in Title 5, Appendix]. The Executive Director shall perform such functions as the President may from time to time direct.

SEC. 2. ESTABLISHMENT OF AN OFFICE OF ADMINISTRATION

There is hereby established in the Executive Office of the President the Office of Administration which shall be headed by the President. There shall be a Director of the Office of Administration. The Director shall be appointed by the President and shall serve as chief administrative officer of the Office of Administration. The President is authorized to fix the compensation and duties of the Director.

The Office of Administration shall provide components of the Executive Office of the President with such administrative services as the President shall from time to time direct.

SEC. 3. ABOLITION OF COMPONENTS

The following components of the Executive Office of the President are hereby abolished:
A. The Domestic Council;
B. The Office of Drug Abuse Policy;
C. The Office of Telecommunications Policy; and
D. The Economic Opportunity Council.

SEC. 4. APPOINTMENT OF THE ASSISTANT SECRETARY OF COMMERCE FOR COMMUNICATIONS AND INFORMATION

There shall be in the Department of Commerce an Assistant Secretary for Communications and Information who shall be appointed by the President, by and with the advice and consent of the Senate. [As amended Pub. L. 97–195, § 1(c)(5), June 16, 1982, 96 Stat. 115.]

SEC. 5. TRANSFERS OF FUNCTIONS

The following functions shall be transferred:
A. All functions vested in the Director of the Office of Science and Technology Policy and in the Office of Science and Technology Policy pursuant to sections 205(a)(2), 206 and 209 of the National Science and Technology Policy, Organization, and Priorities Act of 1976 (Public Law 94–282; 90 Stat. 459) [42 U.S.C. 6614(a)(2), 6615 and 6618], are hereby transferred to the Director of the National Science Foundation. The Intergovernmental Science, Engineering, and Technology Advisory Panel, the President's Committee on Science and Technology, and the Federal Coordinating Council for Science, Engineering and Technology, established in accordance with the provisions of Titles II, III, IV of the National Science and Technology Policy, Organization, and Priorities Act of 1976 [42 U.S.C. 6611 et seq., 6631 et seq., and 6651 et seq.], are hereby abolished, and their functions transferred to the President.
B. Those functions of the Office of Telecommunications Policy and of its Director relating to:
(1) the preparation of Presidential telecommunications policy options including, but not limited to those related to the procurement and management of Federal telecommunications systems, national security, and emergency matters; and
(2) disposition of appeals from assignments of radio frequencies to stations of the United States Government;
are hereby transferred to the President who may delegate such functions within the Executive Office of the President as the President may from time to time deem desirable. All other functions of the Office of Telecommunications Policy and of its Director are hereby transferred to the Secretary of Commerce who shall provide for the performance of such functions.
C. The functions of the Office of Drug Abuse Policy and its Director are hereby transferred to the President, who may delegate such functions within the Executive Office of the President as the President may from time to time deem desirable.
D. The functions of the Domestic Council are hereby transferred to the President, who may delegate such functions within the Executive Office of the President as the President may from time to time deem desirable.
E. Those functions of the Council on Environmental Quality and the Office of Environmental Quality relating to the evaluation provided for by Section 11 of the Federal Nonnuclear Energy Research and Development Act of 1974 (Public Law 93–577, 88 Stat. 1878) [42 U.S.C. 5910], are hereby transferred to the Administrator of the Environmental Protection Agency.
F. Those functions of the Office of Management and Budget and its Director relating to the Committee Management Secretariat (Public Law 92–463, 86 Stat. 770, as amended by Public Law 94–409, 90 Stat. 1247) [see section 7 of the Federal Advisory Committee Act, Pub. L. 92–463, Oct. 6, 1972, 86 Stat. 774, as amended, set out in Title 5, Appendix] are hereby transferred to the Administrator of General Services.
G. The functions of the Economic Opportunity Council are hereby transferred to the President, who may delegate such functions within the Executive Office of the President as the President may from time to time deem desirable.

SEC. 6. INCIDENTAL TRANSFERS

So much of the personnel, property, records, and unexpended balances of appropriations, allocations and other funds employed, used, held, available, or to be made available in connection with the functions transferred under this Plan, as the Director of the Office of Management and Budget shall determine, shall be transferred to the appropriate department, agency, or component at such time or times as the Director of the Office of Management and Budget shall provide, except that no such unexpended balances transferred shall be used for purposes other than those for which the appropriation was originally made. The Director of the Office of Management and Budget shall provide for terminating the affairs of all agencies abolished herein and for such further measures and dispositions as such Director deems necessary to effectuate the purposes of this Reorganization Plan.

SEC. 7. EFFECTIVE DATE

This Reorganization Plan shall become effective at such time or times on or before April 1, 1978, as the President shall specify, but not sooner than the earliest time allowable under Section 906 of Title 5 of the United States Code.

MESSAGE OF THE PRESIDENT

To the Congress of the United States:
I herewith transmit my plan for the Reorganization of the Executive Office of the President (EOP), Reorganization Plan No. 1 of 1977. This plan is the first of a series I intend to submit under the reorganization authority vested in me by the Reorganization Act of 1977 (Public Law 95–17) [5 U.S.C. 901–912]. It adheres to the purposes set forth in Section 901(a) of the Act [5 U.S.C. 901(a)].
This plan in conjunction with the other steps I am taking will:
Eliminate seven of the seventeen units now within the EOP and modify the rest. There were 19 units when I took office; the President's Foreign Intelligence Advisory Board and the Economic Policy Board have already been abolished. Thus with this plan I will have eliminated nine of 19 EOP units.
Reduce EOP staffing by about 250 which includes the White House staff reduction of 134 or 28 percent which I have already ordered.
Improve efficiency by centralizing administrative functions; and
Improve the process by which information is provided for Presidential decisionmaking.

These recommendations arise from a careful, systematic study of the EOP. They are based on the premise that the EOP exists to serve the President and should be structured to meet his needs. They will reduce waste and cost while improving the service the President, and the nation, receive from the EOP.

The EOP now consists of the immediate White House Office, the Vice President's Office, the Office of Management and Budget, and fourteen other agencies. The EOP has a budget authority of about $80,000,000 and 1,712 full time employees.

The White House Office concentrates on close personal support including policy and political advice and administrative and operational services. The Office of the Vice President provides similar support to him. OMB's primary mission is to develop and implement the budget; it also carries out a number of management and reorganization activities.

Three EOP units have responsibility for policy development:

National Security Council.
Domestic Council.
Council on International Economic Policy.

The other 11 are more specialized offices that offer analysis and advice, help develop policy in certain areas, or carry out special projects. These are:

Council of Economic Advisers.
Council on Wage and Price Stability.
Office of the Special Representative for Trade Negotiations.
Council on Environmental Quality.
Office of Science and Technology Policy.
Office of Drug Abuse Policy.
Office of Telecommunications Policy.
Intelligence Oversight Board.
Federal Property Council.
Energy Resources Council.
Economic Opportunity Council.

To make the EOP more effective, four steps are necessary:

I. Strengthen management of policy issues.

II. Limit the EOP, wherever possible, to functions directly related to the President's work.

III. Centralize administrative services.

IV. Reduce size of White House and EOP staffs.

I. STRENGTHEN PROCESS MANAGEMENT OF POLICY ISSUES

Perhaps the most important function of the President's staff is to make sure he has the wide variety of views and facts he needs to make decisions. By building a more orderly system for collecting information and advice, the President can make sure that he will hear all the views he should—and hear them in time. To better insure that this happens, I am taking the following actions to:

Institute for domestic and economic issues, a system similar to the Presidential Review Memorandum process currently used for National Security issues.

Create a committee of Presidential advisers, chaired by the Vice President, to set priorities among issues and oversee their staffing.

Assure that Presidential decision memoranda on policy issues are coordinated with Cabinet and EOP advisers most involved with the issue.

Consolidate under the Staff Secretary the two current White House paper circulation systems.

Appoint a group of advisers to review the decision-making process periodically.

Give the Assistant to the President for Domestic Affairs and Policy clear responsibility for managing the way in which domestic and most economic policy issues are prepared for Presidential decision.

Assign follow-up responsibility for Presidential decisions as follows: immediate follow-up will be handled by the NSC or Domestic Policy Staff most directly involved in the issue; long term follow-up on selected issues will be handled by the Assistant to the President for Intergovernmental Relations.

These actions recognize that the White House and Executive Office staff must use their proximity to the President to insure that the full resources of the government and the public are brought to bear on Presidential decisions in a timely fashion. It is my purpose in instituting these changes to strengthen Cabinet participation in Presidential decisions.

II. RATIONALIZE EOP STRUCTURE BY LIMITING EOP, WHEREVER POSSIBLE, TO FUNCTIONS WHICH BEAR A CLOSE RELATIONSHIP TO THE WORK OF THE PRESIDENT

As the President's principal staff institution, there are several major things the EOP must do:

Provide day-to-day operational support (e.g., scheduling, appointments) and help the President communicate with the public, the Congress, and the press.

Manage the budget and coordinate Administration positions on matters before the Congress.

Manage the Presidential decisionmaking processes efficiently and fairly, and bring the President the widest possible range of opinions.

Help the President: plan and set priorities; monitor and evaluate progress toward achieving the President's objectives; understand and resolve major conflicts among line subordinates; manage crises, especially in national security matters.

In order to restructure the EOP around these basic functions, the functions of seven units should be discontinued or transferred, and ten units, including the White House Office, should be retained but modified.

Seven units should be discontinued or their functions transferred. These are:

1. Office of Drug Abuse Policy.
2. Office of Telecommunications Policy.
3. Council on International Economic Policy.
4. Federal Property Council.
5. Energy Resources Council.
6. Economic Opportunity Council.
7. Domestic Council.

The functions of the Office of Drug Abuse Policy (ODAP) can be performed by a smaller staff reporting to a Presidential adviser in the EOP. The Office itself will be discontinued.

Much of the work done by the Office of Telecommunications Policy (OTP) can be more effectively performed outside the EOP. It is important that the EOP have the capacity to resolve differences and that the President have immediate advice on telecommunications and information policy, especially on national security, emergency preparedness and privacy issues. This only requires a small staff within EOP. The Office of Management and Budget would take responsibility for Federal telecommunications procurement and management policy and arbitration of interagency disputes about frequency allocation. All other functions except developing Presidential policy options would be transferred to a new office within the Department of Commerce, headed by a new Assistant Secretary for Communications and Information, who will perform many of the functions previously performed by the head of the OTP.

I propose that the Economic Opportunity Council be discontinued; it is dormant and its only active function (preparation of the Catalogue of Federal Domestic Assistance) is being performed by OMB. Three other units are also inactive and should be discontinued: Council on International Economic Policy, the Federal Property Council, and the Energy Resources Council.

The Domestic Council should be abolished. It has rarely functioned as a Council, because it is too large and its membership too diverse to make decisions efficiently. Its functions have been performed entirely by its staff. This Domestic Policy Staff should report to the Assistant to the President for Domestic Affairs and Policy. Under the policy process system described earlier, they should manage the process which coordinates the making of domestic and most economic policy. They should work closely with the Cabinet departments and agencies to insure that the views of the Cabinet and agency heads are brought to the President before decisions are made.

The ten EOP units which will continue with some modification are:

1. White House Office.
2. Office of the Vice President.
3. Office of Management and Budget.
4. Council on Environmental Quality.
5. Council of Economic Advisers.
6. Office of Science and Technology Policy.
7. Office of the Special Representative for Trade Negotiations.
8. National Security Council.
9. Intelligence Oversight Board.
10. Council on Wage and Price Stability.

The operations of the Office of the Vice President reflect the combination of constitutional, statutory, and Presidentially assigned duties that make it unique among EOP units. Because his interests and assignments cover the same range as the President's, the Vice President requires a staff with expertise in diverse areas. Its basic functions should not be changed. However, I propose that certain support functions—involving accounting, personnel services, and supply—be transferred to a centralized EOP Administrative Unit.

The Office of Management and Budget would remain as a separate entity in the EOP, but some functional changes should be made. Four functions should be transferred from OMB to other parts of the government:

Administration to the new EOP Central Administrative Unit;

Executive Department/Labor Relations (except for Pay Agent, Executive Level Pools, and Legislative Analysis) to the Civil Service Commission;

Advisory Committee Management Secretariat to the General Services Administration;

Statistical Policy (except Forms Clearance) to the Department of Commerce.

I have asked the OMB to reorganize its management arm to emphasize major Presidential initiatives, such as reorganization, program evaluation, paperwork reduction, and regulatory reform.

The Council on Environmental Quality (CEQ) should remain in the EOP as an environmental adviser to the President. The CEQ's major purpose is to provide an independent assessment of our policies for improving the environment. Toward this end, it will analyze long term trends and conditions in the environment. It will advise OMB on the reorganization of natural resources functions within the Federal government. The Council will retain the functions it now has under NEPA and Executive Order No. 11514 with the exception of routine review of the adequacy of impact statements and the administrative aspects of their receipt and handling. The EPA will take over CEQ's evaluation responsibility under the Federal Nonnuclear Energy Research Development Act of 1974 [section 5901 et seq. of Title 42, The Public Health and Welfare]. The CEQ will continue to review and publish the Annual Report on Environmental Quality.

The strength of the Council of Economic Advisers (CEQ) lies in its economic analysis of current policy choices. It also presents objective economic data, makes macroeconomic forecasts, and analyzes economic trends and their impact on the national economy. It will continue with a small reduction in staff.

The Office of Science and Technology Policy (OSTP) should retain those science, engineering, and technology functions which can be so useful in helping the President and his advisers make decisions about policy and budget issues. Instead of the Intergovernmental Science, Engineering, and Technology Advisory Panels, the President should rely on an intergovernmental relations working group, chaired by the Science Adviser. The Federal Coordinating Council on Science and Technology should operate as a sub-Cabinet working group chaired by the Science Adviser. The reorganization work of the President's Committee on Science and Technology would be part of the overall reorganization effort. The responsibility for preparing certain reports should be transferred to the National Science Foundation.

The proposal places manageable limits on OSTP's broad mandate while emphasizing functions that support the President.

The Office of the Special Representative for Trade Negotiations (STR) is now operating effectively and will be retained essentially as is. With the difficult negotiations now underway in Geneva, the benefits of transferring the STR to another agency are outweighed by the potential reduction in its effectiveness as an international negotiator.

The National Security Council (NSC) will be retained in its present form and its staff slightly reduced.

Intelligence Oversight Board (IOB) should be retained to insure that abuses of the past are not repeated and to emphasize Presidential concerns regarding intelligence issues.

The Council of Wage and Price Stability (COWPS) is a necessary weapon in the continuing fight against inflation and will be retained. To be sure that its work is closely coordinated with the economic analyses performed by the Council of Economic Advisers (CEA), COWPS should be directed by the Chairman of CEA.

III. CENTRALIZE ADMINISTRATIVE FUNCTIONS

About 380 (22 percent) of the full-time, permanent EOP personnel perform administrative support services in EOP units. Most EOP units besides the White House and OMB are too small to provide a full complement of administrative services. They depend on the White House, OMB, GSA, other federal departments, or several of these sources for many of these services. This approach is inefficient; the quality is uneven and the coordination poor. Some services are duplicated, others inconsistently distributed (excess capacity in some units and deficiencies in others), and most too costly.

I propose to combine administrative support operations into a Central Administrative Unit in EOP to provide support in administrative services common to all EOP entities. It should be a separate EOP entity because of the need to assure equal access by all other units.

This consolidation will result in:

Saving of roughly 40 positions and about $1.1 million, improved and more innovative services.

A focus for monitoring the efficiency and responsibility of administrative services.

A base for an effective EOP budget/planning system through which the President can manage an integrated EOP rather than a collection of disparate units.

The EOP has never before been organized as a single, unified entity serving the President. It is only by viewing it as a whole that we can improve efficiency through steps like the Central Administrative Unit.

IV. REDUCE THE SIZE OF WHITE HOUSE AND EOP STAFFS

I am reducing the White House staff by 28 percent, from the 485 I inherited from my predecessor to 351. This involves cuts in my policy and administrative staffs as well as transfers to the Central Administrative Unit.

I estimate that this plan and the other steps I am taking will reduce staff levels in the EOP by about 250, from 1,712 full-time permanent positions to about 1,460 and will save the taxpayers at least $6 million.

As in the rest of the government, I will be reluctant to add staff unless necessary to help me do my job better.

I ask that you support me in improving the operations of the Executive Office of the President by approving the attached reorganization plan.

In summary this plan would:

Abolish the Domestic Council and establish a Domestic Policy Staff.

Establish within the EOP a Central Administrative Unit.

Transfer certain functions of the Council on Environmental Quality to the President for redelegation.

Abolish the Office of Drug Abuse Policy and vest functions in the President for redelegation.

Abolish the Office of Telecommunications Policy and transfer functions to the Department of Commerce and to the President for redelegation.

Create an Assistant Secretary of Commerce for Communications and Information.

Vest some Office of Science and Technology Policy functions in the President for redelegation.

Abolish the Economic Opportunity Council and vest those functions in the President for redelegation.

Transfer the Committee Management Secretariat function of the Office of Management and Budget to the President for redelegation.

Make other incidental transfers attendant to those mentioned above.

Each of the changes set forth in the plan accompanying this message is necessary to accomplish one or more of the purposes set forth in Section 901(a) of Title 5 of the United States Code. I have taken care to determine that all functions abolished by the plan are done so only under statutory authority provided by Section 903(b) of Title 5 of the United States Code. The provisions in the plan for the appointment and pay of any head or officer of any agency have been found by me to be necessary.

As we continue our studies of other parts of the Executive Branch, we will find more ways to improve services in the EOP and elsewhere. This plan is only a beginning, but I am confident that it represents a major step toward a more efficient government that will serve the needs of the people and the President well.

JIMMY CARTER.

THE WHITE HOUSE, July 15, 1977.

ABOLITION OF OFFICE OF TELECOMMUNICATIONS POLICY

For effective date of the abolition of the Office of Telecommunications Policy and its transfer of functions, implementing Reorg. Plan No. 1 of 1977, set out above, see Ex. Ord. No. 12046, Mar. 27, 1978, 43 F.R. 13349, set out as a note under section 305 of Title 47, Telegraphs, Telephones, and Radiotelegraphs.

EX. ORD. NO. 12028. OFFICE OF ADMINISTRATION IN EXECUTIVE OFFICE OF PRESIDENT

Ex. Ord. No. 12028, Dec. 12, 1977, 42 F.R. 62895, as amended by Ex. Ord. No. 12122, Feb. 26, 1979, 44 F.R. 11197, provided:

By virtue of the authority vested in me by the Constitution and statutes of the United States of America, including the National Security Act of 1947, as amended [act July 26, 1947, ch. 343, 61 Stat. 495], Reorganization Plan No. 2 of 1970 (5 U.S.C. App.), Section 202 of the Budget and Accounting Procedures Act of 1950 (31 U.S.C. 581c) [31 U.S.C. 1531], and Reorganization Plan No. 1 of 1977 (42 FR 56101 (October 21, 1977)) [set out above], and as President of the United States of America, in order to effectuate the establishment of the Office of Administration in the Executive Office of the President, it is hereby ordered as follows:

SECTION 1. The establishment, provided by Section 2 of Reorganization Plan No. 1 of 1977 (42 F.R. 56101), of the Office of Administration in the Executive Office of the President shall be effective, as authorized by Section 7 of that Plan, on December 4, 1977.

SEC. 2. The Director of the Office of Administration, hereinafter referred to as the Director, shall report to the President. As the chief administrative officer of the Office of Administration, the Director shall be responsible for ensuring that the Office of Administration provides units within the Executive Office of the President common administrative support and services.

SEC. 3. (a) The Office of Administration shall provide common administrative support and services to all units within the Executive Office of the President, except for such services provided primarily in direct support of the President. The Office of Administration shall, upon request, assist the White House Office in performing its role of providing those administrative services which are primarily in direct support of the President.

(b) The common administrative support and services provided by the Office of Administration shall encompass all types of administrative support and services

that may be used by, or useful to, units within the Executive Office of the President. Such services and support shall include, but not be limited to, providing support services in the following administrative areas:

(1) personnel management services, including equal employment opportunity programs;

(2) financial management services;

(3) data processing, including support and services;

(4) library, records, and information services;

(5) office services and operations, including: mail, messenger, printing and duplication, graphics, word processing, procurement, and supply services; and

(6) any other administrative support or service which will achieve financial savings and increase efficiency through centralization of the supporting service.

(c) Administrative support and services shall be provided to all units within the Executive Office of the President in a manner consistent with available funds and other resources, or in accord with Section 7 of the Act of May 21, 1920 (41 Stat. 613), as amended (31 U.S.C. 686, referred to as the Economy Act) [31 U.S.C. 1535, 1536].

SEC. 4. (a) Subject to such direction or approval as the President may provide or require, the Director shall organize the Office of Administration, contract for supplies and services, and do all other things that the President, as head of the Office of Administration, might do.

(b) The Director is designated to perform the functions of the President under Section 107(b) of Title 3 of the United States Code.

(c) The Director may appoint and fix the pay of employees pursuant to the provisions of Section 107(b)(1)(A) of Title 3 of the United States Code without regard to any other provision of law regulating the employment or compensation of persons in the Government service. Under that section the Director may also fix the pay of an employee serving in a competitive position or in the career service in order to avoid the pay limitation imposed by Section 114 of Title 3 of the United States Code. The provisions of other laws regulating the employment or compensation of persons in the Government service shall continue to apply to such employee.

(d) The Director shall not be accountable for the program and management responsibilities of units within the Executive Office of the President; the head of each unit shall remain responsible for those functions.

SEC. 5. The primary responsibility for performing all administrative support and service functions of units within the Executive Office of the President shall be transferred and reassigned to the Office of Administration; except to the extent those functions are vested by law in the head of such a unit, other than the President; and except to the extent those functions are performed by the White House Office primarily in direct support of the President.

SEC. 6. The records, property, personnel, and unexpended balances of appropriations, available or to be made available, which relate to the functions transferred or reassigned by this Order from units within the Executive Office of the President to the Office of Administration, shall be transferred to the Office of Administration.

SEC. 7. (a) The Director of the Office of Management and Budget shall make such determinations, issue such orders, and take all actions necessary or appropriate to effectuate the transfers or reassignments provided by this Order, including the transfer of funds, records, property, and personnel.

(b) Such transfers shall become effective on April 1, 1978, or at such earlier time or times as the Director of the Office of Management and Budget determines, after consultation with the Director of the Office of Administration and other appropriate units within the Executive Office of the President.

JIMMY CARTER.

Ex. Ord. No. 12045. Implementation of Reorganization Plan Relating to Domestic Council, Domestic Policy Staff, Office of Drug Abuse Policy, and Economic Opportunity Council

Ex. Ord. No. 12045, Mar. 27, 1978, 43 F.R. 13347, provided:

By virtue of the authority vested in me by the Constitution and laws of the United States of America, including Section 7 of Reorganization Plan No. 1 of 1977 (42 F.R. 56101 (October 21, 1977)) [set out above], Section 202 of the Budget and Accounting Procedures Act of 1950 (31 U.S.C. 581c) [31 U.S.C. 1531], and Section 301 of Title 3 of the United States Code, and as President of the United States of America, in order to provide for transfers of the functions of the Office of Drug Abuse Policy, the Domestic Council, and the Economic Opportunity Council, and the abolition of the Office of Drug Abuse Policy, and Domestic Council, and the Economic Opportunity Council, and for other purposes, it is hereby ordered as follows:

Section 1. (a) The transfer of all functions of the Domestic Council, as provided by Section 5D of Reorganization Plan No. 1 of 1977 (42 F.R. 56101), is hereby effective.

(b) The redesignation of the Domestic Council Staff as the Domestic Policy Staff and the other provisions of Section 1 of Reorganization Plan No. 1 of 1977 (42 F.R. 56101), are hereby effective.

(c) The abolition of the Domestic Council, as provided by Section 3A of Reorganization Plan No. 1 of 1977 (42 F.R. 56101), is hereby effective.

(d) The Domestic Policy Staff shall perform such functions as the President may from time to time direct.

Sec. 2. (a) The transfer of all functions of the Office of Drug Abuse Policy and its Director, as provided by Section 5C of Reorganization Plan No. 1 of 1977 (42 F.R. 56101), is hereby effective.

(b) The abolition of the Office of Drug Abuse Policy, as provided by Section 3B of Reorganization Plan No. 1 of 1977 (42 F.R. 56101), is hereby effective.

(c) The Domestic Policy Staff shall assist the President in the performance of the functions transferred by Section 5C of Reorganization Plan No. 1 of 1977 (42 F.R. 56101).

Sec. 3. (a) The transfer of all functions of the Economic Opportunity Council, as provided by Section 5G of Reorganization Plan No. 1 of 1977 (42 F.R. 56101), is hereby effective.

(b) The abolition of the Economic Opportunity Council, as provided by Section 3D Reorganization Plan No. 1 of 1977 (42 F.R. 56101), is hereby effective.

Sec. 4. All provisions of Reorganization Plan No. 1 of 1977 (42 F.R. 56101) not made effective on or prior to the effective date of this Order are hereby effective.

Sec. 5. The records, property, personnel, and unexpended balances of appropriations, available or to be made available, which relate to the functions transferred, assigned, or delegated as provided in this Order are hereby transferred as appropriate.

Sec. 6. The Director of the Office of Management and Budget shall make such determinations, issue such orders, and take all actions necessary or appropriate to effectuate the transfers or reassignments provided in this Order, including the transfer of funds, records, property, and personnel.

Sec. 7. This Order shall be effective March 26, 1978.

Jimmy Carter.

Executive Order No. 12133

Ex. Ord. No. 12133, May 9, 1979, 44 F.R. 27635, which related to the drug policy functions of the Domestic Policy Staff, was revoked by Ex. Ord. No. 12368, June 24, 1982, 47 F.R. 27843, set out as a note under section 1112 of Title 21, Food and Drugs.

Ex. Ord. No. 12134. Transfer of Printing and Duplicating Service Activity of Office of Administration to Department of Navy

Ex. Ord. No. 12134, May 9, 1979, 44 F.R. 27637, provided:

By the authority vested in me as President by the Constitution and laws of the United States of America, including Reorganization Plan No. 2 of 1970 (5 U.S.C. App.), Section 202 of the Budget and Accounting Procedures Act of 1950 (31 U.S.C. 581c) [31 U.S.C. 1531], and Reorganization Plan No. 1 of 1977 (42 F.R. 56101; 5 U.S.C. App.) [also set out above], and in order to provide for the transfer of the printing and duplicating service activity from the Office of Administration in the Executive Office of the President to the Department of the Navy, it is hereby ordered as follows:

1–101. (a) The primary responsibility for performing the common and usual administrative support and services that are related to printing and duplication and that are assigned to the Office of Administration in the Executive Office of the President by Section 3(b)(5) of Executive Order No. 12028, as amended [set out above], is transferred and reassigned to the Department of the Navy.

(b) The Department of the Navy shall be primarily responsible for providing to the Office of Administration, both onsite and offsite, that common and usual administrative support and service related to printing and duplication. It shall be provided in a manner consistent with available funds and other resources, or in accord with Section 7 of the Act of May 21, 1920 (41 Stat. 613), as amended (31 U.S.C. 686, referred to as the Economy Act) [31 U.S.C. 1535, 1536].

1–102. The records, property, personnel, and unexpended balances of appropriations, available or to be made available, which relate to the functions transferred or reassigned by this Order, shall be transferred to the Department of the Navy.

1–103. The Director of the Office of Management and Budget shall make such determinations, issue such orders, and take all actions necessary or appropriate to effectuate the transfers or reassignments provided by this Order, including the transfer of funds, records, property, and personnel.

1–104. Such transfers shall be effective on May 6, 1979.

Jimmy Carter.

Ex. Ord. No. 12859. Establishment of Domestic Policy Council

Ex. Ord. No. 12859, Aug. 16, 1993, 58 F.R. 44101, as amended by Ex. Ord. No. 13284, §10, Jan. 23, 2003, 68 F.R. 4076; Ex. Ord. No. 13500, Feb. 5, 2009, 74 F.R. 6981; Ex. Ord. No. 13569, §3, Apr. 5, 2011, 76 F.R. 19891, provided:

By the authority vested in me as President by the Constitution and the laws of the United States of America, including sections 105, 107, and 301 of title 3, United States Code, it is hereby ordered as follows:

Section 1. *Establishment.* There is established the Domestic Policy Council ("the Council").

Sec. 2. *Membership.* The Council shall comprise the:

(a) President, who shall serve as a Chairman of the Council;

(b) Vice President;

(c) Secretary of Health and Human Services;

(d) Attorney General;

(e) Secretary of Labor;

(f) Secretary of Veterans Affairs;

(g) Secretary of the Interior;

(h) Secretary of Education;

(i) Secretary of Housing and Urban Development;

(j) Secretary of Agriculture;

(k) Secretary of Transportation;

(*l*) Secretary of Commerce;

(m) Secretary of Energy;

(n) Secretary of the Treasury;

(o) Secretary of Homeland Security;

(p) Administrator of the Environmental Protection Agency;

(q) Chair of the Council of Economic Advisers;

(r) Director of the Office of Management and Budget;

(s) Assistant to the President for Economic Policy;

(t) Assistant to the President for Domestic Policy;

(u) Senior Advisor and Assistant to the President for Intergovernmental Affairs and Public Liaison;

(v) Chair of the Council on Environmental Quality;

(w) Director, Office of National Drug Control Policy;

(x) Assistant to the President and Chief Technology Officer;

(y) Chief Executive Officer, Corporation for National and Community Service[;]

(z) Director of the Office of Science and Technology Policy; and

(aa) Such other officials of Executive departments and agencies as the President may, from time to time, designate.

SEC. 3. *Meeting of the Council.* The President, or upon his direction, the Assistant to the President for Domestic Policy ("the Assistant"), may convene meetings of the Council. The President shall preside over the meetings of the Council, provided that in his absence the Vice President, and in his absence the Assistant, will preside.

SEC. 4. *Functions.* (a) The principal functions of the Council are: (1) to coordinate the domestic policy-making process; (2) to coordinate domestic policy advice to the President; (3) to ensure that domestic policy decisions and programs are consistent with the President's stated goals, and to ensure that those goals are being effectively pursued; and (4) to monitor implementation of the President's domestic policy agenda. The Assistant may take such actions, including drafting a Charter, as may be necessary or appropriate to implement such functions.

(b) All executive departments and agencies, whether or not represented on the Council, shall coordinate domestic policy through the Council.

(c) In performing the foregoing functions, the Assistant will, when appropriate, work with the Assistant to the President for National Security Affairs and the Assistant to the President for Economic Policy.

SEC. 5. *Administration.* (a) The Council may function through established or ad hoc committees, task forces or interagency groups.

(b) The Council shall have a staff to be headed by the Assistant to the President for Domestic Policy. The Council shall have such staff and other assistance as may be necessary to carry out the provisions of this order.

(c) All executive departments and agencies shall cooperate with the Council and provide such assistance, information, and advice to the Council as the Council may request, to the extent permitted by law.

EX. ORD. NO. 13199. ESTABLISHMENT OF WHITE HOUSE OFFICE OF FAITH-BASED AND NEIGHBORHOOD PARTNERSHIPS

Ex. Ord. No. 13199, Jan. 29, 2001, 66 F.R. 8499, as amended by Ex. Ord. No. 13498, §1, Feb. 5, 2009, 74 F.R. 6533, provided:

By the authority vested in me as President of the United States by the Constitution and the laws of the United States of America, and in order to help the Federal Government coordinate a national effort to expand opportunities for faith-based and other community organizations and to strengthen their capacity to better meet social needs in America's communities, it is hereby ordered as follows:

SECTION 1. *Policy.* Faith-based and other neighborhood organizations are vital to our Nation's ability to address the needs of low-income and other underserved persons and communities. The American people are key drivers of fundamental change in our country, and few institutions are closer to the people than our faith-based and other neighborhood organizations. It is critical that the Federal Government strengthen the ability of such organizations and other nonprofit providers in our neighborhoods to deliver services effectively in partnership with Federal, State, and local governments and with other private organizations, while preserving our fundamental constitutional commitments guaranteeing the equal protection of the laws and the free exercise of religion and forbidding the establishment of religion. The Federal Government can preserve these fundamental commitments while empowering faith-based and neighborhood organizations to deliver vital services in our communities, from providing mentors and tutors to school children to giving ex-offenders a second chance at work and a responsible life to ensuring that families are fed. The Federal Government must also ensure that any organization receiving taxpayers' dollars must be held accountable for its performance. Through rigorous evaluation, and by offering technical assistance, the Federal Government must ensure that organizations receiving Federal funds achieve measurable results in furtherance of valid public purposes.

SEC. 2. *Establishment.* There is established a White House Office of Faith-Based and Neighborhood Partnerships (Office) within the Executive Office of the President that will have lead responsibility in the executive branch to establish policies, priorities, and objectives for the Federal Government's comprehensive effort to enlist, equip, enable, empower, and expand the work of faith-based and other community organizations to the extent permitted by law.

SEC. 3. *Functions.* The principal functions of the Office are, to the extent permitted by law: (a) to develop, lead, and coordinate the Administration's policy agenda affecting faith-based and other community programs and initiatives, expand the role of such efforts in communities, and increase their capacity through executive action, legislation, Federal and private funding, and regulatory relief;

(b) to ensure that Administration and Federal Government policy decisions and programs are consistent with the President's stated goals with respect to faith-based and other community initiatives;

(c) to ensure that services paid for with Federal Government funds are provided in a manner consistent with fundamental constitutional commitments guaranteeing the equal protection of the laws and the free exercise of religion and prohibiting laws respecting an establishment of religion;

(d) to promote effective training for persons providing federally funded social services in faith-based and neighborhood organizations;

(e) to promote the better use of program evaluation and research, in order to ensure that organizations deliver services as specified in grant agreements, contracts, memoranda of understanding, and other arrangements;

(f) to help integrate the President's policy agenda affecting faith-based and other community organizations across the Federal Government;

(g) to coordinate public education activities designed to mobilize public support for faith-based and community nonprofit initiatives through volunteerism, special projects, demonstration pilots, and public-private partnerships;

(h) to encourage private charitable giving to support faith-based and community initiatives;

(i) to bring concerns, ideas, and policy options to the President for assisting, strengthening, and replicating successful faith-based and other community programs;

(j) to provide policy and legal education to State, local, and community policymakers and public officials seeking ways to empower faith-based and other community organizations and to improve the opportunities, capacity, and expertise of such groups;

(k) to develop and implement strategic initiatives under the President's agenda to strengthen the institutions of civil society and America's families and communities;

(*l*) to showcase and herald innovative grassroots nonprofit organizations and civic initiatives;

(m) to eliminate unnecessary legislative, regulatory, and other bureaucratic barriers that impede effective faith-based and other community efforts to solve social problems;

(n) to monitor implementation of the President's agenda affecting faith-based and other community organizations; and

(*o*) to ensure that the efforts of faith-based and other community organizations meet high standards of excellence and accountability.

SEC. 4. *Administration.* (a) The Office may function through established or ad hoc committees, task forces, or interagency groups.

(b) The Office shall have a staff to be headed by the Special Assistant to the President and Executive Director of the White House Office of Faith-Based and Neighborhood Partnerships (Executive Director). The Office shall have such staff and other assistance, to the extent permitted by law, as may be necessary to carry out the provisions of this order. The Office operations shall begin no later than 30 days from the date of this order.

(c) The Office shall coordinate with the liaison and point of contact designated by each executive department and agency with respect to this initiative.

(d) All executive departments and agencies (agencies) shall cooperate with the Office and provide such information, support, and assistance to the Office as it may request, to the extent permitted by law.

(e) The agencies' actions directed by this Executive Order shall be carried out subject to the availability of appropriations and to the extent permitted by law.

SEC. 5. *Judicial Review.* This order does not create any right or benefit, substantive or procedural, enforceable at law or equity by a party against the United States, its agencies or instrumentalities, its officers or employees, or any other person.

EXECUTIVE ORDER NO. 13283

Ex. Ord. No. 13283, Jan. 21, 2003, 68 F.R. 3371, which established the Office of Global Communications in the White House Office, was revoked by Ex. Ord. No. 13385, § 9, Sept. 29, 2005, 70 F.R. 57991, set out as a note under section 14 of the Federal Advisory Committee Act in the Appendix to Title 5, Government Organization and Employees.

EX. ORD. NO. 13498. AMENDMENTS TO EXECUTIVE ORDER 13199 AND ESTABLISHMENT OF THE PRESIDENT'S ADVISORY COUNCIL FOR FAITH-BASED AND NEIGHBORHOOD PARTNERSHIPS

Ex. Ord. No. 13498, Feb. 5, 2009, 74 F.R. 6533, provided:

By the authority vested in me as President by the Constitution and the laws of the United States of America, and in order to strengthen the ability of faith-based and other neighborhood organizations to deliver services effectively in partnership with Federal, State, and local governments and with other private organizations, while preserving our fundamental constitutional commitments, it is hereby ordered:

SECTION 1. [Amended Ex. Ord. No. 13199, set out as a note above.]

SEC. 2. *President's Advisory Council on Faith-Based and Neighborhood Partnerships.* (a) *Establishment.* There is established within the Executive Office of the President the President's Advisory Council on Faith-Based and Neighborhood Partnerships (Council).

(b) *Mission.* The Council shall bring together leaders and experts in fields related to the work of faith-based and neighborhood organizations in order to: identify best practices and successful modes of delivering social services; evaluate the need for improvements in the implementation and coordination of public policies relating to faith-based and other neighborhood organizations; and make recommendations to the President, through the Executive Director, for changes in policies, programs, and practices that affect the delivery of services by such organizations and the needs of low-income and other underserved persons in communities at home and around the world.

(c) *Membership.* (1) The Council shall be composed of not more than 25 members appointed by the President from among individuals who are not officers or employees of the Federal Government. The members shall be persons with experience and expertise in fields related to the provision of social services by faith-based and other neighborhood organizations.

(2) Members of the Council shall serve for terms of 1 year, and may continue to serve after the expiration of their terms until the President appoints a suc-

cessor. Members shall be eligible for reappointment and serve at the pleasure of the President during their terms.

(3) The President shall designate a member of the Council to serve as Chair for a term of 1 year at the pleasure of the President. The Chair may continue to serve after the expiration of the Chair's term and shall be eligible for redesignation by the President.

(4) The Executive Director of the White House Office of Faith-Based and Neighborhood Partnerships shall also serve as Executive Director of the Council.

(5) The Council shall have a staff headed by the Executive Director.

(d) *Administration.* (1) Upon the request of the Chair, with the approval of the Executive Director, the heads of executive departments and agencies shall, to the extent permitted by law, provide the Council with information it needs for purposes of carrying out its mission.

(2) With the approval of the Executive Director, the Council may request and collect information, hold hearings, establish subcommittees, and establish task forces consisting of members of the Council or other individuals who are not officers or employees of the Federal Government, as necessary to carry out its mission.

(3) With the approval of the Executive Director, the Council may conduct analyses and develop reports or other materials as necessary to perform its mission.

(4) Members of the Council shall serve without compensation, but shall be allowed travel expenses, including per diem in lieu of subsistence, as authorized by law for persons serving intermittently in Government service (5 U.S.C. 5701–5707) to the extent funds are available.

(5) To the extent permitted by law, and subject to the availability of appropriations, the Department of Health and Human Services shall provide the Council with administrative support and with such funds as may be necessary for the performance of the Council's functions.

(e) *General Provisions.* (1) Insofar as the Federal Advisory Committee Act, as amended (5 U.S.C. App.) (Act), may apply to the Council, any functions of the President under that Act, except for those in section 6 of the Act, shall be performed by the Secretary of Health and Human Services in accordance with guidelines issued by the Administrator of General Services.

(2) The Council shall terminate 2 years from the date of this order unless extended by the President.

SEC. 3. *General Provisions.* (a) Nothing in this order shall be construed to impair or otherwise affect:

(1) authority granted by law to a department, agency, or the head thereof; or

(2) functions of the Director of the Office of Management and Budget relating to budget, administrative, or legislative proposals.

(b) This order shall be implemented consistent with applicable law and subject to the availability of appropriations.

(c) In order to ensure that Federal programs and practices involving grants or contracts to faith-based organizations are consistent with law, the Executive Director, acting through the Counsel to the President, may seek the opinion of the Attorney General on any constitutional and statutory questions involving existing or prospective programs and practices.

(d) This order is not intended to, and does not, create any right or benefit, substantive or procedural, enforceable at law or in equity by any party against the United States, its departments, agencies, or entities, its officers, employees, or agents, or any other person.

BARACK OBAMA.

EX. ORD. NO. 13503. ESTABLISHMENT OF THE WHITE HOUSE OFFICE OF URBAN AFFAIRS

Ex. Ord. No. 13503, Feb. 19, 2009, 74 F.R. 8139, provided:

By the authority vested in me as President by the Constitution and the laws of the United States of

America, and in order to take a coordinated and comprehensive approach to developing and implementing an effective strategy concerning urban America, it is hereby ordered as follows:

SECTION 1. *Policy.* About 80 percent of Americans live in urban areas, and the economic health and social vitality of our urban communities are critically important to the prosperity and quality of life for Americans. Vibrant cities spawn innovation, economic growth, and cultural enrichment through the businesses, universities, and civic, cultural, religious, and nonprofit institutions they attract. Forward-looking policies that encourage wise investment and development in our urban areas will create employment and housing opportunities and make our country more competitive, prosperous, and strong. In the past, insufficient attention has been paid to the problems faced by urban areas and to coordinating the many Federal programs that affect our cities. A more comprehensive approach is needed, both to develop an effective strategy for urban America and to coordinate the actions of the many executive departments and agencies whose actions impact urban life.

SEC. 2. *Establishment.* There is established within the Executive Office of the President the White House Office of Urban Affairs (the "Office").

SEC. 3. *Functions.* The principal functions of the Office are, to the extent permitted by law:

(a) to provide leadership for and coordinate the development of the policy agenda for urban America across executive departments and agencies;

(b) to coordinate all aspects of urban policy;

(c) to work with executive departments and agencies to ensure that appropriate consideration is given by such departments and agencies to the potential impact of their actions on urban areas;

(d) to work with executive departments and agencies, including the Office of Management and Budget, to ensure that Federal Government dollars targeted to urban areas are effectively spent on the highest-impact programs; and

(e) to engage in outreach and work closely with State and local officials, with nonprofit organizations, and with the private sector, both in seeking input regarding the development of a comprehensive urban policy and in ensuring that the implementation of Federal programs advances the objectives of that policy.

SEC. 4. *Coordination.* In performing its functions, the Office shall work closely with all relevant executive departments and agencies, and offices and councils within the Executive Office of the President, including but not limited to:

(a) the Department of the Treasury;

(b) the Department of Justice;

(c) the Department of Commerce;

(d) the Department of Labor;

(e) the Department of Health and Human Services;

(f) the Department of Housing and Urban Development;

(g) the Department of Transportation;

(h) the Department of Energy;

(i) the Department of Education; and

(j) the Environmental Protection Agency.

SEC. 5. *Administration.* (a) The Office may work with established or ad hoc committees, task forces, and interagency groups.

(b) The Office shall have a staff headed by the Deputy Assistant to the President and Director of Urban Affairs (Director). The Director shall report jointly to the Assistant to the President for Intergovernmental Affairs and Public Liaison and to the Assistant to the President for Domestic Policy. The Office shall have such staff and other assistance as may be necessary to carry out the provisions of this order.

(c) All executive departments and agencies shall cooperate with the Office and provide such information, support, and assistance to the Office as the Director may request, to the extent permitted by law.

SEC. 6. *General Provisions.* (a) Nothing in this order shall be construed to impair or otherwise affect:

(i) authority granted by law to a department, agency, or the head thereof; or

(ii) functions of the Director of the Office of Management and Budget relating to budgetary, administrative, or legislative proposals.

(b) This order shall be implemented consistent with applicable law and subject to the availability of appropriations.

(c) This order is not intended to, and does not, create any right or benefit, substantive or procedural, enforceable at law or in equity by any party against the United States, its departments, agencies, or entities, its officers, employees, or agents, or any other person.

BARACK OBAMA.

EXECUTIVE ORDER NO. 13509

Ex. Ord. No. 13509, June 23, 2009, 74 F.R. 30903, which established the White House Council on Automotive Communities and Workers, was revoked by Ex. Ord. No. 13578, §3, July 6, 2011, 76 F.R. 40592, set out as a note under section 551 of Title 29, Labor.

EX. ORD. NO. 13569. AMENDMENTS TO EXECUTIVE ORDERS 12824, 12835, 12859, AND 13532, REESTABLISHMENT PURSUANT TO EXECUTIVE ORDER 13498, AND REVOCATION OF EXECUTIVE ORDER 13507

Ex. Ord. No. 13569, Apr. 5, 2011, 76 F.R. 19891, provided:

By the authority vested in me as President by the Constitution and the laws of the United States of America, it is hereby ordered as follows:

SECTION 1. [Amended Ex. Ord. No. 12824, set out as a note under section 492 of Title 14, Coast Guard.]

SEC. 2. [Amended Ex. Ord. No. 12835, set out as a note under section 1023 of Title 15, Commerce and Trade.]

SEC. 3. [Amended Ex. Ord. No. 12859, set out as a note above.]

SEC. 4. [Amended Ex. Ord. No. 13532, set out as a note under section 1060 of Title 20, Education.]

SEC. 5. The President's Advisory Council on Faith-Based and Neighborhood Partnerships, as set forth under the provisions of Executive Order 13498 of February 5, 2009, is hereby reestablished and shall terminate 2 years from the date of this order unless extended by the President.

SEC. 6. [Revoked Ex. Ord. No. 13507, set out as a note under section 201 of Title 42, The Public Health and Welfare.]

SEC. 7. This order is not intended to, and does not, create any right or benefit, substantive or procedural, enforceable at law or in equity by any party against the United States, its departments, agencies, or entities, its officers, employees, or agents, or any other person.

BARACK OBAMA.

WHITE HOUSE TASK FORCE ON MIDDLE-CLASS WORKING FAMILIES

Memorandum of President of the United States, Jan. 30, 2009, 74 F.R. 5979, provided:

Memorandum for the Heads of Executive Departments and Agencies

For many years, middle-class Americans have been working harder, yet not enjoying their fair share of the fruits of a growing economy. While the productivity of the American workforce grew during the decade ending in 2007, middle-income workers saw their real incomes fall. The current economic situation has exacerbated the challenges facing middle-class Americans, with health care coverage, safe and steady employment opportunities, effective and affordable education, owning a home, and saving for retirement slipping out of reach. It is a high priority of my Administration to achieve a secure future for middle-class working families, one in which they share in prosperous times and are cushioned during hard times. To these ends, I hereby direct the following:

SECTION 1. *White House Task Force on Middle-Class Working Families.* There is established within the Office of the Vice President, a White House Task Force on

Middle-Class Working Families (Task Force) to focus on raising the living standards of middle-class working families in the United States of America. The Vice President shall serve as Chair of the Task Force.

(a) MEMBERSHIP OF THE TASK FORCE. In addition to the Vice President, the Task Force shall consist exclusively of the heads of the executive branch departments, agencies, and offices listed below:

(1) the Department of Commerce;

(2) the Department of Labor;

(3) the Department of Health and Human Services;

(4) the Department of Education;

(5) the Office of Management and Budget;

(6) the National Economic Council;

(7) the Domestic Policy Council;

(8) the Council of Economic Advisers; and

(9) such other executive branch departments, agencies, or offices as the President may designate.

A member of the Task Force may designate, to perform the Task Force functions of the member, any person who is a part of the member's department, agency, or office, and who is a full-time officer or employee of the Federal Government. At the direction of the Chair, the Task Force may establish subgroups consisting exclusively of Task Force members or their designees under this section, as appropriate.

(b) ADMINISTRATION OF THE TASK FORCE. The Department of Labor shall provide funding and administrative support for the Task Force to the extent permitted by law and within existing appropriations. The Vice President shall designate an Executive Director of the Task Force, who shall coordinate the work of the Task Force.

SEC. 2. *Mission and Functions of the Task Force.* The Task Force shall work with a wide array of executive departments and agencies that have responsibility for key issues facing middle-class working families, expedite administrative reforms, propose Executive Orders, and develop legislative and policy proposals that can be of special importance to middle-class working families. The functions of the Task Force are advisory only and shall include, but shall not be limited to, producing a detailed set of recommendations to:

(a) expand education and lifelong training opportunities;

(b) improve work and family balance;

(c) restore labor standards, including workplace safety;

(d) protect the incomes of middle-class working families; and

(e) protect retirement security.

SEC. 3. *Outreach.* Consistent with the objectives set out in section 2 of this memorandum, the Task Force, in accordance with applicable law, in addition to regular meetings, shall conduct outreach with representatives of labor, business, nonprofit organizations, State and local government agencies, and other interested persons that will assist with the Task Force's development of a detailed set of recommendations.

SEC. 4. *Transparency and Reports.* The Task Force shall facilitate the posting on the Internet of submissions by outside parties and engage in an open, two-way dialogue with the American people. The Task Force shall present to the President annual reports, beginning 1 year from the date of this memorandum, on its findings and recommendations, which shall be made available to the public and posted on the Internet.

SEC. 5. *General Provisions.* (a) The heads of executive departments and agencies shall assist and provide information to the Task Force, consistent with applicable law, as may be necessary to carry out the functions of the Task Force. Each executive department and agency shall bear its own expense for participating in the Task Force.

(b) Nothing in this memorandum shall be construed to impair or otherwise affect:

(i) authority granted by law to an executive department, agency, or the head thereof; or

(ii) functions of the Director of the Office of Management and Budget relating to budgetary, administrative, or legislative proposals.

(c) This memorandum shall be implemented consistent with applicable law and subject to the availability of appropriations.

(d) This memorandum is not intended to, and does not, create any right or benefit, substantive or procedural, enforceable at law or in equity by any party against the United States, its departments, agencies, or entities, its officers, employees, or agents, or any other person.

SEC. 6. *Publication.* The Secretary of Labor is authorized and directed to publish this memorandum in the Federal Register.

BARACK OBAMA.

§ 101. Commencement of term of office

The term of four years for which a President and Vice President shall be elected, shall, in all cases, commence on the 20th day of January next succeeding the day on which the votes of the electors have been given.

(June 25, 1948, ch. 644, 62 Stat. 678.)

SHORT TITLE OF 2000 AMENDMENT

Pub. L. 106–293, §1, Oct. 12, 2000, 114 Stat. 1035, provided that: "This Act [amending provisions set out as a note under section 102 of this title] may be cited as the 'Presidential Transition Act of 2000'."

DWIGHT D. EISENHOWER EXECUTIVE OFFICE BUILDING

Pub. L. 106–92, Nov. 9, 1999, 113 Stat. 1309, provided that:

"SECTION 1. DESIGNATION OF DWIGHT D. EISENHOWER EXECUTIVE OFFICE BUILDING.

"The Old Executive Office Building located at 17th Street and Pennsylvania Avenue, NW, in Washington, District of Columbia, shall be known and designated as the 'Dwight D. Eisenhower Executive Office Building'.

"SEC. 2. REFERENCES.

"Any reference in a law, map, regulation, document, paper, or other record of the United States to the building referred to in section 1 shall be deemed to be a reference to the 'Dwight D. Eisenhower Executive Office Building'."

Pub. L. 100–461, title V, §590, Oct. 1, 1988, 102 Stat. 2268–52, as amended by Pub. L. 106–92, §2, Nov. 9, 1999, 113 Stat. 1309, provided that:

"(a) ACCEPTANCE OF GIFTS OF MONEY AND PROPERTY.— The Director of the Office of Administration is authorized to—

"(1) accept, hold, administer, utilize and sell gifts and bequests of property, both real and personal, and loans of personal property other than money; and

"(2) accept and utilize voluntary and uncompensated services;

for the purpose of aiding, benefiting, or facilitating the work of preservation, restoration, renovation, rehabilitation, or historic furnishing of the Dwight D. Eisenhower Executive Office Building and the grounds thereof.

"(b) ESTABLISHMENT OF FUND.—There is established in the Treasury a fund for use in accordance with the provisions of this section. Amounts of money and proceeds from the sale of property accepted under subsection (a) shall be deposited in the fund, which shall be available to the Director of the Office of Administration. Such funds shall be held in trust by the Secretary of the Treasury.

"(c) USE OF FUND.—Property accepted pursuant to this section or the proceeds from the sale thereof, shall be used as nearly as possible in accordance with the terms of the gift or bequest. Any use or sale of property accepted pursuant to this section, and any use of proceeds from such sale, shall be subject to the disapproval of the Administrator of General Services within 30 days after the Administrator receives notice of such use or sale. The Director of the Office of Administration shall not accept any gift under this section that is expressly conditioned on any expenditure not to be met from the gift itself unless such expenditure has been approved by an Act of Congress.

"(d) TAXES.—For the purpose of the Federal income, estate, and gift tax laws, property accepted under this section shall be considered as a gift, bequest, or devise to the United States."

PRESIDENT'S ADVISORY COMMISSION ON PRESIDENTIAL OFFICE SPACE

Act Aug. 3, 1956, ch. 925, 70 Stat. 979, as amended by Pub. L. 85–3, Jan. 25, 1957, 71 Stat. 4, created a President's Advisory Commission on Presidential Office Space to study the problem of providing more adequate office space for the White House Office and the other agencies of the Executive Office of the President. Pursuant to section 1(b) of act Aug. 3, 1956, the Commission was required to report to the President its findings and recommendations within 10 months after Aug. 3, 1956, and section 2(g) of act Aug. 3, 1956, provided that the Commission should cease to exist 30 days after the submission of its final report.

§ 102. Compensation of the President

The President shall receive in full for his services during the term for which he shall have been elected compensation in the aggregate amount of $400,000 a year, to be paid monthly, and in addition an expense allowance of $50,000 to assist in defraying expenses relating to or resulting from the discharge of his official duties. Any unused amount of such expense allowance shall revert to the Treasury pursuant to section 1552 of title 31, United States Code. No amount of such expense allowance shall be included in the gross income of the President. He shall be entitled also to the use of the furniture and other effects belonging to the United States and kept in the Executive Residence at the White House.

(June 25, 1948, ch. 644, 62 Stat. 678; Jan. 19, 1949, ch. 2, §1(a), 63 Stat. 4; Oct. 20, 1951, ch. 521, title VI, §619(a), 65 Stat. 569; Pub. L. 91–1, §1, Jan. 17, 1969, 83 Stat. 3; Pub. L. 95–570, §5(a), Nov. 2, 1978, 92 Stat. 2450; Pub. L. 106–58, title VI, §644(a), Sept. 29, 1999, 113 Stat. 478; Pub. L. 108–199, div. F, title III, §301, Jan. 23, 2004, 118 Stat. 326.)

AMENDMENTS

2004—Pub. L. 108–199 substituted ". Any unused amount of such expense allowance shall revert to the Treasury pursuant to section 1552 of title 31, United States Code. No amount of such expense allowance shall be included in the gross income of the President." for ", for which expense allowance no accounting, other than for income tax purposes, shall be made by him."

1999—Pub. L. 106–58 substituted "$400,000" for "$200,000".

1978—Pub. L. 95–570 substituted "Executive Residence at the White House" for "Executive Mansion".

1969—Pub. L. 91–1 substituted "$200,000" for "$100,000".

1951—Act Oct. 20, 1951, made President's expense allowance taxable.

1949—Act Jan. 19, 1949, increased salary from $75,000 to $100,000 per year, and gave President a yearly expense account of $50,000 for which he was to make no accounting and which was tax free.

EFFECTIVE DATE OF 1999 AMENDMENT

Pub. L. 106–58, title VI, §644(b), Sept. 29, 1999, 113 Stat. 478, provided that: "The amendment made by this section [amending this section] shall take effect at noon on January 20, 2001."

EFFECTIVE DATE OF 1978 AMENDMENT

Section 6(a) of Pub. L. 95–570 provided that: "The amendments made by this Act [enacting sections 107, 108, 112, 113, and 114 of this title, amending sections 102, 103, 105, 106, 109, 110, and 202 of this title, repealing section 107 of this title, and enacting provisions set out as a note under section 107 of this title] shall apply to any fiscal year which begins on or after October 1, 1978."

EFFECTIVE DATE OF 1969 AMENDMENT

Section 2 of Pub. L. 91–1 provided that: "The amendment made by this Act [amending this section] shall take effect at noon on January 20, 1969."

EFFECTIVE DATE OF 1951 AMENDMENT

Section 619(e) of act Oct. 20, 1951, provided that: "The amendments made by subsections (a) and (b) of this section [amending this section and section 111 of this title] shall become effective at noon on January 20, 1953, and the amendments made by subsections (c) and (d) [amending sections 31a and 31b of Title 2, The Congress] shall become effective at noon on January 3, 1953."

EFFECTIVE DATE OF 1949 AMENDMENT

Amendment by act Jan. 19, 1949, effective noon, Jan. 19, 1949, see section 3 of that act.

AUTHORIZATION OF TRANSITION ACTIVITIES BY THE INCUMBENT ADMINISTRATION

Pub. L. 111–283, §3, Oct. 15, 2010, 124 Stat. 3048, provided that:

"(a) IN GENERAL.—The President of the United States, or the President's delegate, may take such actions as the President determines necessary and appropriate to plan and coordinate activities by the Executive branch of the Federal Government to facilitate an efficient transfer of power to a successor President, including—

"(1) the establishment and operation of a transition coordinating council comprised of—

"(A) high-level officials of the Executive branch selected by the President, which may include the Chief of Staff to the President, any Cabinet officer, the Director of the Office of Management and Budget, the Administrator of the General Services Administration, the Director of the Office of Personnel Management, the Director of the Office of Government Ethics, and the Archivist of the United States, and

"(B) any other persons the President determines appropriate;

"(2) the establishment and operation of an agency transition directors council which includes career employees designated to lead transition efforts within Executive Departments or agencies;

"(3) the development of guidance to Executive Departments and agencies regarding briefing materials for an incoming administration, and the development of such materials; and

"(4) the development of computer software, publications, contingency plans, issue memoranda, memoranda of understanding, training and exercises (including crisis training and exercises), programs, lessons learned from previous transitions, and other items appropriate for improving the effectiveness and efficiency of a Presidential transition that may be disseminated to eligible candidates (as defined in section 3(h)(4) of the Presidential Transition Act of 1963, as added by section 2(a) [section 3(h)(4) of Pub. L. 88–277, set out in a note below]) and to the President-elect and Vice-President-elect.

Any information and other assistance to eligible candidates under this subsection shall be offered on an equal basis and without regard to political affiliation.

"(b) REPORTS.—

"(1) IN GENERAL.—The President of the United States, or the President's delegate, shall provide to the Committee on Oversight and Government Reform of the House of Representatives and the Committee on Homeland Security and Governmental Affairs of the Senate reports describing the activities undertaken by the President and the Executive Departments and agencies to prepare for the transfer of power to a new President.

"(2) TIMING.—The reports under paragraph (1) shall be provided six months and three months before the date of the general election for the Office of President of the United States."

DISCLOSURE OF IN-KIND CONTRIBUTIONS TO 1988–1989 TRANSITION

Pub. L. 100–398, § 5, Aug. 17, 1988, 102 Stat. 987, provided that:

"(a) DISCLOSURE AS CONDITION OF RECEIPT OF FUNDS.— The President-elect and Vice-President-elect (as a condition for receiving services under section 3 and for funds provided under section 6(a)(1) of the Presidential Transition Act of 1963 [Pub. L. 88–277] (3 U.S.C. 102 note) shall provide an estimate to the Administrator of General Services of the aggregate value of in-kind contributions made during the period beginning on November 9, 1988, through January 20, 1989, received for transition activities for—

"(1) transportation;

"(2) hotel and other accommodations;

"(3) suitable office space; and

"(4) furniture, furnishings, office machines and equipment, and office supplies.

"(b) FORM AND AVAILABILITY OF ESTIMATES.—The estimates made under subsection (a) shall be—

"(1) in the form of a report to the Administrator of General Services within 90 days after January 20, 1989; and

"(2) made available to the public by the Administrator upon receipt by the Administrator."

PRESIDENTIAL TRANSITION ACT OF 1963

Pub. L. 88–277, Mar. 7, 1964, 78 Stat. 153, as amended by Pub. L. 94–499, §§ 1, 2, Oct. 14, 1976, 90 Stat. 2380; Pub. L. 100–398, §§ 2(a), 3, 4, Aug. 17, 1988, 102 Stat. 985, 986; Pub. L. 106–293, § 2, Oct. 12, 2000, 114 Stat. 1035; Pub. L. 108–271, § 8(b), July 7, 2004, 118 Stat. 814; Pub. L. 108–458, title VII, § 7601(a), Dec. 17, 2004, 118 Stat. 3856; Pub. L. 111–283, § 2(a), (b), (d), Oct. 15, 2010, 124 Stat. 3045, 3047, 3048, provided: "That this Act may be cited as the 'Presidential Transition Act of 1963.'

"PURPOSE OF THIS ACT

"SEC. 2. The Congress declares it to be the purpose of this Act to promote the orderly transfer of the executive power in connection with the expiration of the term of office of a President and the inauguration of a new President. The national interest requires that such transitions in the office of President be accomplished so as to assure continuity in the faithful execution of the laws and in the conduct of the affairs of the Federal Government, both domestic and foreign. Any disruption occasioned by the transfer of the executive power could produce results detrimental to the safety and well-being of the United States and its people. Accordingly, it is the intent of the Congress that appropriate actions be authorized and taken to avoid or minimize any disruption. In addition to the specific provisions contained in this Act directed toward that purpose, it is the intent of the Congress that all officers of the Government so conduct the affairs of the Government for which they exercise responsibility and authority as (1) to be mindful of problems occasioned by transitions in the office of President, (2) to take appropriate lawful steps to avoid or minimize disruptions that might be occasioned by the transfer of the executive power, and (3) otherwise to promote orderly transitions in the office of President.

"SERVICES AND FACILITIES AUTHORIZED TO BE PROVIDED TO PRESIDENTS-ELECT AND VICE-PRESIDENTS-ELECT

"SEC. 3. (a) The Administrator of General Services, referred to hereafter in this Act as 'the Administrator,'

is authorized to provide, upon request, to each President-elect and each Vice-President-elect, for use in connection with his preparations for the assumption of official duties as President or Vice President necessary services and facilities, including the following:

"(1) Suitable office space appropriately equipped with furniture, furnishings, office machines and equipment, and office supplies, as determined by the Administrator, after consultation with the President-elect, the Vice-President-elect, or their designee provided for in subsection (e) of this section, at such place or places within the United States as the President-elect or Vice-President-elect shall designate.

"(2) Payment of the compensation of members of office staffs designated by the President-elect or Vice-President-elect at rates determined by them not to exceed the rate provided by the Classification Act of 1949, as amended [chapter 51 and subchapter III of chapter 53 of title 5], for grade GS–18: *Provided*, That any employee of any agency of any branch of the Government may be detailed to such staffs on a reimbursable basis with the consent of the head of the agency; and while so detailed such employee shall be responsible only to the President-elect or Vice-President-elect for the performance of his duties: *Provided further*, That any employee so detailed shall continue to receive the compensation provided pursuant to law for his regular employment, and shall retain the rights and privileges of such employment without interruption. Notwithstanding any other law, persons receiving compensation as members of office staffs under this subsection, other than those detailed from agencies, shall not be held or considered to be employees of the Federal Government except for purposes of the Civil Service Retirement Act [section 8301 et seq. of title 5], the Federal Employees' Compensation Act [section 8501 et seq. of title 5], the Federal Employees' Group Life Insurance Act of 1954 [section 8701 et seq. of title 5], and the Federal Employees Health Benefits Act of 1959 [section 8901 et seq. of title 5].

"(3) Payment of expenses for the procurement of services of experts or consultants or organizations thereof for the President-elect or Vice-President-elect, as authorized for the head of any department by section 15 of the Administrative Expenses Act of 1946, as amended (5 U.S.C. 55a) [section 3109 of title 5].

"(4)(A) Payment of travel expenses and subsistence allowances, including rental of Government or hired motor vehicles, found necessary by the President-elect or Vice-President-elect, as authorized for persons employed intermittently or for persons serving without compensation by section 5 of the Administrative Expenses Act of 1946, as amended (5 U.S.C. 73b–2) [section 5703 of title 5], as may be appropriate;

"(B) When requested by the President-elect or Vice-President-elect or their designee, and approved by the President, Government aircraft may be provided for transition purposes on a reimbursable basis; when requested by the President-elect, the Vice-President-elect, or the designee of the President-elect or Vice-President-elect, aircraft may be chartered for transition purposes; and any collections from the Secret Service, press, or others occupying space on chartered aircraft shall be deposited to the credit of the appropriations made under section 6 of this Act.

"(5) Communications services found necessary by the President-elect or Vice-President-elect.

"(6) Payment of expenses for necessary printing and binding, notwithstanding the Act of January 12, 1895, and the Act of March 1, 1919, as amended (44 U.S.C. 111) [section 501 of title 44].

"(7) Reimbursement to the postal revenues in amounts equivalent to the postage that would otherwise be payable on mail matter referred to in subsection (d) of this section.

"(8)(A)(i) Not withstanding subsection (b), payment of expenses during the transition for briefings, workshops, or other activities to acquaint key prospective Presidential appointees with the types of problems and challenges that most typically confront new political appointees when they make the transition from campaign and other prior activities to assuming the responsibility for governance after inauguration.

"(ii) Activities under this paragraph may include interchange between such appointees and individuals who—

"(I) held similar leadership roles in prior administrations;

"(II) are department or agency experts from the Office of Management and Budget or an Office of Inspector General of a department or agency; or

"(III) are relevant staff from the Government Accountability Office.

"(iii) Activities under this paragraph may include training or orientation in records management to comply with section 2203 of title 44, United States Code, including training on the separation of Presidential records and personal records to comply with subsection (b) of that section.

"(iv) Activities under this paragraph may include training or orientation in human resources management and performance-based management.

"(v) Activities under this paragraph shall include the preparation of a detailed classified, compartmented summary by the relevant outgoing executive branch officials of specific operational threats to national security; major military or covert operations; and pending decisions on possible uses of military force. This summary shall be provided to the President-elect as soon as possible after the date of the general elections held to determine the electors of President and Vice President under section 1 or 2 of title 3, United States Code.

"(B) Activities under this paragraph shall be conducted primarily for individuals the President-elect or eligible candidate (as defined in subsection (h)(4)) for President intends to nominate as department heads or appoint to key positions in the Executive Office of the President.

"(9)(A) Notwithstanding subsection (b), development of a transition directory by the Administrator of General Services Administration, in consultation with the Archivist of the United States (head of the National Archives and Records Administration) for activities conducted under paragraph (8).

"(B) The transition directory shall be a compilation of Federal publications and materials with supplementary materials developed by the Administrator that provides information on the officers, organization, and statutory and administrative authorities, functions, duties, responsibilities, and mission of each department and agency.

"(10) Notwithstanding subsection (b), consultation by the Administrator with any President-elect, Vice-President-elect, or eligible candidate (as defined in subsection (h)(4)) to develop a systems architecture plan for the computer and communications systems of the candidate to coordinate a transition to Federal systems if the candidate is elected.

"(b) The Administrator may not expend funds for the provision of services and facilities under section 3 of this Act in connection with any obligations incurred by the President-elect or Vice-President-elect—

"(1) before the day following the date of the general elections held to determine the electors of President and Vice President under section 1 or 2 of title 3, United States Code; or

"(2) after 30 days after the date of the inauguration of the President-elect as President and the inauguration of the Vice-President-elect as Vice President.

"(c) The terms 'President-elect' and 'Vice-President-elect' as used in this Act shall mean such persons as are the apparent successful candidates for the office of President and Vice President, respectively, as ascertained by the Administrator following the general elections held to determine the electors of President and Vice President in accordance with title 3, United States Code, sections 1 and 2.

"(d) Each President-elect shall be entitled to conveyance within the United States and its territories and possessions of all mail matter, including airmail, sent by him in connection with his preparations for the assumption of official duties as President, and such mail matter shall be transmitted as penalty mail as provided in title 39, United States Code, section 4152 [now section 3202 of title 39]. Each Vice-President-elect shall be entitled to conveyance within the United States and its territories and possessions of all mail matter, including airmail, sent by him under his written autograph signature in connection with his preparations for the assumption of official duties as Vice President.

"(e) Each President-elect and Vice-President-elect, or eligible candidate (as defined in subsection (h)(4)) for President or Vice-President, may designate to the Administrator an assistant authorized to make on his behalf such designations or findings of necessity as may be required in connection with the services and facilities to be provided under this Act. Not more than 10 per centum of the total expenditures under this Act for any President-elect or Vice-President-elect may be made upon the basis of a certificate by him or the assistant designated by him pursuant to this section that such expenditures are classified and are essential to the national security, and that they accord with the provisions of subsections (a), (b), and (d) of this section.

"(f)(1) The President-elect should submit to the Federal Bureau of Investigation or other appropriate agency and then, upon taking effect and designation, to the agency designated by the President under section 115(b) of the National Intelligence Reform Act of 2004 [probably should be section 3001(c) of Pub. L. 108–458, 50 U.S.C. 435b(c)], the names of candidates for high level national security positions through the level of undersecretary of cabinet departments as soon as possible after the date of the general elections held to determine the electors of President and Vice President under section 1 or 2 of title 3, United States Code.

"(2) The responsible agency or agencies shall undertake and complete as expeditiously as possible the background investigations necessary to provide appropriate security clearances to the individuals who are candidates described under paragraph (1) before the date of the inauguration of the President-elect as President and the inauguration of the Vice-President-elect as Vice President.

"(g) In the case where the President-elect is the incumbent President or in the case where the Vice-President-elect is the incumbent Vice President, there shall be no expenditures of funds for the provision of services and facilities to such incumbent under this Act, and any funds appropriated for such purposes shall be returned to the general funds of the Treasury.

"(h)(1)(A) In the case of an eligible candidate, the Administrator—

"(i) shall notify the candidate of the candidate's right to receive the services and facilities described in paragraph (2) and shall provide with such notice a description of the nature and scope of each such service and facility; and

"(ii) upon notification by the candidate of which such services and facilities such candidate will accept, shall, notwithstanding subsection (b), provide such services and facilities to the candidate during the period beginning on the date of the notification and ending on the date of the general elections described in subsection (b)(1).

The Administrator shall also notify the candidate that sections 7601(c) and 8403(b) of the Intelligence Reform and Terrorism Prevention Act of 2004 [Pub. L. 108–458; 50 U.S.C. 435b note and 5 U.S.C. 1101 note] provide additional services.

"(B) The Administrator shall provide the notice under subparagraph (A)(i) to each eligible candidate—

"(i) in the case of a candidate of a major party (as defined in section 9002(6) of the Internal Revenue Code of 1986 [26 U.S.C. 9002(6)]), on one of the first 3 business days following the last nominating convention for such major parties; and

"(ii) in the case of any other candidate, as soon as practicable after an individual becomes an eligible candidate (or, if later, at the same time as notice is provided under clause (i)).

"(C)(i) The Administrator shall, not later than 12 months before the date of each general election for President and Vice-President (beginning with the election to be held in 2012), prepare a report summarizing modern presidential transition activities, including a bibliography of relevant resources.

"(ii) The Administrator shall promptly make the report under clause (i) generally available to the public (including through electronic means) and shall include such report with the notice provided to each eligible candidate under subparagraph (A)(i).

"(2)(A) Except as provided in subparagraph (B), the services and facilities described in this paragraph are the services and facilities described in subsection (a) (other than paragraphs (2), (3), (4), (7), and 8(A)(v) thereof), but only to the extent that the use of the services and facilities is for use in connection with the eligible candidate's preparations for the assumption of official duties as President or Vice-President.

"(B) The Administrator—

"(i) shall determine the location of any office space provided to an eligible candidate under this subsection;

"(ii) shall, as appropriate, ensure that any computers or communications services provided to an eligible candidate under this subsection are secure;

"(iii) shall offer information and other assistance to eligible candidates on an equal basis and without regard to political affiliation; and

"(iv) may modify the scope of any services to be provided under this subsection to reflect that the services are provided to eligible candidates rather than the President-elect or Vice-President-elect, except that any such modification must apply to all eligible candidates.

"(C) An eligible candidate, or any person on behalf of the candidate, shall not use any services or facilities provided under this subsection other than for the purposes described in subparagraph (A), and the candidate or the candidate's campaign shall reimburse the Administrator for any unauthorized use of such services or facilities.

"(3)(A) Notwithstanding any other provision of law, an eligible candidate may establish a separate fund for the payment of expenditures in connection with the eligible candidate's preparations for the assumption of official duties as President or Vice-President, including expenditures in connection with any services or facilities provided under this subsection (whether before such services or facilities are available under this section or to supplement such services or facilities when so provided). Such fund shall be established and maintained in such manner as to qualify such fund for purposes of section 501(c)(4) of the Internal Revenue Code of 1986 [26 U.S.C. 501(c)(4)].

"(B)(i) The eligible candidate may—

"(I) transfer to any separate fund established under subparagraph (A) contributions (within the meaning of section 301(8) of the Federal Election Campaign Act of 1971 (2 U.S.C. 431(8))) the candidate received for the general election for President or Vice-President or payments from the Presidential Election Campaign Fund under chapter 95 of the Internal Revenue Code of 1986 [26 U.S.C. 9001 et seq.] the candidate received for the general election; and

"(II) solicit and accept amounts for receipt by such separate fund.

"(ii) Any expenditures from the separate fund that are made from such contributions or payments described in clause (i)(I) shall be treated as expenditures (within the meaning of section 301(9) of such Act (2 U.S.C. 431(9))) or qualified campaign expenses (within the meaning of section 9002(11) of such Code [26 U.S.C. 9002(11)]), whichever is applicable.

"(iii) An eligible candidate establishing a separate fund under subparagraph (A) shall (as a condition for receiving services and facilities described in paragraph (2)) comply with all requirements and limitations of

section 5 in soliciting or expending amounts in the same manner as the President-elect or Vice-President-elect, including reporting on the transfer and expenditure of amounts described in subparagraph (B)(i) in the disclosures required by section 5.

"(4)(A) In this subsection, the term 'eligible candidate' means, with respect to any presidential election (as defined in section 9002(10) of the Internal Revenue Code of 1986 [26 U.S.C. 9002(10)])—

"(i) a candidate of a major party (as defined in section 9002(6) of such Code [26 U.S.C. 9002(6)]) for President or Vice-President of the United States; and

"(ii) any other candidate who has been determined by the Administrator to be among the principal contenders for the general election to such offices.

"(B) In making a determination under subparagraph (A)(ii), the Administrator shall—

"(i) ensure that any candidate determined to be an eligible candidate under such subparagraph—

"(I) meets the requirements described in Article II, Section 1, of the United States Constitution for eligibility to the office of President;

"(II) has qualified to have his or her name appear on the ballots of a sufficient number of States such that the total number of electors appointed in those States is greater than 50 percent of the total number of electors appointed in all of the States; and

"(III) has demonstrated a significant level of public support in national public opinion polls, so as to be realistically considered among the principal contenders for President or Vice-President of the United States; and

"(ii) consider whether other national organizations have recognized the candidate as being among the principal contenders for the general election to such offices, including whether the Commission on Presidential Debates has determined that the candidate is eligible to participate in the candidate debates for the general election to such offices.

"SEC. 4. The Administrator is authorized to provide, upon request, to each former President and each former Vice President, for a period not to exceed seven months from 30 days before the date of the expiration of his term of office as President or Vice President, for use in connection with winding up the affairs of his office, necessary services and facilities of the same general character as authorized by this Act to be provided to Presidents-elect and Vice-Presidents-elect. Any person appointed or detailed to serve a former President or former Vice President under authority of this section shall be appointed or detailed in accordance with, and shall be subject to, all of the provisions of section 3 of this Act applicable to persons appointed or detailed under authority of that section. The provisions of the Act of August 25, 1958 (72 Stat. 838; 3 U.S.C. 102, note), other than subsections (a) and (e) shall not become effective with respect to a former President until six months after the expiration of his term of office as President.

"SEC. 5. (a)(1) The President-elect and Vice-President-elect (as a condition for receiving services under section 3 and for funds provided under section 6(a)(1)) shall disclose to the Administrator the date of contribution, source, amount, and expenditure thereof of all money, other than funds from the Federal Government, and including currency of the United States and of any foreign nation, checks, money orders, or any other negotiable instruments payable on demand, received either before or after the date of the general elections for use in the preparation of the President-elect or Vice-President-elect for the assumption of official duties as President or Vice President.

"(2) The President-elect and Vice-President-elect (as a condition for receiving such services and funds) shall make available to the Administrator and the Comptroller General all information concerning such contributions as the Administrator or Comptroller General may require for purposes of auditing both the public and private funding used in the activities authorized by this Act.

"(3) Disclosures made under paragraph (1) shall be—

"(A) in the form of a report to the Administrator within 30 days after the inauguration of the President-elect as President and the Vice-President-elect as Vice President; and

"(B) made available to the public by the Administrator upon receipt by the Administrator.

"(b)(1) The President-elect and Vice-President-elect (as a condition for receiving services provided under section 3 and funds provided under section 6(a)(1)) shall make available to the public—

"(A) the names and most recent employment of all transition personnel (full-time or part-time, public or private, or volunteer) who are members of the President-elect or Vice-President-elect's Federal department or agency transition teams; and

"(B) information regarding the sources of funding which support the transition activities of each transition team member.

"(2) Disclosures under paragraph (1) shall be made public before the initial transition team contact with a Federal department or agency and shall be updated as necessary.

"(c) The President-elect and Vice-President-elect (as a condition for receiving services under section 3 and for funds provided under section 6(a)(1)) shall not accept more than $5,000 from any person, organization, or other entity for purposes of carrying out activities authorized by this Act.

"AUTHORIZATION OF APPROPRIATIONS

"SEC. 6. (a) There are hereby authorized to be appropriated to the Administrator such funds as may be necessary for carrying out the purposes of this Act, except that with respect to any one Presidential transition—

"(1) not more than $3,500,000 may be appropriated for the purposes of providing services and facilities to the President-elect and Vice President-elect under section 3, and

"(2) not more than $1,500,000 may be appropriated for the purposes of providing services and facilities to the former President and former Vice President under section 4, except that any amount appropriated pursuant to this paragraph in excess of $1,250,000 shall be returned to the general fund of the Treasury in the case where the former Vice President is the incumbent President.

The President shall include in the budget transmitted to Congress, for each fiscal year in which his regular term of office will expire, a proposed appropriation for carrying out the purposes of this Act.

"(b) The amounts authorized to be appropriated under subsection (a) shall be increased by an inflation adjusted amount, based on increases in the cost of transition services and expenses which have occurred in the years following the most recent Presidential transition, and shall be included in the proposed appropriation transmitted by the President under the last sentence of subsection (a)."

[Pub. L. 108–458, title VII, §7601(d), Dec. 17, 2004, 118 Stat. 3858, provided that: "Notwithstanding section 351 [Pub. L. 108–458 does not contain a section 351], this section [enacting provisions set out as a note under section 435b of Title 50, War and National Defense, and amending section 3 of Pub. L. 88–277, set out above] and the amendments made by this section shall take effect on the date of enactment of this Act [Dec. 17, 2004]."]

[Pub. L. 100–398, §2(b), Aug. 17, 1988, 102 Stat. 985, provided that: "The amendments made by subsection (a) of this section [renumbering and amending section 6 of Pub. L. 88–277, set out above] shall be effective upon enactment [Aug. 17, 1988], except that the amendment made by paragraph (7) of such subsection [enacting subsec. (b) of section 6 of Pub. L. 88–277, set out above] shall take effect on October 1, 1989."]

[Pub. L. 94–499, §3, Oct. 14, 1976, 90 Stat. 2380, provided that amendment of section 5 of Pub. L. 88–277 [set out above] by section 1 of Pub. L. 94–499, respecting revision of appropriation authorization, shall be effective Oct. 14, 1976.]

[For transfer of the functions, personnel, assets, and obligations of the United States Secret Service, including the functions of the Secretary of the Treasury relating thereto, to the Secretary of Homeland Security, and for treatment of related references, see sections 381, 551(d), 552(d), and 557 of Title 6, Domestic Security, and the Department of Homeland Security Reorganization Plan of November 25, 2002, as modified, set out as a note under section 542 of Title 6.]

[References in laws to the rates of pay for GS–16, 17, or 18, or to maximum rates of pay under the General Schedule, to be considered references to rates payable under specified sections of Title 5, Government Organization and Employees, see section 529 [title I, §101(c)(1)] of Pub. L. 101–509, set out in a note under section 5376 of Title 5.]

EXPENSE ALLOWANCE: USE; REVERSION OF UNEXPENDED PORTION; NONTAXABLE

Provisions prohibiting expenditure of funds made available for official expenses for any other purpose and requiring reversion of any unused amount to the Treasury pursuant to 31 U.S.C. 1552 were contained in a paragraph under the headings "EXECUTIVE OFFICE OF THE PRESIDENT AND FUNDS APPROPRIATED TO THE PRESIDENT" and "COMPENSATION OF THE PRESIDENT" in the Executive Office of the President Appropriations Act, 2006, Pub. L. 109–115, div. A, title V, Nov. 30, 2005, 119 Stat. 2472, and were repeated in provisions of subsequent appropriations acts which are not set out in the Code. Similar provisions were also contained in the following prior appropriation acts:

Pub. L. 108–447, div. H, title III, Dec. 8, 2004, 118 Stat. 3246.

Pub. L. 108–199, div. F, title III, Jan. 23, 2004, 118 Stat. 321.

Pub. L. 108–7, div. J, title III, Feb. 20, 2003, 117 Stat. 442.

Pub. L. 107–67, title III, Nov. 12, 2001, 115 Stat. 526.

Pub. L. 106–554, §1(a)(3) [title III], Dec. 21, 2000, 114 Stat. 2763, 2763A–136.

Pub. L. 106–58, title III, Sept. 29, 1999, 113 Stat. 444.

Pub. L. 105–277, div. A, §101(h) [title III], Oct. 21, 1998, 112 Stat. 2681–480, 2681–492.

Pub. L. 105–61, title III, Oct. 10, 1997, 111 Stat. 1290.

Pub. L. 104–208, div. A, title I, §101(f) [title III], Sept. 30, 1996, 110 Stat. 3009–314, 3009–326.

Pub. L. 104–52, title III, Nov. 19, 1995, 109 Stat. 477.

Pub. L. 103–329, title III, Sept. 30, 1994, 108 Stat. 2392.

Pub. L. 103–123, title III, Oct. 28, 1993, 107 Stat. 1235.

Pub. L. 102–393, title III, Oct. 6, 1992, 106 Stat. 1738.

Pub. L. 102–141, title III, Oct. 28, 1991, 105 Stat. 844.

Pub. L. 101–509, title III, Nov. 5, 1990, 104 Stat. 1399.

Pub. L. 101–136, title III, Nov. 3, 1989, 103 Stat. 790.

Pub. L. 100–440, title III, Sept. 22, 1988, 102 Stat. 1728.

Pub. L. 100–202, §101(m) [title III], Dec. 22, 1987, 101 Stat. 1329–390, 1329–398.

Pub. L. 99–500, §101(m) [title III], Oct. 18, 1986, 100 Stat. 1783–308, 1783–315, and Pub. L. 99–591, §101(m) [title III, §301], Oct. 30, 1986, 100 Stat. 3341–308, 3341–315.

Pub. L. 99–190, §101(h) [H.R. 3036, title III], Dec. 19, 1985, 99 Stat. 1291.

Pub. L. 98–473, §101(j) [H.R. 5798, title III], Oct. 12, 1984, 98 Stat. 1963.

Pub. L. 98–151, §101(f) [H.R. 4139, title III], Nov. 14, 1983, 97 Stat. 973.

Pub. L. 97–377, title I, §101(a) [incorporating H.R. 4121, title III, for FY 1982], Dec. 21, 1982, 96 Stat. 1830.

Pub. L. 97–92, §101(a) [H.R. 4121, title III], Dec. 15, 1981, 95 Stat. 1183.

Pub. L. 96–536, §101(a) [incorporating Pub. L. 96–74, title III], Dec. 16, 1980, 94 Stat. 3166.

Pub. L. 96–74, title III, Sept. 29, 1979, 93 Stat. 563.

FORMER PRESIDENTS; ALLOWANCE; SELECTION, COMPENSATION, AND STATUS OF OFFICE STAFF; OFFICE SPACE; WIDOW'S ALLOWANCE, TERMINATION; "FORMER PRESIDENT" DEFINED

Pub. L. 85–745, Aug. 25, 1958, 72 Stat. 838, as amended by Pub. L. 86–682, §12(c), Sept. 2, 1960, 74 Stat. 730; Pub. L. 88–426, title I, §124, Aug. 14, 1964, 78 Stat. 412; Pub. L. 89–554, §8(a), Sept. 6, 1966, 80 Stat. 660; Pub. L. 90–206, title II, §224(c), Dec. 16, 1967, 81 Stat. 642; Pub. L. 91–231, §7, Apr. 15, 1970, 84 Stat. 198; Pub. L. 91–658, §6, Jan. 8, 1971, 84 Stat. 1963; Pub. L. 95–138, §1, Oct. 18, 1977, 91 Stat. 1170; Pub. L. 103–123, title IV, §6(a), Oct. 28, 1993, 107 Stat. 1246; Pub. L. 103–329, title V, §531, Sept. 30, 1994, 108 Stat. 2413; Pub. L. 104–52, title V, §523, Nov. 19, 1995, 109 Stat. 495; Pub. L. 105–61, title IV, §409(a), Oct. 10, 1997, 111 Stat. 1299; Pub. L. 108–447, div. H, title V, §526, Dec. 8, 2004, 118 Stat. 3271, provided that:

"(a) Each former President shall be entitled for the remainder of his life to receive from the United States a monetary allowance at a rate per annum, payable monthly by the Secretary of the Treasury, which is equal to the annual rate of basic pay, as in effect from time to time, of the head of an executive department, as defined in section 101 of title 5, United States Code. However, such allowance shall not be paid for any period during which such former President holds an appointive or elective office or position in or under the Federal Government or the government of the District of Columbia to which is attached a rate of pay other than a nominal rate.

"(b) The Administrator of General Services shall, without regard to the civil-service and classification laws, provide for each former President an office staff. Persons employed under this subsection shall be selected by the former President and shall be responsible only to him for the performance of their duties. Each former President shall fix basic rates of compensation for persons employed for him under this paragraph which in the aggregate shall not exceed $96,000 per annum except that for the first 30-month period during which a former President is entitled to staff assistance under this subsection, such rates of compensation in the aggregate shall not exceed $150,000 per annum. The annual rate of compensation payable to any such person shall not exceed the highest annual rate of basic pay now or hereafter provided by law for positions at level II of the Executive Schedule under section 5313 of title 5, United States Code. Amounts provided for 'Allowances and Office Staff for Former Presidents' may be used to pay fees of an independent contractor who is not a member of the staff of the office of a former President for the review of Presidential records of a former President in connection with the transfer of such records to the National Archives and Records Administration or a Presidential Library without regard to the limitation on staff compensation set forth herein.

"(c) The Administrator of General Services shall furnish for each former President suitable office space appropriately furnished and equipped, as determined by the Administrator, at such place within the United States as the former President shall specify.

"(d) [Repealed. Pub. L. 86–682, §12(c), Sept. 2, 1960, 74 Stat. 730. See sections 3214 and 3216 of title 39.]

"(e) The widow of each former President shall be entitled to receive from the United States a monetary allowance at a rate of $20,000 per annum, payable monthly by the Secretary of the Treasury, if such widow shall waive the right to each other annuity or pension to which she is entitled under any other Act of Congress. The monetary allowance of such widow—

"(1) commences on the day after the former President dies;

"(2) terminates on the last day of the month before such widow—

"(A) dies; or

"(B) remarries before becoming 60 years of age; and

"(3) is not payable for any period during which such widow holds an appointive or elective office or position in or under the Federal Government or the government of the District of Columbia to which is attached a rate of pay other than a nominal rate.

"(f) As used in this section, the term 'former President' means a person—

"(1) who shall have held the office of President of the United States of America;

"(2) whose service in such office shall have terminated other than by removal pursuant to section 4 of article II of the Constitution of the United States of America; and

"(3) who does not then currently hold such office.

"(g) There are authorized to be appropriated to the Administrator of General Services up to $1,000,000 for each former President and up to $500,000 for the spouse of each former President each fiscal year for security and travel related expenses: *Provided*, That under the provisions set forth in section 3056, paragraph (a), subparagraph (3) of title 18, United States Code, the former President and/or spouse was not receiving protection for a lifetime provided by the United States Secret Service under section 3056 paragraph (a) subparagraph (3) of title 18, United States Code; the protection provided by the United States Secret Service expired at its designated time; or the protection provided by the United States Secret Service was declined prior to authorized expiration in lieu of these funds."

[Pub. L. 95–138, §2, Oct. 18, 1977, 91 Stat. 1170, provided that: "The amendment made by the first section of this Act [amending Pub. L. 87–745, set out above] shall take effect October 1, 1977."]

[For transfer of the functions, personnel, assets, and obligations of the United States Secret Service, including the functions of the Secretary of the Treasury relating thereto, to the Secretary of Homeland Security, and for treatment of related references, see sections 381, 551(d), 552(d), and 557 of Title 6, Domestic Security, and the Department of Homeland Security Reorganization Plan of November 25, 2002, as modified, set out as a note under section 542 of Title 6.]

FORMER PRESIDENT EISENHOWER; ALLOWANCE; COMPENSATION OF OFFICE STAFF; WIDOW'S PENSION

Allowance to former President Eisenhower as precluding entitlement to pay of General of the Army, compensation of office staff to former President to be reduced by pay of military assistants to the General of the Army, and benefits of widow of former President unaffected by restoration of military status, see Appointment of General of the Army note under former sections 1691 to 1697 of Title 50, Appendix, War and National Defense.

§ 103. Traveling expenses

There may be expended for or on account of the traveling expenses of the President of the United States such sum as Congress may from time to time appropriate, not exceeding $100,000 per annum, such sum when appropriated to be expended in the discretion of the President and accounted for on his certificate solely.

(June 25, 1948, ch. 644, 62 Stat. 678; Pub. L. 95–570, §4, Nov. 2, 1978, 92 Stat. 2450.)

AMENDMENTS

1978—Pub. L. 95–570 substituted "$100,000" for "$40,000".

EFFECTIVE DATE OF 1978 AMENDMENT

Amendment by Pub. L. 95–570 applicable to any fiscal year beginning on or after Oct. 1, 1978, see section 6(a) of Pub. L. 95–570, set out as a note under section 102 of this title.

§ 104. Salary of the Vice President

(a) The per annum rate of salary of the Vice President of the United States shall be the rate determined for such position under chapter 11 of title 2, as adjusted under this section. Subject to subsection (b), effective at the beginning of the first month in which an adjustment takes effect under section 5303 of title 5 in the rates of pay under the General Schedule, the salary of the Vice President shall be adjusted by an amount, rounded to the nearest multiple of $100 (or if midway between multiples of $100, to the nearest higher multiple of $100), equal to the percentage of such per annum rate which corresponds to the most recent percentage change in the ECI (relative to the date described in the next sentence), as determined under section 704(a)(1) of the Ethics Reform Act of 1989. The appropriate date under this sentence is the first day of the fiscal year in which such adjustment in the rates of pay under the General Schedule takes effect.

(b) In no event shall the percentage adjustment taking effect under the second and third sentences of subsection (a) in any calendar year (before rounding) exceed the percentage adjustment taking effect in such calendar year under section 5303 of title 5 in the rates of pay under the General Schedule.

(June 25, 1948, ch. 644, 62 Stat. 678; Jan. 19, 1949, ch. 2, §1(b), 63 Stat. 4; Mar. 2, 1955, ch. 9, §4(c), 69 Stat. 11; Pub. L. 88–426, title III, §304(a), Aug. 14, 1964, 78 Stat. 422; Pub. L. 91–67, §1, Sept. 15, 1969, 83 Stat. 106; Pub. L. 94–82, title II, §203, Aug. 9, 1975, 89 Stat. 420; Pub. L. 97–257, title I, §105(b), Sept. 10, 1982, 96 Stat. 849; Pub. L. 101–194, title VII, §704(a)(2)(A), Nov. 30, 1989, 103 Stat. 1769; Pub. L. 101–509, title V, §529 [title I, §101(b)(4)(I)], Nov. 5, 1990, 104 Stat. 1427, 1440; Pub. L. 103–356, title I, §101(2), Oct. 13, 1994, 108 Stat. 3410.)

References in Text

The General Schedule, referred to in text, is set out under section 5332 of Title 5, Government Organization and Employees.

Section 704(a)(1) of the Ethics Reform Act of 1989, referred to in subsec. (a), is section 704(a)(1) of Pub. L. 101–194, which is set out as a note under section 5318 of Title 5.

Amendments

1994—Pub. L. 103–356 designated existing provisions as subsec. (a), substituted "Subject to subsection (b), effective" for "Effective" in second sentence, and added subsec. (b).

1990—Pub. L. 101–509 substituted "5303" for "5305".

1989—Pub. L. 101–194 substituted "corresponds to the most recent percentage change in the ECI (relative to the date described in the next sentence), as determined under section 704(a)(1) of the Ethics Reform Act of 1989. The appropriate date under this sentence is the first day of the fiscal year in which such adjustment in the rates of pay under the General Schedule takes effect" for "corresponds to the overall average percentage (as set forth in the report transmitted to the Congress under section 5305 of title 5) of the adjustment in such rates of pay".

1982—Pub. L. 97–257 struck out requirement for payment of salary on a monthly basis.

1975—Pub. L. 94–82 substituted provisions for a rate of salary to be determined under chapter 11 of title 2, as adjusted under this section, with adjustments equal to the percentage of such per annum rate which corresponds to the overall average percentage of the adjustment in such rates of pay for provisions for a per annum rate of salary of $62,500.

1969—Pub. L. 91–67 increased salary from $43,000 to $62,500.

1964—Pub. L. 88–426 increased salary from $35,000 to $43,000.

1955—Act Mar. 2, 1955, increased salary from $30,000 to $35,000.

1949—Act Jan. 19, 1949, increased salary from $20,000 to $30,000.

Effective Date of 1994 Amendment

Section 101 of Pub. L. 101–356 provided that the amendment made by that section is effective Dec. 31, 1994.

Effective Date of 1990 Amendment

Amendment by Pub. L. 101–509 effective on such date as the President shall determine, but not earlier than 90 days, and not later than 180 days, after Nov. 5, 1990, see section 529 [title III, §305] of Pub. L. 101–509, set out as a note under section 5301 of Title 5, Government Organization and Employees.

Effective Date of 1989 Amendment

Amendment by Pub. L. 101–194 effective Jan. 1, 1991, see section 704(b) of Pub. L. 101–194, set out as a note under section 5318 of Title 5, Government Organization and Employees.

Effective Date of 1982 Amendment

Amendment by Pub. L. 97–257 effective in the case of compensation payable for months after December 1981, see section 105(c) of Pub. L. 97–257, set out as a note under section 60c–1 of Title 2, The Congress.

Effective Date of 1969 Amendment

Section 3 of Pub. L. 91–67 provided that: "The amendments made by this Act [amending this section and section 31 of Title 2, The Congress] shall become effective on March 1, 1969."

Effective Date of 1964 Amendment

Amendment by Pub. L. 88–426 effective on first day of first pay period which begins on or after July 1, 1964, except to the extent provided in section 501(c) of Pub. L. 88–426, see section 504 of Pub. L. 88–426.

Effective Date of 1955 Amendment

Amendment by act Mar. 2, 1955, effective Mar. 1, 1955, see section 5 of that act, set out as a note under section 31 of Title 2, The Congress.

Effective Date of 1949 Amendment

Amendment by act Jan. 19, 1949, effective noon, Jan. 20, 1949, see section 3 of that act.

Salary Increases

For adjustment of pay rates under this section, see the executive order detailing the adjustment of certain rates of pay set out as a note under section 5332 of Title 5, Government Organization and Employees.

For prior year salary increases per the recommendation of the President, see Prior Salary Recommendations notes under section 358 of Title 2, The Congress.

For miscellaneous provisions dealing with adjustments of pay and limitations on use of funds to pay salaries in prior years, see notes under section 5318 of Title 5, Government Organization and Employees.

§ 105. Assistance and services for the President

(a)(1) Subject to the provisons[1] of paragraph (2) of this subsection, the President is authorized to appoint and fix the pay of employees in the White House Office without regard to any other provision of law regulating the employ-

---

[1] So in original. Probably should be "provisions".

ment or compensation of persons in the Government service. Employees so appointed shall perform such official duties as the President may prescribe.

(2) The President may, under paragraph (1) of this subsection, appoint and fix the pay of not more than—

(A) 25 employees at rates not to exceed the rate of basic pay then currently paid for level II of the Executive Schedule of section 5313 of title 5; and in addition

(B) 25 employees at rates not to exceed the rate of basic pay then currently paid for level III of the Executive Schedule of section 5314 of title 5; and in addition

(C) 50 employees at rates not to exceed the maximum rate of basic pay then currently paid for GS–18 of the General Schedule of section 5332 of title 5; and in addition

(D) such number of other employees as he may determine to be appropriate at rates not to exceed the minimum rate of basic pay then currently paid for GS–16 of the General Schedule of section 5332 of title 5.

(b)(1) Subject to the provisions of paragraph (2) of this subsection, the President is authorized to appoint and fix the pay of employees in the Executive Residence at the White House without regard to any other provision of law regulating the employment or compensation of persons in the Government service. Employees so appointed shall perform such official duties as the President may prescribe.

(2) The President may, under paragraph (1) of this subsection, appoint and fix the pay of not more than—

(A) 3 employees at rates not to exceed the maximum rate of basic pay then currently paid for GS–18 of the General Schedule of section 5332 of title 5; and in addition

(B) such number of other employees as he may determine to be appropriate at rates not to exceed the minimum rate of basic pay then currently paid for GS–16 of the General Schedule of section 5332 of title 5.

(c) The President is authorized to procure for the White House Office and the Executive Residence at the White House, as provided in appropriation Acts, temporary or intermittent services of experts and consultants, as described in and in accordance with the first two sentences of section 3109(b) of title 5—

(1) in the case of the White House Office, at respective daily rates of pay for individuals which are not more than the daily equivalent of the rate of basic pay then currently paid for level II of the Executive Schedule of section 5313 of title 5; and

(2) in the case of the Executive Residence, at respective daily rates of pay for individuals which are not more than the daily equivalent of the maximum rate of basic pay then currently paid for GS–18 of the General Schedule of section 5332 of title 5.

Notwithstanding such section 3109(b), temporary services of any expert or consultant described in such section 3109(b) may be procured for a period in excess of one year if the President determines such procurement is necessary.

(d) There are authorized to be appropriated each fiscal year to the President such sums as may be necessary for—

(1) the care, maintenance, repair, alteration, refurnishing, improvement, air-conditioning, heating, and lighting (including electric power and fixtures) of the Executive Residence at the White House;

(2) the official expenses of the White House Office;

(3) the official entertainment expenses of the President;

(4) the official entertainment expenses for allocation within the Executive Office of the President; and

(5) the subsistence expenses of persons in the Government service while traveling on official business in connection with the travel of the President.

Sums appropriated under this subsection for expenses described in paragraphs (1), (3), and (5) may be expended as the President may determine, notwithstanding the provisions of any other law. Such sums shall be accounted for solely on the certificate of the President, except that, with respect to such expenses, the Comptroller General may inspect all necessary books, documents, papers, and records relating to any such expenditures solely for the purpose of verifying that all such expenditures related to expenses in paragraph (1), (3), or (5). The Comptroller General shall certify to Congress the fact of such verification, and shall report any such expenses not expended for such purpose.

(e) Assistance and services authorized pursuant to this section to the President are authorized to be provided to the spouse of the President in connection with assistance provided by such spouse to the President in the discharge of the President's duties and responsibilities. If the President does not have a spouse, such assistance and services may be provided for such purposes to a member of the President's family whom the President designates.

(June 25, 1948, ch. 644, 62 Stat. 678; Oct. 15, 1949, ch. 695, § 2(a), 63 Stat. 880; July 31, 1956, ch. 804, title I, § 109, 70 Stat. 740; Pub. L. 87–367, title III, § 303(h), Oct. 4, 1961, 75 Stat. 794; Pub. L. 88–426, title III, § 304(b), Aug. 14, 1964, 78 Stat. 422; Pub. L. 90–222, title I, § 111(c), Dec. 23, 1967, 81 Stat. 726; Pub. L. 95–570, § 1(a), Nov. 2, 1978, 92 Stat. 2445.)

AMENDMENTS

1978—Pub. L. 95–570 inserted provisions relating to appointment and determination of pay by President of employees in the White House Office and the Executive Residence at the White House; procurement by President of temporary or intermittent services of experts and consultants and pay of such experts and consultants; appropriation of sums for the care, maintenance, etc., of the Executive Residence at the White House, the official expenses of the White House Office, the official entertainment expenses of the President, the official entertainment expenses for allocation within the Executive Office, and the subsistence expenses of Government personnel while traveling on official business in connection with the travel of the President; accounting of sums by President; inspection, certification and report to Congress by the Comptroller General concerning expenditures; and allotment of assistance and services to spouse of President or to a member of President's family; struck out provisions which authorized President to fix compensation of six administrative assistants, Executive Secretaries of the National Security Council, the National Aeronautics and Space Council, and the Economic Opportunity Council, and eight other secretaries or other immediate staff assistants in the White House Office, at rates of basic pay not to exceed the rate of Executive level II.

1967—Pub. L. 90–222 inserted position of Executive Secretary of the Economic Opportunity Council.

1964—Pub. L. 88–426 included Executive Secretary of the National Aeronautics and Space Council, and substituted provisions permitting President to fix compensation of enumerated personnel at rates of basic compensation not more than that of level II of the Federal Executive Salary Schedule for provisions which limited compensation of such personnel to two at rates not more than $22,500, three at not more than $21,000, seven at not more than $20,000 and three at not more than $18,500 per annum.

1961—Pub. L. 87–367 authorized President to increase compensation of three assistants to the President from $17,500 to $18,500 per annum.

1956—Act July 31, 1956, authorized President to fix compensation of an additional three secretaries or other immediate staff assistants, substituted "$22,500" for "$20,000", "$21,000" for "$18,000", and "$20,000" for "$15,000", and provided for payment of three at rates not exceeding $17,500 per annum.

1949—Act Oct. 15, 1949, increased compensation of secretaries, and executive, administrative, and staff assistants.

Effective Date of 1978 Amendment

Amendment by Pub. L. 95–570 applicable to any fiscal year beginning on or after Oct. 1, 1978, see section 6(a) of Pub. L. 95–570, set out as a note under section 102 of this title.

Effective Date of 1967 Amendment

Amendment by Pub. L. 90–222 effective immediately on enactment of Pub. L. 90–222, which was approved on Dec. 23, 1967, see section 401 of Pub. L. 90–222, set out as a note under section 2702 of Title 42, The Public Health and Welfare.

Effective Date of 1964 Amendment

Amendment by Pub. L. 88–426 effective on first day of first pay period which begins on or after July 1, 1964, except to the extent provided in section 501(c) of Pub. L. 88–426, see section 501 of Pub. L. 88–426.

Effective Date of 1961 Amendment

Amendment by Pub. L. 87–367 effective at beginning of first pay period which begins on or after sixtieth day following Oct. 4, 1961, see section 305 of Pub. L. 87–367.

Effective Date of 1956 Amendment

Amendment by act July 31, 1956, effective at beginning of first pay period commencing after June 30, 1956, see section 120 of act July 31, 1956.

Effective Date of 1949 Amendment

Amendment by act Oct. 15, 1949, effective on first day of first pay period after Oct. 15, 1949, see section 9 of that act, set out as a note under section 273 of Title 2, The Congress.

Repeals

Act July 31, 1956, ch. 804, title I, § 109, 70 Stat. 740, cited as a credit to this section, was repealed by Pub. L. 88–426, title III, § 305(1), Aug. 14, 1964, 78 Stat. 422.

Abolition of National Aeronautics and Space
Council

National Aeronautics and Space Council, including office of Executive Secretary of Council, together with functions of Council, abolished by section 3(a)(4) of 1973 Reorg. Plan No. 1, effective July 1, 1973, set out in the Appendix to Title 5, Government Organization and Employees.

References in Other Laws to GS–16, 17, or 18 Pay
Rates

References in laws to the rates of pay for GS–16, 17, or 18, or to maximum rates of pay under the General Schedule, to be considered references to rates payable under specified sections of Title 5, Government Organization and Employees, see section 529 [title I, § 101(c)(1)] of Pub. L. 101–509, set out in a note under section 5376 of Title 5.

§ 106. Assistance and services for the Vice President

(a) In order to enable the Vice President to provide assistance to the President in connection with the performance of functions specially assigned to the Vice President by the President in the discharge of executive duties and responsibilities, the Vice President is authorized—

(1) without regard to any other provision of law regulating the employment or compensation of persons in the Government service, to appoint and fix the pay of not more than—

(A) 5 employees at rates not to exceed the rate of basic pay then currently paid for level II of the Executive Schedule of section 5313 of title 5; and in addition

(B) 3 employees at rates not to exceed the rate of basic pay then currently paid for level III of the Executive Schedule of section 5314 of title 5; and in addition

(C) 3 employees at rates not to exceed the maximum rate of basic pay then currently paid for GS–18 of the General Schedule of section 5332 of title 5; and in addition

(D) such number of other employees as he may determine to be appropriate at rates not to exceed the minimum rate of basic pay then currently paid for GS–16 of the General Schedule of section 5332 of title 5; and

(2) to procure, as provided in appropriation Acts, temporary or intermittent services of experts and consultants, as described in and in accordance with the first two sentences of section 3109(b) of title 5, at respective daily rates of pay for individuals which are not more than the daily equivalent of the rate of basic pay then currently paid for level II of the Executive Schedule of section 5313 of title 5.

Notwithstanding such section 3109(b), temporary services of any expert or consultant described in such section 3109(b) may be procured under paragraph (2) of this subsection for a period in excess of one year if the Vice President determines such procurement is necessary.

(b) In order to carry out the executive duties and responsibilities referred to in subsection (a), there are authorized to be appropriated each fiscal year to the Vice President such sums as may be necessary for—

(1) the official expenses of the Office of the Vice President;

(2) the official entertainment expenses of the Vice President; and

(3) the subsistence expenses of persons in the Government service while traveling on official business in connection with the travel of the Vice President.

Sums appropriated under this subsection for expenses described in paragraphs (2) and (3) may be expended as the Vice President may determine, notwithstanding the provisions of any other law. Such sums shall be accounted for solely on the certificate of the Vice President, except that, with respect to such expenses, the Comptroller General may inspect all necessary books, documents, papers, and records relating to any such expenditures solely for the purpose of verifying that all such expenditures related to expenses in paragraph (2) or (3). The Comptroller General shall certify to Congress the fact of such verification, and shall report any such expenses not expended for such purpose.

(c) Assistance and services authorized pursuant to this section to the Vice President are authorized to be provided to the spouse of the Vice President in connection with assistance provided by such spouse to the Vice President in the discharge of the Vice President's executive duties and responsibilities. If the Vice President does not have a spouse, such assistance and services may be provided for such purposes to a member of the Vice President's family whom the Vice President designates.

(June 25, 1948, ch. 644, 62 Stat. 678; Oct. 15, 1949, ch. 695, § 2(b), 63 Stat. 880; Pub. L. 95–570, § 1(a), Nov. 2, 1978, 92 Stat. 2446.)

AMENDMENTS

1978—Pub. L. 95–570 inserted provisions relating to appointment and determination of pay by the Vice President of employees and procurement by the Vice President of temporary or intermittent services of experts and consultants to enable the Vice President to provide assistance to the President; appropriation of sums for the official expenses of the Office of the Vice President, the official entertainment expenses of the Vice President, and subsistence expenses of Government personnel while traveling on official business in connection with the travel of the Vice President; accounting of sums by the Vice President; inspection, certification and report to Congress by the Comptroller General concerning expenditures; and allotment of assistance and services to the spouse of the Vice President or to a member of the Vice President's family; struck out provisions which authorized the President to appoint and fix compensation of not to exceed six administrative assistants and directed that each assistant perform such duties as the President prescribed.

1949—Act Oct. 15, 1949, struck out salary provisions. See section 105 of this title.

EFFECTIVE DATE OF 1978 AMENDMENT

Amendment by Pub. L. 95–570 applicable to any fiscal year beginning on or after Oct. 1, 1978, see section 6(a) of Pub. L. 95–570, set out as a note under section 102 of this title.

EFFECTIVE DATE OF 1949 AMENDMENT

Amendment by act Oct. 15, 1949, effective on first day of first pay period after Oct. 15, 1949, see section 9 of that act, set out as a note under section 273 of Title 2, The Congress.

REFERENCES IN OTHER LAWS TO GS–16, 17, OR 18 PAY RATES

References in laws to the rates of pay for GS–16, 17, or 18, or to maximum rates of pay under the General Schedule, to be considered references to rates payable under specified sections of Title 5, Government Organization and Employees, see section 529 [title I, § 101(c)(1)] of Pub. L. 101–509, set out in a note under section 5376 of Title 5.

FORMER PRESIDENT'S OFFICE STAFF

See note under section 102 of this title.

EX. ORD. NO. 11456. SPECIAL ASSISTANT TO THE PRESIDENT FOR LIAISON WITH FORMER PRESIDENTS

Ex. Ord. No. 11456, Feb. 14, 1969, 34 F.R. 2301, provided:

By virtue of the authority vested in me as President of the United States, it is hereby ordered as follows:

SECTION 1. There shall be in the White House Office a Special Assistant to the President for Liaison with Former Presidents (referred to hereinafter as the Special Assistant).

SEC. 2. (a) On behalf of the President, the Special Assistant shall maintain channels of communication between the President and each former living President of the United States, to the end that (1) each such former President shall be kept abreast of such developments as the President may desire; and (2) the President may avail himself of the counsel and advice of any or all of such former Presidents with respect to major matters, particularly of a national security nature, currently confronting the President.

(b) The Special Assistant shall also—

(1) Keep each former President currently informed of the major aspects of such principal international and domestic problems as the President directs;

(2) Arrange to secure from such former Presidents, or any of them, and convey to the President, their views on such issues as the President may designate; and

(3) Arrange to secure and convey to the President such views as any of the former Presidents may wish to communicate to the President on any issue of current interest or concern.

SEC. 3. (a) The Secretary of State, the Secretary of Defense, the Director of the Central Intelligence Agency, and the Executive Secretary of the National Security Council shall each designate a member of his staff as a point of contact for the Special Assistant. The Special Assistant may call upon such designated staff members to supply information and render such other appropriate assistance as he may require in carrying out his duties under section 2 of this Order.

(b) Upon request of the Special Assistant, the head of any department or agency of the Federal Government shall designate a member of his staff as a point of contact to supply information and assistance for the Special Assistant in the performance of his duties in the same manner as provided in subsection (a) for staff members designated pursuant to that subsection.

SEC. 4. The Special Assistant shall be appointed by the President and shall serve at the pleasure of the President. He shall receive compensation at such rate as the President, consonant with law, may prescribe.

SEC. 5. (a) The Special Assistant shall have such staff and other assistance as may be necessary to carry out his duties under this Order.

(b) The Special Assistant shall be provided with such office space as may be necessary to carry out his duties under this Order, and shall also be provided with such office space, and maintenance thereof, as may be necessary for the use of former Presidents at the seat of Government when they are engaged in any effort of interest or concern to the President.

SEC. 6. (a) The compensation and expenses of the Special Assistant and members of his staff shall be paid from the appropriation under the heading "Special" in the Executive Office Appropriation Act, 1969, or any corresponding appropriation which may be made for subsequent fiscal years, or from such other appropriated funds as may be available under law.

(b) The General Services Administration shall provide, on a reimbursable basis, such administrative services and facilities for the Special Assistant as the White House Office may request.

RICHARD NIXON.

§ 107. Domestic Policy Staff and Office of Administration; personnel

(a) In order to enable the Domestic Policy Staff to perform its functions, the President (or his designee) is authorized—

(1) without regard to any other provision of law regulating the employment or compensation of persons in the Government service, to appoint and fix the pay of not more than—

(A) 6 employees at rates not to exceed the rate of basic pay then currently paid for level III of the Executive Schedule of section 5314 of title 5; and in addition

(B) 18 employees at rates not to exceed the maximum rate of basic pay then currently paid for GS–18 of the General Schedule of section 5332 of title 5; and in addition

(C) such number of other employees as he may determine to be appropriate at rates not to exceed the minimum rate of basic pay then currently paid for GS–16 of the General Schedule of section 5332 of title 5; and

(2) to procure, as provided in appropriation Acts, temporary or intermittent services of experts and consultants, as described in and in accordance with the first two sentences of section 3109(b) of title 5, at respective daily rates of pay for individuals which are not more than the daily equivalent of the rate of basic pay then currently paid for level III of the Executive Schedule of section 5314 of title 5.

(b)(1) In order to enable the Office of Administration to perform its functions, the President (or his designee) is authorized—

(A) without regard to such other provisions of law as the President may specify which regulate the employment and compensation of persons in the Government service, to appoint and fix the pay of not more than—

(i) 5 employees at rates not to exceed the rate of basic pay then currently paid for level III of the Executive Schedule of section 5314 of title 5; and in addition

(ii) 5 employees at rates not to exceed the maximum rate of basic pay then currently paid for GS–18 of the General Schedule of section 5332 of title 5; and

(B) to procure, as provided in appropriation Acts, temporary or intermittent services of experts and consultants, as described in and in accordance with the first two sentences of section 3109(b) of title 5, at respective daily rates of pay for individuals which are not more than the daily equivalent of the maximum rate of basic pay then currently paid for GS–18 of the General Schedule of section 5332 of title 5.

(2) In addition to any authority granted under paragraph (1) of this subsection, the President (or his designee) is authorized to employ individuals in the Office of Administration in accordance with section 3101 of title 5 and provisions relating thereto. Any individual so employed under the authority granted under such section 3101 shall be subject to the limitation specified in section 114 of this title.

(c) There are authorized to be appropriated each fiscal year such sums as may be necessary for the official expenses of the Domestic Policy Staff and the Office of Administration.

(Added Pub. L. 95–570, § 2(a), Nov. 2, 1978, 92 Stat. 2448.)

PRIOR PROVISIONS

A prior section 107, act June 25, 1948, ch. 644, 62 Stat. 679, providing that employees of the executive departments and independent establishments of the executive branch of the Government might be detailed from time to time to the White House Office for temporary assistance, was repealed by section 2(a) of Pub. L. 95–570. See section 112 of this title.

EFFECTIVE DATE

Section applicable to any fiscal year beginning on or after Oct. 1, 1978, see section 6(a) of Pub. L. 95–570, set out as an Effective Date of 1978 Amendment note under section 102 of this title.

REFERENCES IN OTHER LAWS TO GS–16, 17, OR 18 PAY RATES

References in laws to the rates of pay for GS–16, 17, or 18, or to maximum rates of pay under the General Schedule, to be considered references to rates payable under specified sections of Title 5, Government Organization and Employees, see section 529 [title I, § 101(c)(1)] of Pub. L. 101–509, set out in a note under section 5376 of Title 5.

APPLICABILITY OF SUBSEC. (b) TO CURRENT EMPLOYEES OF OFFICE OF ADMINISTRATION

Section 6(b) of Pub. L. 95–570 provided that: "In the case of an individual—

"(1) who is an employee of the Office of Administration as of the date of the enactment of this Act [Nov. 2, 1978], and

"(2) whose position would be terminated or whose rate of basic pay would be reduced (but for this subsection) by reason of section 107(b) of title 3, United States Code (as amended by this Act) [subsec. (b) of this section],

such employee may be allowed to continue to hold such position and receive basic pay at the rate in effect on the effective date of this Act [see Effective Date of 1978 Amendment note set out under section 102 of this title] during the period which begins on such date and ends 2 years after such date so long as such employee continues as an employee of the Office of Administration."

§ 108. Assistance to the President for unanticipated needs

(a) There is authorized to be appropriated to the President an amount not to exceed $1,000,000 each fiscal year to enable the President, in his discretion, to meet unanticipated needs for the furtherance of the national interest, security, or defense, including personnel needs and needs for services described in section 3109(b) of title 5, and administrative expenses related thereto, without regard to any provision of law regulating the employment or compensation of persons in the Government service or regulating expenditures of Government funds.

(b) The President shall transmit a report to each House of the Congress for each fiscal year beginning on or after the effective date of this subsection which sets forth the purposes for which expenditures were made under this section for such fiscal year and the amount expended for each such purpose. Each such report shall be transmitted no later than 60 days after the close of the fiscal year covered by such report.

(c) An individual may not be paid under the authority of this section at a rate of pay in excess of the rate of basic pay then currently paid for level II of the Executive Schedule of section 5313 of title 5.

(Added Pub. L. 95–570, § 2(a), Nov. 2, 1978, 92 Stat. 2449.)

REFERENCES IN TEXT

For the effective date of this subsection, referred to in subsec. (b), see section 6(a) of Pub. L. 95–570, set out as an Effective Date of 1978 Amendment note under section 102 of this title.

PRIOR PROVISIONS

A prior section 108, act June 25, 1948, ch. 644, 62 Stat. 679, directing the Quartermaster General of the Army to provide suitable accommodations for the horses, carriages, and other vehicles of the President and of the Executive Office, was repealed by act June 28, 1950, ch. 383, title IV, § 401(j), 64 Stat. 271.

Insofar as prior section 108, by virtue of a former proviso in section 401 of act June 28, 1950, continued to remain in effect to the extent that it was applicable to the Department of the Air Force, and the United States Air Force, it was additionally repealed by act Sept. 19, 1951, ch. 407, title IV, § 401(a)(1), 65 Stat. 333.

Act Oct. 31, 1951, ch. 654, § 1(2), 65 Stat. 701, repealed that part of act Mar. 4, 1911, ch. 285, § 1, 36 Stat. 1404, from which prior section 108, as enacted by act June 25, 1948, ch. 644, § 1, 62 Stat. 672, had been derived. That part of the 1911 act had previously been repealed by section 3 of the 1948 act.

EFFECTIVE DATE

Section applicable to any fiscal year beginning on or after Oct. 1, 1978, see section 6(a) of Pub. L. 95–570, set out as an Effective Date of 1978 Amendment note under section 102 of this title.

§ 109. Public property in and belonging to the Executive Residence at the White House

The steward, housekeeper, or such other employee of the Executive Residence at the White House as the President may designate, shall under the direction of the President, have the charge and custody of and be responsible for the plate, furniture, and public property therein. A complete inventory, in proper books, shall be made annually in the month of June, under the direction of the Director of the National Park Service, of all the public property in and belonging to the Executive Residence at the White House, showing when purchased, its cost, condition, and final disposition. This inventory shall be submitted to the President for his approval, and shall then be kept for reference in the office of the Director of the National Park Service, which shall furnish a copy thereof to the steward, housekeeper, or other employee responsible for the property.

(June 25, 1948, ch. 644, 62 Stat. 679; Pub. L. 92–310, title II, § 201, June 6, 1972, 86 Stat. 202; Pub. L. 95–570, § 5(b)(1), Nov. 2, 1978, 92 Stat. 2450.)

AMENDMENTS

1978—Pub. L. 95–570 substituted in section catchline "the Executive Residence at the White House" for "Executive Mansion" and in text "Executive Residence at the White House" for "Executive Mansion" in two places.

1972—Pub. L. 92–310 struck out provisions which required a bond in the sum of $10,000 from the person having charge and custody of the plate, furniture, and public property.

EFFECTIVE DATE OF 1978 AMENDMENT

Amendment by Pub. L. 95–570 applicable to any fiscal year beginning on or after Oct. 1, 1978, see section 6(a)

of Pub. L. 95–570, set out as a note under section 102 of this title.

TRANSFER OF FUNCTIONS

Functions of all other officers of Department of the Interior and functions of all agencies and employees of such Department, with two exceptions, transferred to Secretary of the Interior, with power vested in him to authorize their performance or performance of any of his functions by any of such officers, agencies, and employees, by 1950 Reorg. Plan No. 3, §§ 1, 2, eff. May 24, 1950, 15 F.R. 3174, 64 Stat. 1262, set out in the Appendix to Title 5, Government Organization and Employees.

§ 110. Furniture for the Executive Residence at the White House

All furniture purchased for the use of the Executive Residence at the White House shall be, as far as practicable, of domestic manufacture. With a view to conserving in the Executive Residence at the White House the best specimens of the early American furniture and furnishings, and for the purpose of maintaining the interior of the Executive Residence at the White House in keeping with its original design, the Director of the National Park Service is authorized and directed, with the approval of the President, to accept donations of furniture and furnishings for use in the Executive Residence at the White House, all such articles thus donated to become the property of the United States and to be accounted for as such. The said Director of the National Park Service is further authorized and directed, with the approval of the President, to appoint a temporary committee composed of one representative of the American Federation of Arts, one representative of the National Commission of Fine Arts, one representative of the National Academy of Design, one member of the American Institute of Architects, and five members representing the public at large; the said committee to have full power to select and pass on the articles in question and to recommend the same for acceptance.

(June 25, 1948, ch. 644, 62 Stat. 679; Pub. L. 95–570, § 5(c)(1), Nov. 2, 1978, 92 Stat. 2451.)

AMENDMENTS

1978—Pub. L. 95–570 inserted in section catchline "the Executive Residence at the" before "White House" and substituted in text "Executive Residence at the White House" for "President's House" and "Executive Residence at the White House" for "White House" wherever appearing.

EFFECTIVE DATE OF 1978 AMENDMENT

Amendment by Pub. L. 95–570 applicable to any fiscal year beginning on or after Oct. 1, 1978, see section 6(a) of Pub. L. 95–570, set out as a note under section 102 of this title.

TRANSFER OF FUNCTIONS

Functions of officers of Department of the Interior and functions of all agencies and employees of such Department, with two exceptions, transferred to Secretary of the Interior, see Transfer of Functions note set out under section 109 of this title.

COMMISSION ON RENOVATION OF THE EXECUTIVE MANSION

Act Apr. 14, 1949, ch. 51, 63 Stat. 45, authorized appointment of a commission of six to supervise and approve all construction plans and work necessary to remedy the present unsafe conditions in the Executive Mansion and to modernize same.

WHITE HOUSE; ADMINISTRATION; PRESERVATION OF MUSEUM CHARACTER; ARTICLES OF HISTORIC OR ARTISTIC INTEREST

Pub. L. 87–286, Sept. 22, 1961, 75 Stat. 586, provided: "That all of that portion of reservation numbered 1 in the city of Washington, District of Columbia, which is within the President's park enclosure, comprising eighteen and seven one-hundredths acres, shall continue to be known as the White House and shall be administered pursuant to the Act of August 25, 1916 (39 Stat. 535; 16 U.S.C. 1–3), and Acts supplementary thereto and amendatory thereof. In carrying out this Act primary attention shall be given to the preservation and interpretation of the museum character of the principal corridor on the ground floor and the principal public rooms on the first floor of the White House, but nothing done under this Act shall conflict with the administration of the Executive offices of the President or with the use and occupancy of the buildings and grounds as the home of the President and his family and for his official purposes.

"SEC. 2. Articles of furniture, fixtures, and decorative objects of the White House, when declared by the President to be of historic or artistic interest, together with such similar articles, fixtures, and objects as are acquired by the White House in the future when similarly so declared, shall thereafter be considered to be inalienable and the property of the White House. Any such article, fixture, or object when not in use or on display in the White House shall be transferred by direction of the President as a loan to the Smithsonian Institution for its care, study, and storage or exhibition and such articles, fixtures, and objects shall be returned to the White House from the Smithsonian Institution on notice by the President.

"SEC. 3. Nothing in this Act shall alter any privileges, powers, or duties vested in the White House Police and the United States Secret Service, Treasury Department, by [former] section 202 of title 3, United States Code, and section 3056 of title 18, United States Code."

[For transfer of the functions, personnel, assets, and obligations of the United States Secret Service, including the functions of the Secretary of the Treasury relating thereto, to the Secretary of Homeland Security, and for treatment of related references, see sections 381, 551(d), 552(d), and 557 of Title 6, Domestic Security, and the Department of Homeland Security Reorganization Plan of November 25, 2002, as modified, set out as a note under section 542 of Title 6.]

EX. ORD. NO. 11145. CURATOR OF WHITE HOUSE; COMMITTEE FOR PRESERVATION OF WHITE HOUSE

Ex. Ord. No. 11145, Mar. 7, 1964, 29 F.R. 3189, as amended by Ex. Ord. No. 11565, Oct. 13, 1970, 35 F.R. 16155, provided:

WHEREAS the White House, as the home of the highest elective officer of the United States

—symbolizes the American ideal of responsible self-government

—is emblematic of our democracy and our national purpose

—has been intimately associated with the personal and social life of the Presidents of the United States and many of their official acts

—occupies a particular place in the heart of every American citizen, and

WHEREAS certain historic rooms and entranceways in the White House

—possess great human interest and historic significance

—traditionally have been open to visitors

—have provided pleasure and patriotic inspiration to millions of our citizens

—have come to be regarded as a public museum and the proud possession of all Americans, and

WHEREAS the Congress by law (Act of September 22, 1961), (75 Stat. 586) [set out as a note under this section] has authorized the care and preservation of the historic and artistic contents of the White House and has given the President certain responsibilities with regard thereto:

NOW, THEREFORE, by virtue of the authority vested in me as President of the United States, it is ordered as follows:

SECTION 1. (a) There shall be in the White House a Curator of the White House. The Curator shall assist in the preservation and protection of the articles of furniture, fixtures, and decorative objects used or displayed in the principal corridor on the ground floor and the principal public rooms on the first floor of the White House, and in such other areas in the White House as the President may designate.

(b) The Curator shall report to the President and shall make recommendations with respect to the articles, fixtures, and objects to be declared by the President, under section 2 of the Act of September 22, 1961, to be of historic or artistic interest.

SEC. 2. There is hereby established the Committee for the Preservation of the White House, hereinafter referred to as the "Committee". The Committee shall be composed of the Director of the National Park Service, the Curator of the White House, the Secretary of the Smithsonian Institution, the Chairman of the Commission of Fine Arts, the Director of the National Gallery of Art, the Chief Usher of the White House, and so many other members as the President may from time to time appoint. The Director of the National Park Service shall serve as Chairman of the Committee and shall designate an employee of that Service to act as Executive Secretary of the Committee. Members of the Committee shall serve without compensation.

SEC. 3. (a) The Committee shall report to the President and shall advise the Director of the National Park Service with respect to the discharge of his responsibility under the Act of September 22, 1961, for the preservation and the interpretation of the museum character of the principal corridor on the ground floor and the principal public rooms on the first floor of the White House. Among other things, the Committee shall make recommendations as to the articles of furniture, fixtures, and decorative objects which shall be used or displayed in the aforesaid areas of the White House and as to the decor and arrangements therein best suited to enhance the historic and artistic values of the White House and of such articles, fixtures, and objects.

(b) The Committee shall cooperate with the White House Historical Association, a nonprofit organization heretofore formed under the laws of the District of Columbia.

(c) The Committee is authorized to invite individuals who are distinguished or interested in the fine arts to attend its meetings or otherwise to assist in carrying out its functions.

SEC. 4. Consonant with law, each Federal department and agency represented on the Committee shall furnish necessary assistance to the Committee in accordance with section 214 of the Act of May 3, 1945, 59 Stat. 134 (31 U.S.C. 691) [31 U.S.C. 1346(b)]. The Department of the Interior shall furnish necessary administrative services for the Committee.

EXTENSION OF TERM OF COMMITTEE FOR THE PRESERVATION OF THE WHITE HOUSE

Term of the Committee for the Preservation of the White House extended until Dec. 31, 1978, by Ex. Ord. No. 11948, Dec. 20, 1976, 41 F.R. 55705, formerly set out as a note under section 14 of the Federal Advisory Committee Act in the Appendix to Title 5, Government Organization and Employees.

Term of the Committee for the Preservation of the White House extended until Dec. 31, 1980, by Ex. Ord. No. 12110, Dec. 28, 1978, 44 F.R. 1069, formerly set out as a note under section 14 of the Federal Advisory Committee Act in the Appendix to Title 5.

Term of the Committee for the Preservation of the White House extended until Dec. 31, 1982, by Ex. Ord.

No. 12258, Dec. 31, 1980, 46 F.R. 1251, formerly set out as a note under section 14 of the Federal Advisory Committee Act in the Appendix to Title 5.

Term of the Committee for the Preservation of the White House extended until Sept. 30, 1984, by Ex. Ord. No. 12399, Dec. 31, 1982, 48 F.R. 379, formerly set out as a note under section 14 of the Federal Advisory Committee Act in the Appendix to Title 5.

Term of the Committee for the Preservation of the White House extended until Sept. 30, 1985, by Ex. Ord. No. 12489, Sept. 28, 1984, 49 F.R. 38927, formerly set out as a note under section 14 of the Federal Advisory Committee Act in the Appendix to Title 5.

Term of the Committee for the Preservation of the White House extended until Sept. 30, 1987, by Ex. Ord. No. 12534, Sept. 30, 1985, 50 F.R. 40319, formerly set out as a note under section 14 of the Federal Advisory Committee Act in the Appendix to Title 5.

Term of the Committee for the Preservation of the White House extended until Sept. 30, 1989, by Ex. Ord. No. 12610, Sept. 30, 1987, 52 F.R. 36901, formerly set out as a note under section 14 of the Federal Advisory Committee Act in the Appendix to Title 5.

Term of the Committee for the Preservation of the White House extended until Sept. 30, 1991, by Ex. Ord. No. 12692, Sept. 29, 1989, 54 F.R. 40627, formerly set out as a note under section 14 of the Federal Advisory Committee Act in the Appendix to Title 5.

Term of the Committee for the Preservation of the White House extended until Sept. 30, 1993, by Ex. Ord. No. 12774, Sept. 27, 1991, 56 F.R. 49835, formerly set out as a note under section 14 of the Federal Advisory Committee Act in the Appendix to Title 5.

Term of the Committee for the Preservation of the White House extended until Sept. 30, 1995, by Ex. Ord. No. 12869, Sept. 30, 1993, 58 F.R. 51751, formerly set out as a note under section 14 of the Federal Advisory Committee Act in the Appendix to Title 5.

Term of the Committee for the Preservation of the White House extended until Sept. 30, 1997, by Ex. Ord. No. 12974, Sept. 29, 1995, 60 F.R. 51875, formerly set out as a note under section 14 of the Federal Advisory Committee Act in the Appendix to Title 5.

Term of the Committee for the Preservation of the White House extended until Sept. 30, 1999, by Ex. Ord. No. 13062, Sept. 29, 1997, 62 F.R. 51755, formerly set out as a note under section 14 of the Federal Advisory Committee Act in the Appendix to Title 5.

Term of the Committee for the Preservation of the White House extended until Sept. 30, 2001, by Ex. Ord. No. 13138, Sept. 30, 1999, 64 F.R. 53879, formerly set out as a note under section 14 of the Federal Advisory Committee Act in the Appendix to Title 5.

Term of the Committee for the Preservation of the White House extended until Sept. 30, 2003, by Ex. Ord. No. 13225, Sept. 28, 2001, 66 F.R. 50291, formerly set out as a note under section 14 of the Federal Advisory Committee Act in the Appendix to Title 5.

Term of the Committee for the Preservation of the White House extended until Sept. 30, 2005, by Ex. Ord. No. 13316, Sept. 17, 2003, 68 F.R. 55255, formerly set out as a note under section 14 of the Federal Advisory Committee Act in the Appendix to Title 5.

Term of the Committee for the Preservation of the White House extended until Sept. 30, 2007, by Ex. Ord. No. 13385, Sept. 29, 2005, 70 F.R. 57989, formerly set out as a note under section 14 of the Federal Advisory Committee Act in the Appendix to Title 5.

Term of the Committee for the Preservation of the White House extended until Sept. 30, 2009, by Ex. Ord. No. 13446, Sept. 28, 2007, 72 F.R. 56175, formerly set out as a note under section 14 of the Federal Advisory Committee Act in the Appendix to Title 5.

Term of the Committee for the Preservation of the White House extended until Sept. 30, 2011, by Ex. Ord. No. 13511, Sept. 29, 2009, 74 F.R. 50909, formerly set out as a note under section 14 of the Federal Advisory Committee Act in the Appendix to Title 5.

Term of the Committee for the Preservation of the White House extended until Sept. 30, 2013, by Ex. Ord.

No. 13585, Sept. 30, 2011, 76 F.R. 62281, set out as a note under section 14 of the Federal Advisory Committee Act in the Appendix to Title 5.

§ 111. Expense allowance of Vice President

There shall be paid to the Vice President in equal monthly installments an expense allowance of $20,000 per annum to assist in defraying expenses relating to or resulting from the discharge of his official duties, for which no accounting, other than for income tax purposes, shall be made by him.

(Added Jan. 19, 1949, ch. 2, § 1(c), 63 Stat. 4; amended Oct. 20, 1951, ch. 521, title VI, § 619(b), 65 Stat. 570; Pub. L. 108–7, div. H, title I, § 1(a), Feb. 20, 2003, 117 Stat. 348.)

AMENDMENTS

2003—Pub. L. 108–7 substituted "$20,000" for "$10,000".

1951—Act Oct. 20, 1951, made Vice President's expense allowance taxable.

EFFECTIVE DATE OF 2003 AMENDMENT

Amendment by Pub. L. 108–7 applicable to fiscal year 2003 and each fiscal year thereafter, see section 1(f) of Pub. L. 108–7, set out as a note under section 31a–1 of Title 2, The Congress.

EFFECTIVE DATE OF 1951 AMENDMENT

Amendment by act Oct. 20, 1951, effective at noon on Jan. 20, 1953, see section 619(e) of that act, set out as a note under section 102 of this title.

EFFECTIVE DATE

Section effective noon, Jan. 20, 1949, see section 3 of act Jan. 19, 1949.

OFFICIAL TEMPORARY RESIDENCE OF THE VICE PRESIDENT

Pub. L. 93–346, July 12, 1974, 88 Stat. 340, as amended by Pub. L. 93–552, title VI, § 609(a), Dec. 27, 1974, 88 Stat. 1764; Pub. L. 107–67, title VI, §§ 635, 636, Nov. 12, 2001, 115 Stat. 553, provided: "That effective July 1, 1974, the Government-owned house together with furnishings, associated grounds (consisting of twelve acres, more or less), and related facilities which have heretofore been used as the residence of the Chief of Naval Operations, Department of the Navy, shall, on and after such date be available for, and are hereby designated as, the temporary official residence of the Vice President of the United States.

"SEC. 2. The temporary official residence of the Vice President shall be adequately staffed and provided with such appropriate equipment, furnishings, dining facilities, services, and other provisions as may be required, under the supervision and direction of the Vice President, to enable him to perform and discharge appropriately the duties, functions, and obligations associated with his high office.

"SEC. 3. The Secretary of the Navy shall, subject to the supervision and control of the Vice President, provide for the military staffing, utilities (including electrical) for, and the care and maintenance of the grounds of the temporary official residence of the Vice President and, subject to reimbursement therefor out of funds appropriated for such purposes, provide for the civilian staffing, care, maintenance, repair, improvement, alteration, and furnishing of such residence.

"SEC. 4. There is hereby authorized to be appropriated such sums as may be necessary from time to time to carry out the foregoing provisions of this joint resolution. During any interim period until and before any such funds are so appropriated, the Secretary of the Navy shall make provision for staffing and other appropriate services in connection with the temporary official residence of the Vice President from funds available to the Department of the Navy, subject to reimbursement therefor from funds subsequently appropriated to carry out the purposes of this joint resolution.

"SEC. 5. After the date on which the Vice President moves into the temporary official residence provided for in this joint resolution no funds may be expended for the maintenance, care, repair, furnishing, or security of any residence for the Vice President other than the temporary official residence provided for in this joint resolution unless the expenditure of such funds is specifically authorized by law enacted after such date.

"SEC. 6. The Secretary of the Navy is authorized and directed, with the approval of the Vice President, to accept donations of money or property for the furnishing of or making improvements in or about, or for use at official functions in or about, the temporary official residence of the Vice President, all such donations to become the property of the United States and to be accounted for as such.

"SEC. 7. [Amended former section 202 of this title].

"SEC. 8. [Amended section 3056(a) of title 18].

"SEC. 9. It is the sense of Congress that living accommodations, generally equivalent to those available to the highest ranking officer on active duty in each of the other military services, should be provided for the Chief of Naval Operations."

OFFICIAL RESIDENCE FOR THE VICE PRESIDENT; DESIGN AND CONSTRUCTION; AUTHORIZATION OF APPROPRIATION

Pub. L. 89–386, Apr. 9, 1966, 80 Stat. 106, provided: "That the Administrator of General Services is hereby authorized to plan, design, and construct an official residence for the Vice President of the United States in the District of Columbia.

"SEC. 2. The Administrator is further authorized to use as a site for such residence Federal land and property comprising approximately ten acres at the United States Naval Observatory, the specific area and boundaries thereof to be determined jointly by the General Services Administration and the Department of the Navy: *Provided*, That any roads and improvements thereon for which there is a continued need may be relocated and reconstructed.

"SEC. 3. The Administrator is further authorized to provide for the care, maintenance, repair, improvement, alteration, and furnishing of the official residence and grounds, including heating, lighting, and air conditioning, which services shall be provided at the expense of the United States.

"SEC. 4. The Administrator of General Services is further authorized to accept cash gifts, furniture, and furnishings and other types of gifts on behalf of the United States for use in constructing and furnishing the official residence but without further conditions on use, all such articles thus given to become the property of the United States.

"SEC. 5. There is authorized to be appropriated to the General Services Administration, the sum of $750,000 for planning, design, construction, and costs incidental thereto, including the cost of initial furnishings.

"SEC. 6. There is further authorized to be appropriated to the General Services Administration, annually, such amounts as may be necessary to carry out the purposes of section 3."

§112. Detail of employees of executive departments

The head of any department, agency, or independent establishment of the executive branch of the Government may detail, from time to time, employees of such department, agency, or establishment to the White House Office, the Executive Residence at the White House, the Office of the Vice President, the Domestic Policy Staff, and the Office of Administration. Any such office to which an employee has been detailed for service to such office shall reimburse the detailing department, agency, or establishment for the pay of each employee thereof—

(1) who is so detailed, and

(2) who is performing services which have been or would otherwise be performed by an employee of such office,

for any period occurring during any fiscal year after 180 calendar days after the employee is detailed in such year.

(Added Pub. L. 95–570, §3(a), Nov. 2, 1978, 92 Stat. 2449.)

EFFECTIVE DATE

Section applicable to any fiscal year beginning on or after Oct. 1, 1978, see section 6(a) of Pub. L. 95–570, set out as an Effective Date of 1978 Amendment note under section 102 of this title.

AUTHORITY WITH RESPECT TO DETAILED EMPLOYEES

Pub. L. 107–67, title VI, §637, Nov. 12, 2001, 115 Stat. 553, provided that: "During fiscal year 2002 and thereafter, the head of an entity named in 3 U.S.C. 112 may, with respect to civilian personnel of any branch of the Federal Government performing duties in such entity, exercise authority comparable to the authority that may by law (including chapter 57 and sections 8344 and 8468 of title 5, United States Code) be exercised with respect to the employees of an Executive agency (as defined in 5 U.S.C. 105) by the head of such Executive agency, and the authority granted by this section shall be in addition to any other authority available in law."

§113. Personnel report

(a) The President shall transmit to each House of the Congress, and make available to the public, reports containing information described in subsection (b) for each fiscal year beginning on or after the effective date of this section. Each such report shall be transmitted no later than 60 days after the close of the fiscal year covered by such report and shall contain a statement of such information for such year.

(b) Each report required under subsection (a) shall contain—

(1) the number of employees who are paid at a rate of basic pay equal to or greater than the rate of basic pay then currently paid for level V of the Executive Schedule of section 5316 of title 5 and who are employed in the White House Office, the Executive Residence at the White House, the Office of the Vice President, the Domestic Policy Staff, or the Office of Administration, and the aggregate amount paid to such employees;

(2) the number of employees employed in such offices who are paid at a rate of basic pay which is equal to or greater than the minimum rate of basic pay then currently paid for GS–16 of the General Schedule of section 5332 of title 5 but which is less than the rate then currently paid for level V of the Executive Schedule of section 5316 of title V[1] and the aggregate amount paid to such employees;

(3) the number of employees employed in such offices who are paid at a rate of basic pay which is less than the minimum rate then currently paid for GS–16 of the General Schedule of section 5332 of title V[1], and the aggregate amount paid to such employees;

---

[1] So in original. Probably should be title "5".

(4) the number of individuals detailed under section 112 of this title for more than 30 days to each such office, the number of days in excess of 30 each individual was detailed, and the aggregate amount of reimbursement made as provided by the provisions of section 112 of this title; and

(5) the number of individuals whose services as experts or consultants are procured under this chapter for service in any such office, the total number of days employed, and the aggregate amount paid to procure such services.

The information required under this subsection to be in any report shall be shown both in the aggregate and by office involved.

(Added Pub. L. 95–570, § 3(a), Nov. 2, 1978, 92 Stat. 2449.)

REFERENCES IN TEXT

For the effective date of this section, referred to in subsec. (a), see section 6(a) of Pub. L. 95–570, set out as an Effective Date of 1978 Amendment note under section 102 of this title.

EFFECTIVE DATE

Section applicable to any fiscal year beginning on or after Oct. 1, 1978, see section 6(a) of Pub. L. 95–570, set out as an Effective Date of 1978 Amendment note under section 102 of this title.

TERMINATION OF REPORTING REQUIREMENTS

For termination, effective May 15, 2000, of provisions of law requiring submittal to Congress of any annual, semiannual, or other regular periodic report listed in House Document No. 103–7 (in which the report required by subsec. (a) of this section is listed on page 21), see section 3003 of Pub. L. 104–66, as amended, set out as a note under section 1113 of Title 31, Money and Finance.

REFERENCES IN OTHER LAWS TO GS–16, 17, OR 18 PAY RATES

References in laws to the rates of pay for GS–16, 17, or 18, or to maximum rates of pay under the General Schedule, to be considered references to rates payable under specified sections of Title 5, Government Organization and Employees, see section 529 [title I, § 101(c)(1)] of Pub. L. 101–509, set out in a note under section 5376 of Title 5.

REPORT ON WHITE HOUSE OFFICE PERSONNEL

Pub. L. 103–270, § 6, June 30, 1994, 108 Stat. 737, provided that:

"(a) SUBMISSION OF REPORT.—On July 1 of each year, the President shall submit a report described in subsection (b) to the Committee on Governmental Affairs [now Committee on Homeland Security and Governmental Affairs] of the Senate and the Committee on Government Operations of the House of Representatives.

"(b) CONTENTS.—A report under subsection (a) shall, except as provided in subsection (c), include—

"(1) a list of each individual—

"(A) employed by the White House Office; or

"(B) detailed to the White House Office; and

"(2) with regard to each individual described in paragraph (1), the individual's—

"(A) name;

"(B) position and title; and

"(C) annual rate of pay.

"(c) EXCLUSION FROM REPORT.—If the President determines that disclosure of any item of information described in subsection (b) with respect to any particular individual would not be in the interest of the national defense or foreign policy of the United States—

"(1) a report under subsection (a) shall—

"(A) exclude such information with respect to that individual; and

"(B) include a statement of the number of individuals with respect to whom such information has been excluded; and

"(2) at the request of the Committee on Governmental Affairs [now Committee on Homeland Security and Governmental Affairs] of the Senate or the Committee on Government Operations of the House of Representatives, the information that was excluded from the report shall be made available for inspection by such committee."

[Committee on Government Operations of House of Representatives treated as referring to Committee on Government Reform and Oversight of House of Representatives by section 1(a) of Pub. L. 104–14, set out as a note under section 21 of Title 2, The Congress. Committee on Government Reform and Oversight of House of Representatives changed to Committee on Government Reform of House of Representatives by House Resolution No. 5, One Hundred Sixth Congress, Jan. 6, 1999. Committee on Government Reform of House of Representatives changed to Committee on Oversight and Government Reform of House of Representatives by House Resolution No. 6, One Hundred Tenth Congress, Jan. 5, 2007.]

[Section 6 of Pub. L. 103–270, set out above, effective Jan. 1, 1995, see section 7(i) of Pub. L. 103–270, set out as an Effective Date of 1994 Amendment; Transition Provisions note under section 591 of Title 28, Judiciary and Judicial Procedure.]

§ 114. General pay limitation

Notwithstanding any provision of law, other than the provisions of this chapter, no employee of the White House Office, the Executive Residence at the White House, the Domestic Policy Staff, or the Office of Administration, nor any employee under the Vice President appointed under section 106 of this title, may be paid at a rate of basic pay in excess of the minimum rate of basic pay then currently paid for GS–16 of the General Schedule of section 5332 of title 5.

(Added Pub. L. 95–570, § 3(a), Nov. 2, 1978, 92 Stat. 2450.)

EFFECTIVE DATE

Section applicable to any fiscal year beginning on or after Oct. 1, 1978, see section 6(a) of Pub. L. 95–570, set out as an Effective Date of 1978 Amendment note under section 102 of this title.

REFERENCES IN OTHER LAWS TO GS–16, 17, OR 18 PAY RATES

References in laws to the rates of pay for GS–16, 17, or 18, or to maximum rates of pay under the General Schedule, to be considered references to rates payable under specified sections of Title 5, Government Organization and Employees, see section 529 [title I, § 101(c)(1)] of Pub. L. 101–509, set out in a note under section 5376 of Title 5.

§ 115. Veterans' preference

(a) Subject to subsection (b), appointments under sections 105, 106, and 107 shall be made in accordance with section 2108, and sections 3309 through 3312, of title 5.

(b) Subsection (a) shall not apply to any appointment to a position the rate of basic pay for which is at least equal to the minimum rate established for positions in the Senior Executive Service under section 5382 of title 5 and the duties of which are comparable to those described in section 3132(a)(2) of such title or to any other position if, with respect to such position, the President makes certification—

(1) that such position is—
(A) a confidential or policy-making position; or
(B) a position for which political affiliation or political philosophy is otherwise an important qualification; and

(2) that any individual selected for such position is expected to vacate the position at or before the end of the President's term (or terms) of office.

Each individual appointed to a position described in the preceding sentence as to which the expectation described in paragraph (2) applies shall be notified as to such expectation, in writing, at the time of appointment to such position.

(Added Pub. L. 105–339, §4(b)(1), Oct. 31, 1998, 112 Stat. 3185.)

[CHAPTER 3—REPEALED]

[§ 201. Repealed. July 16, 1951, ch. 226, § 5(a), 65 Stat. 122]

Section, act June 25, 1948, ch. 644, 62 Stat. 680, related to protection of President and family. See section 3056 of Title 18, Crimes and Criminal Procedure.

[§§ 202 to 204. Repealed. Pub. L. 109–177, title VI, § 605(c), Mar. 9, 2006, 120 Stat. 255]

Section 202, acts June 25, 1948, ch. 644, 62 Stat. 680; Pub. L. 87–481, §1, June 8, 1962, 76 Stat. 95; Pub. L. 91–217, §1(2), (3), Mar. 19, 1970, 84 Stat. 74; Pub. L. 93–346, §7, July 12, 1974, as added Pub. L. 93–552, title VI, §609(a), Dec. 27, 1974, 88 Stat. 1765; Pub. L. 94–196, §1(a), (b), Dec. 31, 1975, 89 Stat. 1109; Pub. L. 95–179, Nov. 15, 1977, 91 Stat. 1371; Pub. L. 95–570, §5(d), Nov. 2, 1978, 92 Stat. 2451; Pub. L. 97–418, §1(a), Jan. 4, 1983, 96 Stat. 2089; Pub. L. 99–500, §101(m) [title VI, §622], Oct. 18, 1986, 100 Stat. 1783–308, 1783–333; Pub. L. 99–591, §101(m) [title VI, §622], Oct. 30, 1986, 100 Stat. 3341–308, 3341–333; Pub. L. 102–138, title I, §135(b)(1)–(3), Oct. 28, 1991, 105 Stat. 666, 667; Pub. L. 102–499, §3(a), Oct. 24, 1992, 106 Stat. 3264; Pub. L. 107–296, title XVII, §1703(a)(1), Nov. 25, 2002, 116 Stat. 2313, related to establishment, control, supervision, privileges, powers, and duties of United States Secret Service Uniformed Division.

Section 203, acts June 25, 1948, ch. 644, 62 Stat. 680; Aug. 15, 1950, ch. 715, §2, 64 Stat. 448; June 28, 1952, ch. 481, 66 Stat. 283; Pub. L. 87–481, §2, June 8, 1962, 76 Stat. 95; Pub. L. 91–217, §1(1), (4)–(6), Mar. 19, 1970, 84 Stat. 74, 75; Pub. L. 94–196, §1(c), Dec. 31, 1975, 89 Stat. 1109; Pub. L. 95–179, Nov. 15, 1977, 91 Stat. 1371; Pub. L. 104–208, div. A, title I, §101(f) [title I], Sept. 30, 1996, 110 Stat. 3009–314, 3009–324, related to personnel, appointment, and vacancies in the United States Secret Service Uniformed Division.

Section 204, acts June 25, 1948, ch. 644, 62 Stat. 680; June 20, 1953, ch. 146, title IV, §402, 67 Stat. 76; Pub. L. 85–584, title V, §502(a), Aug. 1, 1958, 72 Stat. 485; Pub. L. 91–217, §1(1), Mar. 19, 1970, 84 Stat. 74; Pub. L. 95–179, Nov. 15, 1977, 91 Stat. 1371, related to grades, salaries, and transfers of appointees to the United States Secret Service Uniformed Division.

See section 3056A of Title 18, Crimes and Criminal Procedure.

[§ 205. Repealed. Pub. L. 91–217, § 1(7), Mar. 19, 1970, 84 Stat. 75]

Section, act June 25, 1948, ch. 644, 62 Stat. 680, provided for appointment of members of White House Police force in accordance with civil service laws.

[§§ 206 to 209. Repealed. Pub. L. 109–177, title VI, § 605(c), Mar. 9, 2006, 120 Stat. 255]

Section 206, acts June 25, 1948, ch. 644, 62 Stat. 681; Pub. L. 91–217, §1(8), Mar. 19, 1970, 84 Stat. 75; Pub. L. 95–179, Nov. 15, 1977, 91 Stat. 1371, related to privileges of civil-service appointees.

Section 207, acts June 25, 1948, ch. 644, 62 Stat. 681; Pub. L. 91–217, §1(1), Mar. 19, 1970, 84 Stat. 74; Pub. L. 95–179, Nov. 15, 1977, 91 Stat. 1371, related to participation in police and firemen's relief fund.

Section 208, added Pub. L. 94–196, §1(d)(1), Dec. 31, 1975, 89 Stat. 1109; amended Pub. L. 97–418, §1(b), Jan. 4, 1983, 96 Stat. 2089; Pub. L. 99–93, title I, §126(c), Aug. 16, 1985, 99 Stat. 418; Pub. L. 99–399, title IV, §410, Aug. 27, 1986, 100 Stat. 866; Pub. L. 102–138, title I, §135(a)(1), (2), (c), Oct. 28, 1991, 105 Stat. 666, 667; Pub. L. 107–296, title XVII, §1703(a)(2), Nov. 25, 2002, 116 Stat. 2313, related to reimbursement of State and local governments.

Section 209, acts June 25, 1948, ch. 644, 62 Stat. 681, §208; renumbered §209, Pub. L. 94–196, §1(d)(1), Dec. 31, 1975, 89 Stat. 1109, related to authorization of appropriations to carry out provisions.

See section 3056A of Title 18, Crimes and Criminal Procedure.

CHAPTER 4—DELEGATION OF FUNCTIONS

Sec.	
301.	General authorization to delegate functions; publication of delegations.
302.	Scope of delegation of functions.
303.	Definitions.

SIMILAR PROVISIONS; REPEAL; SAVING CLAUSE

Similar provisions were contained in former chapter 4, comprising former sections 301 to 303 of this title, which was set out here but which was not a part of this title. Former sections 301 to 303 were derived from act Aug. 8, 1950, ch. 646, §§1–3, 64 Stat. 419, and were repealed by section 56(j) of act Oct. 31, 1951. Subsec. (*l*) of section 56 provided that the repeal should not affect any rights or liabilities existing under the repealed sections on the effective date of the repeal (Oct. 31, 1951).

§ 301. General authorization to delegate functions; publication of delegations

The President of the United States is authorized to designate and empower the head of any department or agency in the executive branch, or any official thereof who is required to be appointed by and with the advice and consent of the Senate, to perform without approval, ratification, or other action by the President (1) any function which is vested in the President by law, or (2) any function which such officer is required or authorized by law to perform only with or subject to the approval, ratification, or other action of the President: *Provided*, That nothing contained herein shall relieve the President of his responsibility in office for the acts of any such head or other official designated by him to perform such functions. Such designation and authorization shall be in writing, shall be published in the Federal Register, shall be subject to such terms, conditions, and limitations as the President may deem advisable, and shall be revocable at any time by the President in whole or in part.

(Added Oct. 31, 1951, ch. 655, § 10, 65 Stat. 712.)

TRANSFER OF FUNCTIONS

Functions vested by law (including reorganization plan) in Bureau of the Budget or Director of Bureau of the Budget transferred to President by section 101 of

1970 Reorg. Plan No. 2, eff. July 1, 1970, 35 F.R. 7959, 84 Stat. 2085. Section 102 of 1970 Reorg. Plan No. 2, redesignated Bureau of the Budget as Office of Management and Budget and Director of Bureau of the Budget as Director of Office of Management and Budget. See Reorganization Plan No. 2 of 1970, set out in the Appendix to Title 5, Government Organization and Employees.

SIMILAR PROVISIONS; REPEAL; SAVING CLAUSE

For similar provisions contained in prior law, and saving clause in connection therewith, see note preceding this section.

EX. ORD. NO. 10250. DELEGATION OF FUNCTIONS TO THE SECRETARY OF THE INTERIOR

Ex. Ord. No. 10250, June 5, 1951, 16 F.R. 5385, as amended by Ex. Ord. No. 10732, Oct. 10, 1957, 22 F.R. 8135; Ex. Ord. No. 10752, Feb. 12, 1958, 23 F.R. 973; Pub. L. 101–509, title V, § 529 [title I, § 112(c)], Nov. 5, 1990, 104 Stat. 1427, 1454, provided:

1. The Secretary of the Interior is hereby designated and empowered to perform the following-described functions of the President without the approval, ratification, or other action of the President:

(a) The authority vested in the President by section 1 of the act of July 10, 1935, ch. 375, 49 Stat. 477 [see 16 U.S.C. 19e to 19n], to appoint members of the National Park Trust Fund Board.

(b) The authority vested in the President by section 2059 of the Revised Statutes [25 U.S.C. 62] to discontinue any Indian agency, or transfer the same, from the place or tribe designated by law to such other place or tribe as the public service may require.

(c) The authority vested in the President by section 6 of the act of May 17, 1882, ch. 168, 22 Stat. 88, as amended [25 U.S.C. 63], to consolidate two or more Indian agencies into one, to consolidate one or more Indian tribes, and to abolish such agencies as are thereby rendered unnecessary.

(d) The authority vested in the President by the act of March 1, 1907, ch. 2285, 34 Stat. 1016 [25 U.S.C. 140], to divert appropriations made for certain purposes to other uses for the benefit of the several Indian tribes: *Provided,* That the Secretary of the Interior shall make to the Congress reports required in connection with action taken by him under this provision.

(e) The authority vested in the President by section 5 of the act of February 8, 1887, ch. 119, 24 Stat. 389, as amended [25 U.S.C. 348], by the act of December 24, 1942, ch. 814, 56 Stat. 1081 [25 U.S.C. 348a], by the act of June 21, 1906, ch. 3504, 34 Stat. 326 [25 U.S.C. 391], and by section 3 of the act of January 12, 1891, 26 Stat. 712, as amended by section 3 of the act of March 2, 1917, ch. 146, 39 Stat. 976, to extend trust periods on land patents issued to Indians and to continue restrictions on alienation.

(f) The authority vested in the President by section 4705(b) of the Internal Revenue Code of 1954 [former 26 U.S.C. 4705(b)] to authorize certain persons in the Virgin Islands to obtain certain drugs for legitimate medical purposes without regard to order forms, and by section 4762(b) of such Code [former 26 U.S.C. 4762(b)] to provide for the registration of and the imposition of special and transfer taxes upon persons in the Virgin Islands who import, manufacture, produce, compound, sell, deal in, dispense, prescribe, administer, or give away marihuana: *Provided,* That the Secretary of the Interior shall perform the functions referred to in this subsection in consultation with the Department of the Treasury.

(g) The authority vested in the President by section 2343 of the Revised Statutes [30 U.S.C. 46] to establish additional land districts and to appoint necessary officers under existing laws when deemed necessary for the public convenience in executing certain provisions of law with respect to mineral lands and mining.

(h) The authority vested in the President by section 2252 of the Revised Statutes as affected by section 403 of Reorganization Plan No. 3 of 1946, 60 Stat. 1100 [43 U.S.C. 121], to order the discontinuance of any land office and the transfer of any of its business and archives to any other land office within the same State or Territory.

(i) The authority vested in the President by section 2250 of the Revised Statutes [43 U.S.C. 125] to discontinue a land office in a land district under certain circumstances and to annex the same to some other adjoining land district.

(j) The authority vested in the President by section 2251 of the Revised Statutes [43 U.S.C. 126] to change the location of the land offices in the several land districts established by law and to relocate the same from time to time at such point in the district as may be deemed expedient.

(k) The authority vested in the President by section 2253 of the Revised Statutes [43 U.S.C. 127], to change and reestablish the boundaries of land districts.

(*l*) The authority vested in the President by section 2 of the act of March 2, 1917, ch. 145, 39 Stat. 951, as amended [48 U.S.C. 737], to approve the payment out of the Treasury for other purposes of money derived from any tax levied or assessed for a special purpose in Puerto Rico.

(m) The authority vested in the President by section 7 of the act of March 2, 1917, ch. 145, 39 Stat. 954, as amended [48 U.S.C. 748], to convey to the people of Puerto Rico lands, buildings, or interests in lands, or other property owned by the United States, and to accept lands, buildings, or other interests or property by legislative grant from Puerto Rico.

(n) The authority vested in the President by section 3(b) of the act of March 3, 1925, ch. 426, 43 Stat. 1111, as amended [see 50 U.S.C. 167d], to approve regulations governing the production and sale of helium for medical, scientific, and commercial use.

(o) The authority vested in the President by section 6 of the act of April 26, 1906, ch. 1876, 34 Stat. 139, to remove from office the principal chief of the Choctaw, Cherokee, Creek, or Seminole tribe or the governor of the Chickasaw tribe, to declare any such office vacant, and to fill any vacancy in any such office arising from removal, disability, or death of the incumbent.

(p) The authority vested in the President by section 28 of the act of April 26, 1906, ch. 1876, 34 Stat. 148, to approve acts, ordinances, or resolutions of the tribal council or legislature of the Choctaw, Chickasaw, Cherokee, Creek, and Seminole tribes or nations, and to approve contracts, involving the payment or expenditure of money or affecting property belonging to any of the said tribes or nations, made by them or any of them or by any officer thereof.

(q) [Superseded by section 3 of Ex. Ord. No. 10752, Feb. 12, 1958, 23 F.R. 973, set out as a note under 15 U.S.C. 715j].

(r) The authority vested in the President by section 55 of the act of April 30, 1900, 31 Stat. 150, as amended [48 U.S.C. 562], and by section 4 of the act of August 24, 1954, 68 Stat. 785, as amended [48 U.S.C. 562o], to approve the issuance of bonds or other instruments of indebtedness by the Territory of Hawaii.

2. The Secretary of the Interior is hereby designated and empowered to perform, without the approval, ratification, or other action of the President, the following functions which have heretofore, under the respective provisions of law cited, required the approval, ratification, or other action of the President in connection with their performance by the Secretary of the Interior:

(a) The authority vested in the Secretary of the Interior by section 1 of the act of June 6, 1942, ch. 380, 56 Stat. 326 [16 U.S.C. 459r], to convey or lease to the States or to the political subdivisions thereof any or all of certain recreational demonstration projects and lands and equipment comprised within such projects or any parts of such projects; and to transfer to other Federal agencies any of the said recreational demonstration areas that may be of use to such agencies.

(b) The authority vested in the Secretary of the Interior by section 3 of the act of July 3, 1918, ch. 128, 40

Stat. 755, as amended, and as affected by section 4(f) of Reorganization Plan No. II, effective July 1, 1939, 53 Stat. 1433 [16 U.S.C. 704], to promulgate regulations permitting and governing the hunting, taking, capture, killing, possession, sale, purchase, shipment, transportation, carriage, or export of any migratory bird included in the terms of certain conventions, or any part, nest, or egg thereof.

3. As used in this order, the term "functions" embraces duties, powers, responsibilities, authority, or discretion, and the term "perform" may be construed to mean "exercise".

4. All actions heretofore taken by the President in respect of the matters affected by this order and in force at the time of the issuance of this order, including regulations prescribed by the President in respect of such matters, shall, except as they may be inconsistent with the provisions of this order, remain in effect until modified or revoked pursuant to the authority conferred by this order.

5. The Secretary of the Interior is hereby authorized to redelegate to the Deputy Secretary of the Interior any of the authority delegated to the Secretary of the Interior by section 1 of this order.

EX. ORD. NO. 10289. DELEGATION OF FUNCTIONS TO SECRETARY OF THE TREASURY

Ex. Ord. No. 10289, Sept. 17, 1951, 16 F.R. 9499, as amended by Ex. Ord. No. 10583, Dec. 18, 1954, 19 F.R. 8725; Ex. Ord. No. 10882, July 18, 1960, 25 F.R. 6869; Ex. Ord. No. 11110, June 4, 1963, 28 F.R. 5605; Ex. Ord. No. 11825, Dec. 31, 1974, 40 F.R. 1003; Ex. Ord. No. 12608, Sept. 9, 1987, 52 F.R. 34617, provided:

1. The Secretary of the Treasury is hereby designated and empowered to perform the following-described functions of the President without the approval, ratification, or other action of the President:

(a) The authority vested in the President by section 1 of the act of August 1, 1914, ch. 223, 38 Stat. 609, 623, as amended [19 U.S.C. 2], (1) to rearrange, by consolidation or otherwise, the several customs-collection districts, (2) to discontinue ports of entry by abolishing the same and establishing others in their stead, and (3) to change from time to time the location of the headquarters in any customs-collection district as the needs of the service may require.

(b) The authority vested in the President by section 1 of the Anti-Smuggling Act of August 5, 1935, c. 438, 49 Stat. 517 [19 U.S.C. 1701], (1) to find and declare that at any place or within any area on the high seas adjacent to but outside customs waters any vessel or vessels hover or are being kept off the coast of the United States and that, by virtue of the presence of any such vessel or vessels at such place or within such area, the unlawful introduction or removal into or from the United States of any merchandise or person is being, or may be, occasioned, promoted, or threatened, (2) to find and declare that certain waters on the high seas are in such proximity to such vessel or vessels that such unlawful introduction or removal of merchandise or persons may be carried on by or to or from such vessel or vessels, and (3) to find and declare that, within any customs-enforcement area, the circumstances no longer exist which gave rise to the declaration of such area as a customs-enforcement area.

(c) The authority vested in the President by section 1 of the Act of August 26, 1985 [1983], Public Law 98–89, 97 Stat. 510 (46 U.S.C. 3101); to suspend the provisions of law requiring the inspection of foreign-built vessels admitted to American registry.

(d) The authority vested in the President by section 5 of the act of May 28, 1908, ch. 212, 35 Stat. 425, as amended (46 U.S.C. Appendix 104) [now 46 U.S.C. 60504], to determine (as a prerequisite to the extension of reciprocal privileges by the Commissioner of Customs) that yachts used and employed exclusively as pleasure vessels and belonging to any resident of the United States are allowed to arrive at and depart from any foreign port and to cruise in the waters of such port without entering or clearing at the custom-house thereof and without the payment of any charges for entering or clearing, dues, duty per ton, tonnage taxes, or charges for cruising licenses.

(e) The authority vested in the President by section 2 of the act of March 24, 1908, ch. 96, 35 Stat. 46 ([former] 46 U.S.C. Appendix 134) [see 46 U.S.C. 60311], to name the hospital ships to which section 1 of the said act [former 46 U.S.C. Appendix 133; see 46 U.S.C. 60311], shall apply and to indicate the time when the exemptions thereby provided for shall begin and end.

(f) The authority vested in the President by section 4228 of the Revised Statutes, as amended (46 U.S.C. Appendix 141) [now 46 U.S.C. 60503], (1) to declare that— upon satisfactory proof being given by the government of any foreign nation that no discriminating duties of tonnage or imports are imposed or levied in the ports of such nation upon vessels wholly belonging to citizens of the United States, or upon the produce, manufactures or merchandise imported in the same from the United States or from any foreign country—the foreign discriminating duties of tonnage and impost within the United States are suspended and discontinued, so far as respect the vessels of such foreign nation, and the produce, manufactures, or merchandise imported into the United States from such foreign nation, or from any other foreign country, and (2) to suspend in part the operation of section 4219 of the Revised Statutes, as amended ([former] 46 U.S.C. Appendix 121) [see 46 U.S.C. 60301, 60302, 60304–60306, 60312], and section IV, J, subsection 1 of the act of October 3, 1913, c. 16 38 Stat. 195, as amended ([former] 46 U.S.C. Appendix 146) [see 46 U.S.C. 60502(a)], so that foreign vessels from a country imposing partial discriminating tonnage duties upon American vessels, or partial discriminating import duties upon American merchandise, may enjoy in our ports the identical privileges which the same class of American vessels and merchandise may enjoy in such country: *Provided,* That prior to the issuance of an order of the Secretary of the Treasury suspending and discontinuing (wholly or in part) discriminating tonnage duties, imposts, and import duties within the United States, the Department of State shall obtain and furnish to the Secretary of the Treasury the proof required by the said sections 4228, as amended, as the basis for that order.

(g) The authority vested in the President by section 3650 of the Internal Revenue Code [section 3650 of the Internal Revenue Code of 1939] [see 26 U.S.C. 7621], to establish convenient collection districts (for the purpose of assessing, levying, and collecting the taxes provided by the internal revenue laws), and from time to time to alter such districts.

(h) The authority which is now vested in the President by section 2564(b) of the Internal Revenue Code [section 2564(b) of the Internal Revenue Code of 1939], and which on and after January 1, 1955, will be vested in the President by section 4735(b) of the Internal Revenue Code of 1954 [former 26 U.S.C. 4735(b)], to issue, in accordance with the provisions of the said section 2564(b) or 4735(b), as the case may be, orders providing for the registration and the imposition of a special tax upon all persons in the Canal Zone who produce, import, compound, deal in, dispense, sell, distribute, or give away narcotic drugs.

(i) The authority vested in the President by Section 5318 of the Revised Statutes, as amended (19 U.S.C. 540), to employ suitable vessels other than Coast Guard cutters in the execution of laws providing for the collection of duties on imports and tonnage;[.]

2. The Secretary of the Treasury is hereby designated and empowered to perform without the approval, ratification, or other action of the President the following functions which have heretofore, under the respective provisions of law cited, required the approval of the President in connection with their performance by the Secretary of the Treasury:

(a) The authority vested in the Secretary of the Treasury by section 6 of the act of July 8, 1937, ch. 444, 50 Stat. 480 [now 40 U.S.C. 17309], to make rules and regulations necessary for the execution of the functions vested in the Secretary of the Treasury by the said act, as amended.

(b), (c) [Revoked by Ex. Ord. No. 11110, June 4, 1963, 28 F.R. 5605.]

(d) [Revoked by Ex. Ord. No. 11825, Dec. 31, 1974, 40 F.R. 1003.]

(e) The authority vested in the Secretary of the Treasury by section 1 of Title II of the act of June 15, 1917, ch. 30, 40 Stat. 220 [50 U.S.C. 191], to make rules and regulations governing the anchorage and movement of any vessel, foreign or domestic, in the territorial waters of the United States.

3. (a) The Secretary of the Treasury and the Postmaster General [now United States Postal Service] are hereby designated and empowered jointly to prescribe without the approval of the President regulations, under section 1 of the act of July 8, 1937, ch. 444, 50 Stat. 479 [now 40 U.S.C. 17302], governing the shipment of valuables by the executive departments, independent establishments, agencies, wholly-owned corporations, officers, and employees of the United States.

(b) The Postmaster General [now United States Postal Service] is hereby designated and empowered to exercise without the approval, ratification, or other action of the President the authority vested in the President by section 504(b) of Title 18 of the United States Code to approve regulations issued by the Secretary of the Treasury under the authority of the said section 504(b) (relating to the printing, publishing, or importation, or the making or importation of the necessary plates for such printing or publishing, of postage stamps for philatelic purposes) [see section 504(2) of title 18], and to approve any amendment or repeal of any of such regulations by the Secretary of the Treasury.

4. As used in this order, the term "functions" embraces duties, powers, responsibilities, authority, or discretion, and the term "perform" may be construed to mean "exercise".

5. All actions heretofore taken by the President in respect of the matters affected by this order and in force at the time of the issuance of this order, including regulations prescribed by the President in respect of such matters, shall, except as they may be inconsistent with the provisions of this order, remain in effect until amended, modified, or revoked pursuant to the authority conferred by this order.

Ex. Ord. No. 10530. Delegation of Miscellaneous Functions

Ex. Ord. No. 10530, May 10, 1954, 19 F.R. 2709, as amended by Ex. Ord. No. 10573, Oct. 26, 1954, 19 F.R. 6899; Ex. Ord. No. 10682, Oct. 22, 1956, 21 F.R. 8129; Ex. Ord. No. 10759, Mar. 17, 1958, 23 F.R. 1803; Ex. Ord. No. 10790, Nov. 20, 1958, 23 F.R. 9051; Ex. Ord. No. 10836, Sept. 8, 1959, 24 F.R. 7269; Ex. Ord. No. 10852, Nov. 27, 1959, 24 F.R. 9565; Ex. Ord. No. 10889, Oct. 5, 1960, 25 F.R. 9633; Ex. Ord. No. 10903, Jan. 9, 1961, 26 F.R. 217; Ex. Ord. No. 10960, Aug. 21, 1961, 26 F.R. 7823; Ex. Ord. No. 10970, Oct. 27, 1961, 26 F.R. 10149; Ex. Ord. No. 11012, Mar. 27, 1962, 27 F.R. 2983; Ex. Ord. No. 11116, Aug. 5, 1963, 28 F.R. 8075; Ex. Ord. No. 11164, Aug. 1, 1964, 29 F.R. 11257; Ex. Ord. No. 11184, Oct. 13, 1964, 29 F.R. 14155; Ex. Ord. No. 11196, Feb. 2, 1965, 30 F.R. 1171; Ex. Ord. No. 11222, May 8, 1965, 30 F.R. 6469; Ex. Ord. No. 11228, June 14, 1965, 30 F.R. 7739; Ex. Ord. No. 11230, § 2(1), (3), (5) to (14), June 28, 1965, 30 F.R. 8447; Ex. Ord. No. 12107, Dec. 28, 1978, 44 F.R. 1055; Pub. L. 98–497, title I, § 103(b)(1), Oct. 19, 1984, 98 Stat. 2283; Ex. Ord. No. 12608, Sept. 9, 1987, 52 F.R. 34617, provided:

Part I—Director of the Bureau of the Budget

[Superseded by Ex. Ord. No. 11230, § 2(1), (3), (5)–(14), June 28, 1965, 30 F.R. 8447]

Part II—The Office of Personnel Management

[Superseded by Ex. Ord. No. 11228, § 3(1), (2), (5), June 14, 1965, 30 F.R. 7739]

Part III—The Housing and Home Finance Administrator

[Superseded by Ex. Ord. No. 11196, Feb. 2, 1965, 30 F.R. 1171]

Part IV

THE FEDERAL COMMUNICATIONS COMMISSION

Sec. 5. (a) The Federal Communications Commission is hereby designated and empowered to exercise, without the approval, ratification, or other action of the President, all authority vested in the President by the act of May 27, 1921, ch. 12, 42 Stat. 8 [47 U.S.C. 34 to 39], including the authority to issue, withhold, or revoke licenses to land or operate submarine cables in the United States: *Provided*, That no such license shall be granted or revoked by the Commission except after obtaining approval of the Secretary of State and such advice from any executive department or establishment of the Government as the Commission may deem necessary. The Commission is authorized and directed to receive all applications for the said licenses.

(b) Executive Order No. 3513 of July 9, 1921, as amended by Executive Order No. 6779 of June 30, 1934, is hereby revoked.

Part V

THE ATTORNEY GENERAL AND THE ARCHIVIST OF THE UNITED STATES

Sec. 6. The Attorney General and the Archivist of the United States are hereby designated and empowered jointly to perform the following-described functions without the approval, ratification, or other action of the President:

(a) The authority vested in the President by section 5(a) of the act of July 26, 1935, ch. 417, 49 Stat. 501, as amended (44 U.S.C. 1505(a)), to determine from time to time the documents or classes of documents having general applicability and legal effect.

(b) The authority vested in the President by sections 6, 11(a), and 11(f) of said act, as amended (44 U.S.C. 1506; 1510(a) and 1510(f)), to approve (or disapprove), respectively, (1) regulations, prescribed by the Administrative Committee of the Federal Register, for carrying out the provisions of that act (including the regulations referred to in section 5(b) of the act (44 U.S.C. 1505(b)), authorizing publication in the Federal Register of certain documents or classes of documents), (2) actions of the Administrative Committee of the Federal Register requiring, from time to time, the preparation and publication in special or supplemental editions of the Federal Register of complete codifications of the documents, described in the said section 11(a) (44 U.S.C. 1510(a)), of each agency of the Government, and (3) regulations, prescribed by the Administrative Committee of the Federal Register, for carrying out the provisions of section 11 (44 U.S.C. 1510) of the said act, as amended.

Part VI

GENERAL PROVISIONS

Sec. 7. All actions heretofore taken by the President in respect of the matters affected by this order and in force at the time of the issuance of this order, including any regulations prescribed or approved by the President in respect of such matters, shall, except as they may be inconsistent with the provisions of this order, remain in effect until amended, modified, or revoked pursuant to the authority conferred by this order.

Sec. 8. As used in this order, the term "functions" embraces duties, powers, responsibilities, authority, or discretion, and the term "perform" may be construed to mean "exercise."

Ex. Ord. No. 10621. Delegation of Functions to Secretary of Defense

Ex. Ord. No. 10621, July 1, 1955, 20 F.R. 4759, as amended by Ex. Ord. No. 11294, Aug. 4, 1966, 31 F.R. 10601; Ex.

Ord. No. 12396, Dec. 9, 1982, 47 F.R. 55897; Ex. Ord. No. 12561, July 1, 1986, 51 F.R. 24299, provided:

Section 1. The Secretary of Defense, and, as designated by the said Secretary for this purpose, any of the Secretaries, Under Secretaries, and Assistant Secretaries of the military departments, are hereby designated and empowered to perform the following-described functions of the President without the approval, ratification, or other action of the President:

(a) The authority vested in the President by the act of March 3, 1901, ch. 852, 31 Stat. 1107, 1133 [10 U.S.C. 5941, 7291], to establish and modify, as the needs of the service may require, a classification of vessels of the Navy, and to formulate appropriate rules governing assignments to command of vessels and squadrons.

(b) The authority vested in the President by the act of August 22, 1912, ch. 335, 37 Stat. 382, 331 [see 10 U.S.C. 509, 1171], to approve regulations of the Secretary of the Navy under which any enlisted man may be discharged within three months before the expiration of the term of his enlistment, and under which an enlisted man may voluntarily extend the term of his enlistment.

(c) The authority vested in the President by the act of May 22, 1928, ch. 688, 45 Stat. 712 [10 U.S.C. 6152], to approve regulations governing the advancement of public funds to naval personnel when required to meet expenses of officers and men detailed on emergency shore duty.

(d) The authority vested in the President by the act of June 22, 1938, ch. 567, 52 Stat. 839, as amended [10 U.S.C. 5083, 5133, 5148, 5201], section 201(a) of the act of August 25, 1941, ch. 409, 55 Stat. 680 [10 U.S.C. 5063, 5064], section 3 of the act of December 28, 1945, ch. 604, 59 Stat. 666, as amended [10 U.S.C. 5138], section 2 of the act of August 1, 1946, ch. 727, 60 Stat. 779 [10 U.S.C. 5150], and section 7(a) of the act of March 5, 1948, ch. 98, 62 Stat. 68 [see Department of Defense Reorganization Order set out as a note under 10 U.S.C. 5111], to authorize, in his discretion, for any officer of the Regular Navy or Marine Corps who retires while serving as Chief of Naval Operations, as Chief of a Bureau of the Navy Department, as Judge Advocate General of the Navy, as Commandant of the Marine Corps, as Director of Budgets and Reports, as Chief of the Dental Division, as Chief of Naval Research, or as Chief of Naval Material, or while serving in a lower rank if he has previously served in any of such offices two and one-half years or more, retirement in the highest grade or rank in which he so served and with retired pay based on that rank.

(e) The authority vested in the President by the act of June 15, 1940, ch. 374, 54 Stat. 400, to prescribe from time to time the number of warrant and commissioned warrant officers for the Marine Corps.

(f) The authority vested in the President by the act of June 24, 1941, ch. 231, 55 Stat. 260 [10 U.S.C. 7306], to approve the use for experimental purposes of vessels of the United States Navy stricken from the Navy Register pursuant to the act of August 5, 1882, 22 Stat. 296, as amended [10 U.S.C. 7304].

(g) The authority vested in the President by section 302 of the act of June 22, 1944, ch. 268, 58 Stat. 287 [see 10 U.S.C. 1554], to approve or disapprove the proceedings and decisions of boards of review established under that section by the Secretary of the Army, the Secretary of the Air Force, or the Secretary of the Navy, and to issue orders in such cases.

(h) The authority vested in the President by Section 102(a) of the Federal Civilian Employee and Contractor Travel Expenses Act of 1985, 5 U.S.C. 5702(a), to establish maximum rates of per diem allowances and reimbursements for the actual and necessary expenses of official travel for employees of the Government in the extent that such authority pertains to travel status in localities in Alaska, Hawaii, the Commonwealth of Puerto Rico, and possessions of the United States.

Sec. 2. The Secretary of Defense, and, as designated by the said Secretary for this purpose, the Deputy Secretary of Defense and any of the Assistant Secretaries of Defense, are hereby designated and empowered to perform the following-described functions of the President without the approval, ratification, or other action of the President:

(a) The authority vested in the President by section 1547 of the Revised Statutes of the United States [10 U.S.C. 6011], to approve alterations made by the Secretary of the Navy in Navy Regulations.

(b) The authority vested in the President by section 1 of the act of April 9, 1906, ch. 1370, 34 Stat. 104 [10 U.S.C. 6961], to approve the dismissal by the Secretary of the Navy of a midshipman from the United States Naval Academy.

Sec. 3. All actions heretofore taken by the President with respect to the matters affected by this order and in force and effect at the time of the issuance of this order, including any regulations prescribed or approved by the President with respect to such matters, shall, except as they may be inconsistent with the provisions of this order, remain in force and effect until amended, modified, or revoked pursuant to the authority conferred by this order.

Sec. 4. As used in this order, the term "functions" includes duties, powers, responsibilities, authority, and discretion, and the term "perform" may be construed to mean "exercise".

Ex. Ord. No. 10637. Delegation of Functions to Secretary of Homeland Security

Ex. Ord. No. 10637, Sept. 16, 1955, 20 F.R. 7025, as amended by Ex. Ord. No. 13286, §75, Feb. 28, 2003, 68 F.R. 10631, provided:

Section 1. The Secretary of Homeland Security is hereby designated and empowered to perform the following- described functions without the approval, ratification, or other action of the President:

(a) The authority vested in the President by section 149 of title 14 of the United States Code, in his discretion, to detail officers and enlisted men of the Coast Guard to assist foreign governments in matters concerning which the Coast Guard may be of assistance.

(b) The authority vested in the President by section 229 of title 14 of the United States Code [see 14 U.S.C. 281 et seq.], to revoke the commission of any officer on the active list of the Coast Guard who, at the date of such revocation, has had less than three years of continuous service as a commissioned officer in the Coast Guard, and to prescribe regulations relating to such revocations.

(c) The authority vested in the President by section 232 of title 14 of the United States Code [see 14 U.S.C. 291], in his discretion, to retire from active service any commissioned officer of the Coast Guard, upon his own application, who has completed twenty years of active service in the Coast Guard, Navy, Army, Air Force, or Marine Corps, or the Reserve Components thereof.

(d) The authority vested in the President by section 235 of title 14 of the United States Code [see 14 U.S.C. 251 et seq.], to retire, to approve the retirement of, to place out of line of promotion, and to approve the placing out of line of promotion of, officers of the Coast Guard.

(e) The authority vested in the President by section 492 of title 14 of the United States Code to present a distinguished service medal (including incidental items) to any person who, while serving in any capacity with the Coast Guard, distinguishes himself by exceptionally meritorious service to the Government in a duty of great responsibility.

(f) The authority vested in the President by section 493 of title 14 of the United States Code to present the Coast Guard medal (including incidental items) to any person who, while serving in any capacity with the Coast Guard, distinguishes himself by heroism not involving actual conflict with an enemy.

(g) The authority vested in the President by section 494 of title 14 of the United States Code to award emblems, insignia, rosettes, and other devices, to the extent that such authority relates to the awarding of such items to be worn with the distinguished service medal or the Coast Guard medal.

(h) The authority vested in the President by section 498 of title 14 of the United States Code to make posthumous awards of decorations and to designate representatives to receive such awards, to the extent that such authority relates to the awarding of the distinguished service medal or the Coast Guard medal, or ribbons, emblems, insignia, rosettes, or other devices corresponding thereto.

(i) The authority vested in the President by section 499 of title 14 of the United States Code to make rules, regulations, and orders to the extent that they shall relate to the authority described in sections 1(f), 1(g), and 1(h) above.

(j) The authority vested in the President by the first paragraph of section 806 of the act of September 8, 1916, ch. 463, 39 Stat. 799 [15 U.S.C. 77], to direct the detention of any vessel, American or foreign, by withholding clearance or by formal notice forbidding departure; but such authority shall be exercised by the Secretary of Homeland Security only upon a finding by the President that there is reasonable ground to believe that the vessel concerned is making or giving undue or unreasonable preference or advantage to any party, or is subjecting any party to undue or unreasonable prejudice, disadvantage, injury, or discrimination, as described in the said paragraph; and the authority so vested to revoke, modify, or renew any such direction.

(k) The authority vested in the President by the second paragraph of the said section 806 of the act of September 8, 1916 [15 U.S.C. 77], to withhold clearance from one or more vessels of a belligerent country or government until such belligerent shall restore to American vessels and American citizens reciprocal liberty of commerce and equal facilities for trade, and the authority to direct that similar privileges and facilities, if any, enjoyed by vessels and citizens of such belligerent in the United States or its possessions be refused to vessels or citizens of such belligerent; but such authority shall not, in either instance, be exercised by the Secretary of Homeland Security with respect to any vessel or citizen of such belligerent unless and until the President proclaims that the belligerent nation concerned is denying privileges and facilities to American vessels as described in the said paragraph.

(*l*) The authority vested in the President by section 963(a) of title 18 of the United States Code to detain, in accordance with the provisions of such section, any armed vessel, or any vessel, domestic or foreign (other than one which has entered the ports of the United States as a public vessel), which is manifestly built for warlike purposes or has been converted or adapted from a private vessel to one suitable for warlike use, and to determine, in each case, whether the proof required by such section is satisfactory.

(m) The authority vested in the President by section 967(a) of title 18 of the United States Code, during a war in which the United States is a neutral nation, to withhold clearance from or to any vessel, domestic or foreign, or, by service of formal notice upon the owner, master, or person in command or in charge of any domestic vessel not required to secure clearances, and to forbid its departure from port or from the United States, whenever there is reasonable cause to believe that such vessel is about to carry fuel, arms, ammunition, men, supplies, dispatches, or information to any warship, tender, or supply ship of a foreign belligerent nation in violation of the laws, treaties, or obligations of the United States under the law of nations.

(n) The authority vested in the President by section 10(a) of the act of November 4, 1939, ch. 2, 54 Stat. 9 [22 U.S.C. 450(a)], to require the owner, master, or person in command of a vessel to give a bond to the United States, as prescribed by the said section 10(a).

(o) The authority vested in the President by section 10(b) of the act of November 4, 1939, ch. 2, 54 Stat. 9 [22 U.S.C. 450(b)], to prohibit the departure of a vessel from a port of the United States, in accordance with the provisions of the said section 10(b).

(p) The authority vested in the President by section 2 of the act of August 18, 1914, ch. 256, 38 Stat. 699 [46 U.S.C. 8103(h)(2)], to suspend, in his discretion, by order, so far and for such length of time as he may deem desirable, the provisions of law prescribing that all watch officers of vessels of the United States registered for foreign trade shall be citizens of the United States.

(q) The authority vested in the President by section 2 of the act of October 17, 1940, ch. 896, 54 Stat. 1201 [former 46 U.S.C. 643b], to extend, whenever in his judgment the national interest requires, the provisions of subsection (b) of section 4551, Revised Statutes, as amended [46 U.S.C. 7304], to such additional class or classes of vessels and to such waters as he may designate.

(r) The authority vested in the President by section 6 of the act of July 24, 1941, ch. 320, 55 Stat. 604, as amended (34 U.S.C. 350e) [see Historical and Revision Notes set out under 10 U.S.C. 5501], to make appointments of officers below flag rank without the advice and consent of the Senate, to the extent that such authority relates, pursuant to section 11(b) of the said act, as amended (34 U.S.C. 350j) [see 14 U.S.C. 214, 275], to officers of the United States Coast Guard.

SEC. 2. The Secretary of Homeland Security is hereby designated and empowered to perform without the approval, ratification, or other action of the President the following described functions to the extent that they relate to the United States Coast Guard:

(a) The authority vested in the President by Article 4(a) of the Uniform Code of Military Justice (section 1 of the act of May 5, 1950, ch. 169, 64 Stat. 110) [10 U.S.C. 804], to convene a general court-martial to try any dismissed officer, upon application by the officer concerned for trial by court-martial.

(b) The authority vested in the President by Articles 4(c) and 75 of the Uniform Code of Military Justice (64 Stat. 110, 132) [10 U.S.C. 804, 875], to reappoint a discharged officer to such commissioned rank and precedence as the former officer would have attained had he not been dismissed, and to direct the extent to which any such reappointment shall affect the promotion status of other officers.

(c) The authority vested in the President by section 10 of the act of May 5, 1950, ch. 169, 64 Stat. 146 [10 U.S.C. 1161, 6408], to drop from the rolls any officer who has been absent without authority from his place of duty for a period of three months or more, or who, having been found guilty by the civil authorities of any offense, is finally sentenced to confinement in a Federal or State penitentiary or correctional institution.

(d) The authority vested in the President by section 219 of the Armed Forces Reserve Act, approved July 9, 1952 (66 Stat. 487) [10 U.S.C. 12203], to make appointments of Reserves in commissioned grades below flag officer grades.

(e) The authority vested in the President by section 221 of the said Armed Forces Reserve Act [10 U.S.C. 12203], to determine the tenure in office of commissioned officers of the reserve.

(f) The authority vested in the President by section 248 of the said Armed Forces Reserve Act [see 10 U.S.C. 12681, 12682], to effect the discharge of commissioned officers of the reserve.

(g) The authority vested in the President by section 6 of the act of February 21, 1946, ch. 34, 60 Stat. 27 [10 U.S.C. 6323], as made applicable to the Coast Guard Reserve by section 755(a) of Title 14 of the United States Code, in his discretion, to place upon the retired list any officer of the Coast Guard Reserve, upon his own application, who has completed more than twenty years of active service as described in the said section 6.

SEC. 3. All actions heretofore taken by the President with respect to the matters affected by this order and in force at the time of issuance of this order, including any regulations prescribed or approved by the President with respect to such matters, shall, except as they may be inconsistent with the provisions of this order, remain in effect until amended, modified, or revoked pursuant to the authority conferred by this order.

SEC. 4. As used in this order, the term "functions" embraces duties, powers, responsibilities, authority, or discretion, and the term "perform" may be construed to mean "exercise".

SEC. 5. Whenever the entire Coast Guard operates as a service in the Navy, the references to the Secretary of Homeland Security in the introductory portions of sections 1 and 2 of this order shall be deemed to be references to the Secretary of the Navy.

EX. ORD. NO. 10661. DELEGATION OF FUNCTIONS TO SECRETARY OF DEFENSE AND SECRETARY OF COMMERCE

Ex. Ord. No. 10661, Feb. 27, 1956, 21 F.R. 1315, provided:

SECTION 1. The Secretary of Defense, and, when designated by the Secretary of Defense for such purpose, the Secretary of the Army are hereby designated and empowered to exercise, without the approval, ratification, or other action of the President, the authority vested in the President by the first section of the act of June 26, 1946, ch. 493, 60 Stat. 311, as amended [10 U.S.C. 4344, 9344], to designate persons from the American Republics (other than the United States) and Canada who may be permitted to receive instruction at the United States Military Academy at West Point, New York.

SEC. 2. The Secretary of Defense, and, when designated by the Secretary of Defense for such purpose, the Secretary of the Navy are hereby designated and empowered to exercise, without the approval, ratification, or other action of the President, the following-described authority to designate persons who may be permitted to receive instruction at the United States Naval Academy at Annapolis, Maryland:

(a) The authority vested in the President by the act of July 14, 1941, ch. 292, 55 Stat. 589, as amended [10 U.S.C. 6957], with respect to persons from the American Republics (other than the United States) and Canada.

(b) The authority vested in the President by the act of June 24, 1948, ch. 616, 62 Stat. 583 [10 U.S.C. 6957], with respect to Filipinos.

SEC. 3. The Secretary of Defense, and, when designated by the Secretary of Defense for such purpose, the Secretary of the Air Force are hereby designated and empowered to exercise, without the approval, ratification, or other action of the President, the authority vested in the President by the first section of the said act of June 26, 1946, as made applicable to the United States Air Force Academy by section 5 of the act of April 1, 1954, ch. 127, 68 Stat. 48 [10 U.S.C. 9344], to designate persons from the American Republics (other than the United States) and Canada who may be permitted to receive instruction at the United States Air Force Academy.

SEC. 4. The Secretary of Commerce is hereby designated and empowered to exercise, without the approval, ratification, or other action of the President, the authority vested in the President by the act of August 9, 1946, ch. 928, 60 Stat. 961 [former 46 U.S.C. 1126b], to designate persons from the American Republics (other than the United States) who may be permitted to receive instruction in the United States Merchant Marine Cadet Corps and at the United States Merchant Marine Academy at Kings Point, New York.

SEC. 5. No person shall be designated under the authority of this order to receive instruction except after consultation by the designating officer with the Secretary of State.

DWIGHT D. EISENHOWER.

EX. ORD. NO. 10950. DELEGATION OF FUNCTIONS TO SECRETARY OF THE INTERIOR

Ex. Ord. No. 10950, June 27, 1961, 26 F.R. 5787, as amended by Pub. L. 101–509, title V, §529 [title I, §112(c)], Nov. 5, 1990, 104 Stat. 1427, 1454, provided:

By virtue of the authority vested in me by section 6(b) of the Alaska Statehood Act of July 7, 1958 (72 Stat. 339) [set out as a note preceding 48 U.S.C. 21], and as President of the United States, I hereby designate the Secretary of the Interior as my representative to exercise the authority vested in me by section 6(b) of the act to approve selections of land made by the State of Alaska under the provisions of section 6(b) in instances in which those selections include land lying north and west of the line described in section 10(b) of the act: *Provided*, That no selection by the State shall be approved pursuant to this order, in whole or in part, without the concurrence of the Secretary of Defense or his designated representative.

As the Secretary of the Interior may direct, the Deputy Secretary of the Interior, an Assistant Secretary of the Interior, the Director of the Bureau of Land Management, or the Operations Supervisors of the Bureau of Land Management in Alaska are severally authorized to exercise the authority vested in the Secretary by this order.

EX. ORD. NO. 11012. DELEGATION OF FUNCTIONS TO ADMINISTRATOR OF GENERAL SERVICES

Ex. Ord. No. 11012, Mar. 27, 1962, 27 F.R. 2983, as amended by Ex. Ord. No. 11230, §2(11), June 28, 1965, 30 F.R. 8447; Ex. Ord. No. 12608, Sept. 9, 1987, 52 F.R. 34617, provided:

By virtue of the authority vested in me by Section 301 of Title 3 of the United States Code, and as President of the United States, it is hereby ordered as follows:

SECTION 1. [Superseded by Ex. Ord. No. 11230, §2(11), June 28, 1965, 30 F.R. 8447.]

SEC. 2. The Administrator of General Services is hereby designated and empowered to exercise, without the approval, ratification, or other action of the President, so much of the authority vested in the President by Section 1(b) of the Act of August 2, 1946, ch. 744, 60 Stat. 807 (5 U.S.C. 73b–1(b)) [5 U.S.C. 5724], as pertains to the establishment of the rates to be used in reimbursing civilian officers or employees of the Government on a commuted basis in lieu of the payment of actual expenses of transportation, packing, crating, temporary storage, drayage, and unpacking of their household goods and personal effects in the case of transfers from one official station to another within the continental United States for permanent duty.

SEC. 3. The initial regulations to be issued by the Director of the Office of Management and Budget and by the Administrator of General Services under the authority delegated to each of them by this order shall be effective on the same date and effective as of that date the following-described Executive orders are revoked:

(a) Executive Order No. 9778 of September 10, 1946.

(b) Executive Order No. 9805 of November 25, 1946.

(c) Executive Order No. 9933 of February 27, 1948.

(d) Executive Order No. 9997 of September 8, 1948.

(e) Executive Order No. 10069 of July 14, 1949.

(f) Executive Order No. 10177 of October 27, 1950.

(g) Executive Order No. 10196 of December 20, 1950.

(h) Executive Order No. 10274 of July 18, 1951.

(i) Executive Order No. 10381 of August 6, 1952.

(j) Executive Order No. 10507 of December 10, 1953.

SEC. 4. Existing regulations prescribed by the Director of the Office of Management and Budget under the authority of Section 1(b) of Executive Order No. 10530, as amended and in effect immediately prior to the issuance of this order, shall remain in effect until they are superseded in pursuance of the provisions of this order.

EX. ORD. NO. 11023. DELEGATION OF FUNCTIONS TO SECRETARY OF COMMERCE

Ex. Ord. No. 11023, May 28, 1962, 27 F.R. 5131, as amended by Ex. Ord. No. 12608, Sept. 9, 1987, 52 F.R. 34617; Ex. Ord. No. 13341, May 20, 2004, 69 F.R. 29843, provided:

By virtue of the authority vested in me by section 301 of title 3, of the United States Code, and as President of the United States, it is ordered as follows:

SECTION 1. The Secretary of Commerce is hereby designated and empowered to perform the following-described functions without the approval, ratification, or other action of the President:

(a) The authority contained in section 223(b) of the National Oceanic and Atmospheric Administration Commissioned Officer Corps Act of 2002 (Public Law 107–372; 33 U.S.C. 3023(b)) to revoke the commissions of ensigns of the National Oceanic and Atmospheric Administration who are found not fully qualified and to separate such ensigns from the commissioned service.

(b) The authority vested in the President by section 229(a) of the National Oceanic and Atmospheric Administration Commissioned Officer Corps Act of 2002 (Public Law 107–372; 33 U.S.C. 3029(a)), to make temporary appointments in the grade of ensign in the National Oceanic and Atmospheric Administration.

(c) The authority vested in the President by section 229(b) of the National Oceanic and Atmospheric Administration Commissioned Officer Corps Act of 2002 (Public Law 107–372; 33 U.S.C. 3029(b)), to temporarily promote officers in the permanent grade of ensign in the National Oceanic and Atmospheric Administration, and to appoint such officers to the grade of lieutenant junior grade whenever vacancies exist in higher grades.

(d) The authority vested in the President by section 229(c) of the National Oceanic and Atmospheric Administration Commissioned Officer Corps Act of 2002 (Public Law 107–372; 33 U.S.C. 3029(c)), to temporarily promote any officer one grade.

(e) The authority vested in the President by section 243(b) of the National Oceanic and Atmospheric Administration Commissioned Officer Corps Act of 2002 (Public Law 107–372; 33 U.S.C. 3043(b)), to defer the retirement of an officer of the National Oceanic and Atmospheric Administration serving in a rank above that of captain who has attained 62 years of age, but such a deferment may not extend beyond the first day of the month in which the officer becomes 64 years of age.

(f) The authority vested in the President by section 244 of the National Oceanic and Atmospheric Administration Commissioned Officer Corps Act of 2002 (Public Law 107–372; 33 U.S.C. 3044), to retire from the active service any commissioned officer of the National Oceanic and Atmospheric Administration, upon his own application, who has completed 20 years of active service, of which at least 10 years was service as a commissioned officer.

(g) The authority vested in the President by section 221(a)(4) of the National Oceanic and Atmospheric Administration Commissioned Officer Corps Act of 2002 (Public Law 107–372; 33 U.S.C. 3021(a)(4)), (1) to find that any officer appointed under section 23 is not qualified for service, (2) to revoke the commissions of officers in respect of whom such findings are made, and (3) to prescribe the regulations referred to in that section.

(h) The authority contained in section 230(b)(1) of the National Oceanic and Atmospheric Administration Commissioned Officer Corps Act of 2002 (Public Law 107–372; 33 U.S.C. 3030(b)(1)) to temporarily promote to higher ranks or grades, upon recommendation of the Secretary of the military department concerned, commissioned officers of the National Oceanic and Atmospheric Administration transferred to the military departments.

(i) The authority contained in section 230(b)(2) of the National Oceanic and Atmospheric Administration Commissioned Officer Corps Act of 2002 (Public Law 107–372; 33 U.S.C. 3030(b)(2)) to temporarily promote commissioned officers of the National Oceanic and Atmospheric Administration to fill vacancies in ranks and grades caused by transfer of commissioned officers to the service and jurisdiction of the military departments.

(j) The authority contained in section 230(b)(3) of the National Oceanic and Atmospheric Administration Commissioned Officer Corps Act of 2002 (Public Law 107–372; 33 U.S.C. 3030(b)(3)), to appoint temporarily in all grades to which original appointments in the National Oceanic and Atmospheric Administration are authorized to fill vacancies caused by transfer of officers to the military departments.

(k) The authority vested in the President by section 251 of the National Oceanic and Atmospheric Administration Commissioned Officer Corps Act of 2002 (Public Law 107–372; 33 U.S.C. 3061), to transfer to service and jurisdiction of the Department of Defense, as he may deem to be to the best interest of the country, vessels, equipment, stations, and officers of the National Oceanic and Atmospheric Administration; but the Secretary of Commerce may effect such transfers only during the existence of a state of national emergency proclaimed by President. Commissioned officers so transferred shall serve under their commissions in the National Oceanic and Atmospheric Administration and while so serving shall constitute a part of the active armed forces of the United States and shall be under the direct orders of, and shall be subject to the applicable laws, regulations, and orders for the government of, the armed forces to which they are transferred, respectively. The Secretary of Commerce may return such vessels, equipment, stations, and officers to the jurisdiction of the Department of Commerce, but in time of national emergency such return shall be effected only with the concurrence of the Secretary of Defense.

(*l*) The authority vested in the President by section 8 of the Act of August 6, 1947 (61 Stat. 788; 33 U.S.C. 883h) to employ public vessels, and to give instructions for regulating their conduct, to carry out the provisions of the Act of August 6, 1947 [33 U.S.C. 883a et seq.]; but the employment by the Secretary of Commerce of vessels, except those of the Department of Commerce or of any subordinate entity thereof, shall require the concurrence of the head of the department or other executive agency having custody or control of the vessel.

(m) The authority vested in the President by Public Law 96–215, as amended (10 U.S.C. 716(a)), to transfer any commissioned officer with his consent from his uniformed service to, and appoint him in, the National Oceanic and Atmospheric Administration, provided consent for the transfer is given by the Secretary of Defense, the Secretary of Homeland Security, or the Secretary of Health and Human Services, as applicable, in accordance with joint regulations issued under that statute establishing the policies and procedures for such transfers and appointments.

Sec. 2. Upon receipt by the Secretary of Commerce from the President or from the President's representative of information showing that the Senate has confirmed nominees of the President for appointment as commissioned officers of the National Oceanic and Atmospheric Administration, and without any further action on the part of the President, (1) the Secretary of Commerce or an officer of the Department of Commerce designated by the Secretary may, upon completion of statutory requirements for such appointments, tender offers of appointment to the nominees and upon acceptance such persons shall be deemed to be appointed accordingly, (2) the Secretary of Commerce, in the name of the President, shall issue to each such person a commission evidencing the appointment of such persons accordingly, and (3) the commissions of such persons shall be deemed to have been signed by the President. The effective date specified in any commission so issued shall be deemed, for all purposes, to be the date of the appointment evidenced by such commission.

Sec. 3. In connection with making appointments or promotions under authority delegated to him by subsections (b), (c), (d), (h), (i), and (j) of section 1 of this order, the Secretary of Commerce shall issue to each person appointed or promoted by him thereunder a certificate evidencing the appointment or promotion of such person. Such certificate may be issued in the name of the President.

Sec. 4. Any requirement of any provision of law that commissions of officers under the direction and control of the Secretary of Commerce be signed by the President before the seal of the Department of Commerce may be affixed thereto shall, in the case of officers appointed under the procedure set forth in section 2 of this order and in the case of officers appointed or promoted under authority delegated by subsections (b), (c), (d), (h), (i), and (j) of section 1 of this order, be deemed to be satisfied by signature of the commission or certificate by the Secretary of Commerce, before the departmental seal is affixed thereto.

SEC. 5. The Secretary of Commerce is hereby authorized to accept, in the name of the President, the resignation of a commissioned officer, either permanent or temporary, of the National Oceanic and Atmospheric Administration.

SEC. 6. The authority delegated by the provisions of subsections (b), (c), (d), (h), (i), and (j) of section 1 of this order shall be deemed to include the authority to terminate any appointment or promotion made under the provisions of law referred to in those subsections.

SEC. 7. All actions heretofore taken by the President with respect to the matters affected by this order and in force at the time of issuance of this order, including any regulations prescribed or approved by the President with respect to such matters shall, except as they may be inconsistent with the provisions of this order, remain in effect until amended, modified or revoked pursuant to the authority conferred by this order. The following are hereby superseded: (1) Letter of the President to the Secretary of Commerce, dated April 23, 1929, and relating to the general subject of section 2 of this order, and (2) letter of the Secretary to the President, dated July 1, 1919, and directed to the Secretary of Commerce, relating to the general subject of section 5 of this order.

SEC. 8. As used in this order the term "functions" embraces duties, powers, responsibilities, authority or discretion, and the term "perform" may be construed to mean "exercise".

EX. ORD. NO. 11110. AMENDMENT OF EXECUTIVE ORDER NO. 10289, RELATING TO PERFORMANCE OF CERTAIN FUNCTIONS OF DEPARTMENT OF THE TREASURY

Ex. Ord. No. 11110, June 4, 1963, 28 F.R. 5605, provided:

By virtue of the authority vested in me by section 301 of Title 3 of the United States Code, it is ordered as follows:

SECTION 1. Executive Order No. 10289 of September 19, 1951, as amended [set out as a note under this section], is hereby further amended—

(a) By adding at the end of paragraph 1 thereof the following subparagraph (j):

"(j) The authority vested in the President by paragraph (b) of section 43 of the Act of May 12, 1933, as amended (31 U.S.C. 821(b)) [31 U.S.C. 5301(a), (b)] to issue silver certificates against any silver bullion, silver, or standard silver dollars in the Treasury not then held for redemption of any outstanding silver certificates, to prescribe the denominations of such silver certificates, and to coin standard silver dollars and subsidiary silver currency for their redemption," and

(b) By revoking subparagraphs (b) and (c) of paragraph 2 thereof.

SEC. 2. The amendments made by this order shall not affect any act done, or any right accruing or accrued or any suit or proceeding had or commenced in any civil or criminal cause prior to the date of this order but all such liabilities shall continue and may be enforced as if said amendments had not been made.

JOHN F. KENNEDY.

EX. ORD. NO. 11228. DELEGATION OF FUNCTIONS TO OFFICE OF PERSONNEL MANAGEMENT

Ex. Ord. No. 11228, June 14, 1965, 30 F.R. 7739, as amended by Ex. Ord. No. 11257, Nov. 13, 1965, 30 F.R. 14353; Ex. Ord. No. 12107, Dec. 28, 1978, 44 F.R. 1055, provided:

By virtue of the authority vested in me by Section 301 of Title 3 of the United States Code, and as President of the United States, it is hereby ordered as follows—

SECTION 1. The Office of Personnel Management is hereby designated and empowered to exercise, without the approval, ratification, or other action of the President, the following:

(1) The authority vested in the Office of Personnel Management by Section 605 of the Federal Employees Pay Act of 1945, 59 Stat. 304 (5 U.S.C. 945) [5 U.S.C. 5504(c), 5548, 6101(c)], to issue, subject to the approval of the President, regulations necessary for the administration of certain provisions of that Act insofar as the Act affects officers and employees in or under the executive branch of the Government.

(2) The authority vested in the President by Section 203(f) of the Annual and Sick Leave Act of 1951, 65 Stat. 680 (5 U.S.C. 2062(f)) [5 U.S.C. 6305(a)], to prescribe regulations governing the granting of leave of absence as described in that Section.

(3) Except as to Presidential appointees, the authority vested in the President (A) by Section 204 of the Act of June 30, 1932, 47 Stat. 404 [5 U.S.C. 3323(a)], to exempt from automatic separation from the service under that Section any person when, in his judgment, the public interest so requires and (B) by Section 5(c) of the Civil Service Retirement Act, 70 Stat. 748 (5 U.S.C. 2255(c)) [5 U.S.C. 8335(c)], to exempt from automatic separation from the service under Section 5 of that Act [5 U.S.C. 8335] any employee when, in his judgment, the public interest so requires.

(4) The authority vested in the President by Section 9(b) (8) of the Federal Employees Salary Act of 1965 (approved October 29, 1965) [5 U.S.C. 5595(a)(2)] to prescribe rules and regulations excluding officers or employees from the application of Section 9 of that Act [5 U.S.C. 5595].

(5) The authority vested in the President by Section 9(c) of the Federal Employees Salary Act of 1965 [5 U.S.C. 5595(b)(2)] to prescribe rules and regulations governing severance pay.

SEC. 2. The Director of the Office of Personnel Management is hereby designated and empowered to exercise, without the approval, ratification, or other action of the President, the authority vested in the President by Section 304(e) of the Government Employees' Incentive Awards Act, 68 Stat. 1113 (5 U.S.C. 2123(e)) [5 U.S.C. 4502(d)], to determine the activity primarily benefiting, or the various activities benefiting, from any suggestion, invention, superior accomplishment, or other personal effort of any civilian officer or employee of the Government which constitutes the basis of any Presidential award or honorary recognition made or granted under Section 304(b) of that Act (5 U.S.C. 2123(b)) [5 U.S.C. 4501(2)(A), 4504].

SEC 3. The following are hereby superseded:

(1) Part II of Executive Order No. 10530 of May 10, 1954.

(2) Executive Order No. 10682 of October 22, 1956.

(3) Section 5 of Executive Order No. 10800 of January 15, 1959.

(4) Executive Order No. 10835 of August 21, 1959.

(5) So much of Section 2 of Executive Order No. 10903 of January 9, 1961, as added paragraph (e) of Section 2 of Executive Order No. 10530 of May 10, 1954.

SEC. 4. (a) Unless inappropriate, references in this Order to any statute or to any provision of any statute shall be deemed to include references thereto as amended from time to time.

(b) Unless inappropriate, any reference in any Executive order to any Executive order which is superseded by this Order, or to any Executive order provision so superseded, shall hereafter be deemed to refer to this Order or to the provision of Section 1 or Section 2 of this Order, if any, which corresponds to the superseded provision.

SEC. 5. All actions heretofore taken by the President or by his delegates in respect of the matters affected by Sections 1 and 2 of this Order and in force at the time of the issuance of this Order, including any regulations prescribed or approved by the President or by his delegates in respect of such matters, shall, except as they may be inconsistent with the provisions, of this Order, remain in effect until amended, modified, or revoked pursuant to the authority conferred by this Order unless sooner terminated by operation of law.

EXECUTIVE ORDER NO. 11230

Ex. Ord. No. 11230, June 28, 1965, 30 F.R. 8847, as amended by Ex. Ord. No. 11275, Mar. 31, 1966, 31 F.R.

5283; Ex. Ord. No. 11290, July 21, 1966, 31 F.R. 10067; Ex. Ord. No. 11294, Aug. 4, 1966, 31 F.R. 10601, delegating certain functions of the President to the Director of the Bureau of the Budget, was superseded by Ex. Ord. No. 11609, July 22, 1971, 36 F.R. 13747, set out as a note under this section.

EXECUTIVE ORDER NO. 11294

Ex. Ord. No. 11294, Aug. 4, 1966, 31 F.R. 10601, as amended by Ex. Ord. No. 11609, July 22, 1971, 36 F.R. 13747, which delegated functions of the President to establish maximum rates of per diem allowances for certain travel, was revoked by Ex. Ord. No. 12561, July 1, 1986, 51 F.R. 24299, set out as a note under section 5702 of Title 5, Government Organization and Employees.

EX. ORD. NO. 11390. DELEGATION OF FUNCTIONS TO SECRETARY OF DEFENSE

Ex. Ord. No. 11390, Jan. 22, 1968, 33 F.R. 841, as amended by Ex. Ord. No. 11601, June 29, 1971, 36 F.R. 12473; Ex. Ord. No. 12396, Dec. 9, 1982, 47 F.R. 55897; Ex. Ord. No. 12608, Sept. 9, 1987, 52 F.R. 34617, provided:

By virtue of the authority vested in me by section 301 of title 3 of the United States Code, and as President of the United States, it is ordered as follows:

SECTION 1. The Secretary of Defense, and, as designated by the said Secretary for this purpose, any of the Secretaries, Under Secretaries, and Assistant Secretaries of the military departments, are hereby designated and empowered to perform the following-described functions of the President without the approval, ratification, or other action of the President:

(1) [Revoked by Ex. Ord. No. 12608, Sept. 9, 1987, 52 F.R. 34617.]

(2), (3) [Revoked by Ex. Ord. No. 12396, Dec. 9, 1982, 47 F.R. 55897.]

(4) The authority vested in the President by sections 565 and 599 [now 12243] of title 10, United States Code, to suspend, in time of war or emergency, any provision of law relative to promotion and mandatory retirement or separation of warrant officers of the armed forces.

(5) The authority vested in the President by sections 4337 and 9337 of title 10, United States Code, to appoint the chaplains at the United States Military and Air Force Academies.

(6) The authority vested in the President by sections 4302(a) and 9302(a) of title 10, United States Code, to approve regulations concerning instruction of enlisted members of the Army and Air Force.

(7) [Revoked by Ex. Ord. No. 12608, Sept. 9, 1987, 52 F.R. 34617.]

(8) The authority vested in the President by sections 5139 and 5149 of title 10, United States Code, relating to the retirement of the Chief of the Medical Service Corps, the Deputy Judge Advocate General, and the Assistant Judge Advocate General, of the Navy.

(9) [Revoked by Ex. Ord. No. 12396, Dec. 9, 1982, 47 F.R. 55897.]

(10) The authority vested in the President by section 2102(a) of title 10, United States Code, to prescribe regulations governing the establishment and maintenance of senior reserve officers' Training Corps units at civilian educational institutions.

(11) The authority vested in the President by section 123 of title 10, and section 111 of title 32, United States Code, to suspend in time of war or national emergency those provisions cited therein relating to promotion of reserve officers.

(12) [Revoked by Ex. Ord. No. 12396, Dec. 9, 1982, 47 F.R. 55897.]

(13) The authority vested in the President by section 6223(b) of title 10, United States Code, relating to members of the Marine Corps Band.

(14) The authority vested in the President by section 425 of title 37, United States Code, to approve concert tours of the Navy Band and the Marine Corps Band.

(15) [Revoked by Ex. Ord. No. 12396, Dec. 9, 1982, 47 F.R. 55897.]

SEC. 2. All actions heretofore taken by or for the President with respect to the matters affected by this order and in force and effect at the time of the issuance of this order, including any regulations prescribed or approved by the President with respect to such matters, shall, except as they may be inconsistent with the provisions of this order, remain in force and effect until amended, modified, or revoked pursuant to the authority conferred by this order.

EX. ORD. NO. 11423. DELEGATION OF FUNCTIONS TO SECRETARY OF STATE RESPECTING CERTAIN FACILITIES CONSTRUCTED AND MAINTAINED ON UNITED STATES BORDERS

Ex. Ord. No. 11423, Aug. 16, 1968, 33 F.R. 11741, as amended by Ex. Ord. No. 12847, May 17, 1993, 58 F.R. 29511; Ex. Ord. No. 13284, § 14, Jan. 23, 2003, 68 F.R. 4076; Ex. Ord. No. 13337, § 2, Apr. 30, 2004, 69 F.R. 25300, provided:

WHEREAS the proper conduct of the foreign relations of the United States requires that executive permission be obtained for the construction and maintenance at the borders of the United States of facilities connecting the United States with a foreign country; and

WHEREAS such executive permission has from time to time been sought and granted in the form of Presidential permits for the construction, connection, operation, and maintenance at the borders of the United States of such border crossing facilities as water supply and oil pipelines, aerial tramways and cable cars, submarine cables, and lines for the transmission of electric energy; and

WHEREAS Executive Order No. 10485 of September 3, 1953 [15 U.S.C. 717b note], empowers the Federal Power Commission [Secretary of Energy] to issue permits for the construction, operation, maintenance, or connection, at the borders of the United States, of facilities for the transmission of electric energy between the United States and a foreign country and for the importation or exportation of natural gas to or from a foreign country; and

WHEREAS Executive Order No. 10530 of May 10, 1954 [set out above], empowers the Federal Communications Commission to issue and revoke licenses to land submarine cables in the United States; and

WHEREAS it is desirable to provide a systematic method in connection with the issuance of permits for the construction and maintenance of other such facilities connecting the United States with a foreign country:

NOW, THEREFORE, by virtue of the authority vested in me as President of the United States and Commander in Chief of the Armed Forces of the United States and in conformity with the provisions of section 301 of title 3, United States Code, it is ordered as follows:

SECTION 1. (a) Except with respect to facilities covered by Executive Order Nos. 10485 [15 U.S.C. 717b note] and 10530 [set out above], and by section 1(a) of the Executive Order of April 30, 2004, entitled "Issuance of Permits with Respect to Certain Energy-Related Facilities and Land Transportation Crossings on the International Boundaries of the United States" (the order of April 30, 2004) [Ex. Ord. No. 13337, set out below], the Secretary of State is hereby designated and empowered to receive all applications for Presidential permits for the construction, connection, operation, or maintenance, at the borders of the United States, of:

(i) pipelines, conveyor belts, and similar facilities for the exportation or importation of all products, except those specified in section 1(a) of the order of April 30, 2004, to or from a foreign country;

(ii) facilities for the exportation or importation of water or sewage to or from a foreign country;

(iii) facilities for the transportation of persons or things, or both, to or from a foreign country;

(iv) bridges, to the extent that congressional authorization is not required;

(v) similar facilities above or below ground; and

(vi) border crossings for land transportation, including motor and rail vehicles, to or from a foreign country, whether or not in conjunction with the facilities identified in (iii) above.

(b) With respect to applications received pursuant to subsection (a)(i) above, the Secretary of State shall request the views of the Secretary of the Treasury, the Secretary of Defense, the Attorney General, the Secretary of the Interior, the Secretary of Commerce, the Secretary of Transportation, the Secretary of Homeland Security, the Interstate Commerce Commission, and the Director of the Office of Emergency Planning. With respect to applications received pursuant to subsection (a)(ii) above, the Secretary of State shall request the views of the Secretary of Defense and the Secretary of the Interior. With respect to applications received pursuant to subsection (a)(iii), (iv), (v), or (vi) above, the Secretary of State shall request the views of the Secretary of the Treasury, the Secretary of Defense, the Attorney General, and the Secretary of Transportation.

(c) The Secretary of State may also consult with such other department and agency heads and with such state and local government officials as he deems appropriate with respect to each application. All federal government officials consulted by the Secretary of State pursuant to this section shall provide such information and render such assistance as he may request, consistent with their competence and authority.

(d) If the Secretary of State finds, after consideration of the views obtained pursuant to subsections (b) and (c), that issuance of a permit to the applicant would serve the national interest, he shall prepare a permit, in such form and with such terms and conditions as the national interest may in his judgment require, and shall notify the officials required to be consulted under subsection (b) above of his proposed determination that the permit be issued.

(e) If the Secretary of State finds, after consideration of the views obtained pursuant to subsections (b) and (c), that issuance of a permit to the applicant would not serve the national interest, he shall notify the officials required to be consulted under subsection (b) above of his proposed determination that the application be denied.

(f) The Secretary of State shall issue or deny the permit in accordance with his proposed determination unless, within fifteen days after notification pursuant to subsection (d) or (e) above, an official required to be consulted under subsection (b) above shall notify the Secretary of State that he disagrees with the Secretary's proposed determination and requests the Secretary to refer the application to the President. In the event of such a request, the Secretary of State shall refer the application, together with statements of the views of the several officials involved, to the President for his consideration and final decision.

SEC. 2. (a) The Secretary of State may provide for the publication in the Federal Register of notice of receipt of applications, for the receipt of public comments on applications, and for publication in the Federal Register of notice of issuance or denial of applications.

(b) The Secretary of State is authorized to issue such further rules and regulations, and to prescribe such further procedures, as he may from time to time deem necessary or desirable for the exercise of the authority conferred upon him by this order.

SEC. 3. The authority of the Secretary of State hereunder is supplemental to, and does not supersede, existing authorities or delegations relating to importation, exportation, transmission, or transportation to or from a foreign country. All permits heretofore issued with respect to matters described in section 1 of this order, and in force at the time of issuance of this order, and all permits issued hereunder, shall remain in effect in accordance with their terms unless and until modified, amended, suspended, or revoked by the President or, upon compliance with the procedures provided for in this order, by the Secretary of State.

[Interstate Commerce Commission abolished and functions of Commission transferred, except as otherwise provided in Pub. L. 104–88, to Surface Transpor-

tation Board effective Jan. 1, 1996, by section 702 of Title 49, Transportation, and section 101 of Pub. L. 104–88, set out as a note under section 701 of Title 49. References to Interstate Commerce Commission deemed to refer to Surface Transportation Board, a member or employee of the Board, or Secretary of Transportation, as appropriate, see section 205 of Pub. L. 104–88, set out as a note under section 701 of Title 49.]

EX. ORD. NO. 11592. DELEGATION OF FUNCTIONS TO DIRECTOR OF OFFICE OF MANAGEMENT AND BUDGET

Ex. Ord. No. 11592, May 6, 1971, 36 F.R. 8555, provided:

By virtue of the authority vested in me by section 301 of title 3 of the United States Code, and as President of the United States, the Director of the Office of Management and Budget is hereby designated and empowered to exercise, without the approval, ratification, or other action of the President, the function of granting the approvals authorized or required to be granted by the President by any of the provisions of the River and Harbor Act of 1970 and the Flood Control Act of 1970, Public Law 91–611, approved December 31, 1970.

RICHARD NIXON.

EX. ORD. NO. 11609. DELEGATION OF CERTAIN FUNCTIONS VESTED IN THE PRESIDENT TO OTHER OFFICERS OF THE GOVERNMENT

Ex. Ord. No. 11609, July 22, 1971, 36 F.R. 13747, as amended by Ex. Ord. No. 11713, Apr. 21, 1973, 38 F.R. 10069; Ex. Ord. No. 11779, Apr. 19, 1974, 39 F.R. 14185; Ex. Ord. No. 12107, Dec. 28, 1978, 44 F.R. 1055; Ex. Ord. No. 12215, May 27, 1980, 45 F.R. 36043; Ex. Ord. No. 12466, Feb. 27, 1984, 49 F.R. 7349, eff. Nov. 14, 1983; Ex. Ord. No. 12522, June 24, 1985, 50 F.R. 26337, eff. Oct. 12, 1984; Ex. Ord. No. 12608, Sept. 9, 1987, 52 F.R. 34617; Ex. Ord. No. 12822, Nov. 16, 1992, 57 F.R. 54289, eff. Jan. 1, 1992, provided:

By virtue of the authority vested in me by section 301 of title 3 of the United States Code, and as President of the United States, it is hereby ordered as follows:

SECTION 1. *General Services Administration.* The Administrator of General Services is hereby designated and empowered to exercise, without the approval, ratification, or other action of the President, the following:

(1) The authority of the President under 5 U.S.C. 4111(b) to prescribe regulations with respect to reductions to be made from payments by the Government to employees for travel, subsistence, or other expenses incident to training in a non-Government facility or to attendance at a meeting.

(2) The authority of the President under the last sentence of 5 U.S.C. 5702(a) to establish maximum rates of per diem allowances to the extent that such authority pertains to travel status of employees (as defined in 5 U.S.C. 5701) while enroute to, from, or between localities situated outside the 48 contiguous States of the United States and the District of Columbia.

(3) The authority of the President under 5 U.S.C. 5707 to prescribe regulations necessary for the administration of subchapter I of chapter 57 of title 5 of the United States Code [section 5701 et seq. of title 5] (relating to travel and subsistence expenses and mileage allowances).

(4) The authority of the President under 5 U.S.C. 5722(a) to prescribe regulations with respect to the payment of travel expenses and transportation expenses of household goods and personal effects.

(5) The authority of the President under 5 U.S.C. 5723(a) to prescribe regulations with respect to the payment of travel expenses and transportation expenses.

(6) The authority of the President under 5 U.S.C. 5724 to prescribe the regulations provided for therein (relating to travel and transportation expenses and other matters).

(7)(a) The authority of the President under 5 U.S.C. 5724(a) to prescribe the regulations provided for therein, relating to (i) the availability of appropriations or other funds of agencies for the reimbursement of described expenses of employees for whom the Government pays expenses of travel and transportation under

5 U.S.C. 5724(a), (ii) the entitlement of employees to amounts related to their basic pay, and (iii) the allowance, payment, and receipt of expenses and benefits to former employees who are reemployed by non-temporary appointments.

(b) In consultation with the Secretary of the Treasury, the authority of the President under 5 U.S.C. 5724b to prescribe the regulations provided for therein relating to reimbursement of Federal, State, and city income taxes for travel, transportation, and relocation expenses of employees, transferred at Government expense, furnished in kind or for which reimbursement or an allowance is provided.

(c) The authority of the President under 5 U.S.C. 5724c to prescribe the regulations provided for therein pursuant to which each agency shall carry out its responsibilities under 5 U.S.C. 5724c; *provided*, that the Director of Central Intelligence, after consultation with the Administrator of General Services, shall prescribe such regulations for the Central Intelligence Agency.

(8) The authority of the President under 5 U.S.C. 5726 to prescribe the regulations provided for therein, relating to (i) the definition of "household goods and personal effects", (ii) allowable storage expenses and related transportation, and (iii) the allowance of non-temporary storage expenses or storage at Government expense in Government-owned facilities (including related transportation and other expenses).

(9) The authority of the President under 5 U.S.C. 5727 to prescribe the regulations provided for therein, relating to the transportation at Government expense of privately owned motor vehicles.

(10) The authority of the President under 5 U.S.C. 5728 (a) and (b) to prescribe the regulations provided for therein, relating to the payment by an agency from its appropriations of the expenses of round trip travel of an employee, and the transportation of his immediate family, in described circumstances.

(11) The authority of the President under 5 U.S.C. 5729(a) and (b) to prescribe the regulations provided for therein, relating to (i) the payment by an agency from its appropriations of the expenses of transporting the immediate family of an employee and of shipping his household goods and personal effects, and (ii) the reimbursement from its appropriations by an agency of an employee for the proper transportation expense of returning his immediate family and household goods and personal effects, both in described circumstances.

(12) The authority of the President under 5 U.S.C. 5731(a) to prescribe the regulations provided for therein, relating to certifications respecting transportation accommodations.

(13) The authority of the President under 5 U.S.C. 5742(b) to prescribe regulations with respect to the payment of expenses when an employee dies.

(14) The authority of the President under the last sentence of paragraph (c) of section 32 of title III of the Act of July 22, 1937, c. 517, 50 Stat. 525 (7 U.S.C. 1011(c)), to transfer to Federal, State, or Territorial agencies lands acquired by the Secretary of Agriculture under section 32(a) of that Act.

(15) The authority of the President under section 340 of the Consolidated Farmers Home Administration Act of 1961, 75 Stat. 318 (7 U.S.C. 1990), in his discretion to transfer to the Secretary of Agriculture any right, interest or title held by the United States in any lands acquired in the program of national defense and no longer needed for that program, and to determine the suitability of the lands to be transferred, for the purposes referred to in that section: *Provided*, That the exercise by the Administrator of the authority delegated to him by this paragraph (15) shall require the concurrence of the Secretary of Defense as to the absence of further need of the lands for the national defense program.

(16) The authority of the President under section 4(k) of the Tennessee Valley Authority Act, 55 Stat. 599 (16 U.S.C. 831c(k)), to approve transfers under paragraphs (a) and (c) of that section, other than leases for terms of less than 20 years and conveyances of property having a value not in excess of $500.

(17) The authority of the President under section 7(b) of the Tennessee Valley Authority Act of May 18, 1933, 48 Stat. 63 (16 U.S.C. 831f(b)), to provide for the transfer to the Tennessee Valley Authority of the use, possession, and control of real or personal property of the United States deemed by the Administrator of General Services to be necessary and proper for the purposes of that Authority as stated in that Act.

(18) The authority of the President under section 1 of the Act of March 4, 1927, c. 505, 44 Stat. 1422 (20 U.S.C. 191), to transfer to the jurisdiction of the Secretary of Agriculture for the purposes of that Act any land belonging to the United States within or adjacent to the District of Columbia located along the Anacostia River North of Benning Bridge.

(19) That part of the authority of the President under section 7(a) of the Act of July 17, 1959, P.L. 86–91, 73 Stat. 216, as amended (20 U.S.C. 905(a)), which consists of authority to prescribe regulations relating to storage (including packing, drayage, unpacking, and transportation to and from storage) of household effects and personal possessions.

(20) The authority of the Administrator of General Services under section 210(i) of the Federal Property and Administrative Services Act of 1949, as amended (40 U.S.C. 490(i)) [now 40 U.S.C. 589] to prescribe regulations relating to the installation, repair, and replacement of sidewalks.

(21) The authority of the President under section 108 of the Housing Act of July 15, 1949, c. 338, 63 Stat. 419, as amended (42 U.S.C. 1458), to transfer, or cause to be transferred, to the Secretary of Housing and Urban Development any right, title or interest held by the Federal Government or any department or agency thereof in any land (including buildings thereon) which is surplus to the needs of the Government and which a local public agency certifies will be within the area of a project being planned by it.

(22), (23) [Revoked by Ex. Ord. No. 12215, May 27, 1980, 45 F.R. 36043.]

Sec. 2. *Department of the Treasury.* The Secretary of the Treasury is hereby designated and empowered to exercise, without the approval, ratification, or other action of the President, the following:

(1) The authority under 5 U.S.C. 5943(a) to make recommendations to the President concerning the meeting of losses sustained by employees and members of the uniformed services while serving in a foreign country due to appreciation of foreign currency in its relation to the American dollar.

(2) The authority under 5 U.S.C. 5943(d) to report annually to the Congress on expenditures made under 5 U.S.C. 5943(d).

Sec. 3. *Department of Health and Human Services.* The Secretary of Health and Human Services is hereby designated and empowered to exercise, without the approval, ratification, or other action of the President, the following:

(1) The authority of the President under the first section of the Act entitled "An Act to authorize the operation of stands in Federal buildings by blind persons, to enlarge the economic opportunities of the blind, and for other purposes," approved June 20, 1936, 49 Stat. 1559, as amended (20 U.S.C. 107), to approve regulations prescribed by the heads of the respective departments and agencies thereunder.

(2) The authority of the Secretary of Health and Human Services under section 2 of the Act of August 4, 1947, c. 478, 61 Stat. 751, as amended (24 U.S.C. 168a) to fix per diem rates for care of patients in Saint Elizabeths Hospital.

Sec. 4. (a) *Department of State.* The Secretary of State is hereby designated and empowered to exercise his authority under section 12 of the Act of August 1, 1956, 70 Stat. 892 (22 U.S.C. 2679) (being authority to prescribe certain maximum rates of per diem in lieu of subsistence (or of similar allowances therefor)), without the approval, ratification, or other action of the President.

(b) The Secretary of State is hereby designated and empowered to exercise the authority of the President under section 9 of the United Nations Participation Act of 1945 (59 Stat. 619), as amended by section 15 of Public Law 93–126 (87 Stat. 454–455) [22 U.S.C. 287e–1].

SEC. 5. *Department of Defense.* The Secretary of Defense is hereby designated and empowered to exercise the authority of the President under the last sentence of section 4 of the Act of May 10, 1943, c. 95, 57 Stat. 81 (24 U.S.C. 34) to prescribe from time to time uniform rates of charges for hospitalization and dispensary services: *Provided,* That the authority hereby delegated may not be redelegated to any officer in the Department of the Navy, Department of the Air Force, or Department of the Army.

SEC. 6. *Department of Health and Human Services; Department of Defense.* The following are hereby designated and empowered to exercise, without the approval, ratification, or other action of the President, the authority of the President under 10 U.S.C. 1085 to establish uniform rates of reimbursement for inpatient medical or dental care:

(1) The Secretary of Health and Human Services in respect of such care in a facility under his jurisdiction.

(2) The Secretary of Defense in respect of such care in a facility of an armed force under the jurisdiction of a military department.

SEC. 7. *Veterans Administration.* (a) The Administrator of Veterans Affairs is hereby designated and empowered to exercise the authority of the President under 10 U.S.C. 1074(b) to approve uniform rates of reimbursement for care provided in facilities operated by the Administrator.

(b) Section 2 of Executive Order No. 11302 of September 6, 1966, as amended by Executive Order No. 11429 of September 9, 1968 [set out as a note under section 111 of Title 38, Veterans' Benefits], is hereby further amended by substituting for the words "allowance of not more than six cents a mile" the following: "allowance, in such amount per mile as the Administrator shall from time to time fix pursuant to 38 U.S.C. 111 as affected by this order,".

SEC. 8. *Office of Personnel Management.* The Office of Personnel Management is hereby designated and empowered to exercise, without the approval, ratification, or other action of the President, the following:

(1) The authority of the President under 5 U.S.C. 5514(b) to approve regulations prescribed by the head of each agency to carry out 5 U.S.C. 5514 and section 3(a) of the Act of July 15, 1954, c. 509, 68 Stat. 483, 31 U.S.C. 581d [31 U.S.C. 3530(d)] (relating to installment deductions from pay for indebtedness because of erroneous payment).

(2) The authority of the President under 5 U.S.C. 5903 to prescribe regulations necessary for the uniform administration of subchapter I of chapter 59 of title 5 of the United States Code [5 U.S.C. 5901 et seq.] (relating to uniform allowances).

(3) The authority of the President under 5 U.S.C. 5942 to prescribe regulations establishing rates at which an allowance based on duty (except temporary duty) at remote work sites will be paid and defining and designating the sites, areas and groups of positions to which the rates apply.

(4) The authority of the President under 5 U.S.C. 5942a to prescribe regulations governing the payment of allowances to employees assigned to duty at Johnston Island for the purposes of maintaining the employees' spouses or dependents, or both, at a location other than Johnston Island.

SEC. 9. *Office of Management and Budget.* The Director of the Office of Management and Budget is hereby designated and empowered to exercise, without the approval, ratification, or other action of the President, the following:

(1) The authority of the President under 5 U.S.C. 5911(f) to issue the regulations provided for therein (relating to the provision, occupancy, and availability of quarters and facilities, the determination of rates and charges therefor, and other related matters, as are nec-

essary and appropriate to carry out the provision of section 5911).

(2) The authority of the President under 10 U.S.C. 126(a) to approve the transfers of balances of appropriations provided for therein.

(3) The authority of the President under section 202 of the Budget and Accounting Procedures Act of September 12, 1950, 64 Stat. 833 (31 U.S.C. 581c) [31 U.S.C. 1531] to approve the transfers of balances of appropriations provided for in subsections (a) and (b) of that section.

(4) The authority of the President under the last sentence of section 11 of the Act of June 6, 1924, c. 270, 43 Stat. 463 (40 U.S.C. 72) [now 40 U.S.C. 8731(d)], to approve (i) the designation of lands to be acquired by condemnation, (ii) contracts for purchase of lands, and (iii) agreements between the National Capital Planning Commission and officials of the States of Maryland and Virginia.

(5) The authority of the President under section 1 of the Act of December 22, 1928, c. 48, 45 Stat. 1070 (40 U.S.C. 72a) [now 40 U.S.C. 8732], to approve contracts for acquisition of land subject to limited rights reserved to the grantor and for the acquisition of limited permanent rights in land adjoining park property.

(6) The authority of the President under section 407(b) of the Act of August 30, 1957, 71 Stat. 556 (42 U.S.C. 1594j(b)) [see 10 U.S.C. 2830], to approve regulations (relating to the rental of substandard housing for members of the uniformed services) prescribed pursuant to that section. The Secretaries referred to in section 407(c) of that Act shall furnish the Director of the Office of Management and Budget such reports with respect to matters within the scope of the regulations so approved as he may require and at such times as he may specify.

(7) The authority of the President under 44 U.S.C. 1108 to approve the use, from the appropriations available for printing and binding, of such sums as are necessary for the printing of journals, magazines, periodicals, and similar publications.

(8) The authority of the President under the paragraph appearing under the heading "Expenses of Management Improvement" in title III of the Treasury, Post Office, and Executive Office Appropriation Act, 1971, P.L. 91–422, 84 Stat. 877, or by any reenactment of the provisions of that paragraph in the same or in a different amount of funds, to allocate to any agency or office of the executive branch (including the Office of Management and Budget) funds appropriated by that paragraph or by any such reenactment of it. The Director of the Office of Management and Budget shall from time to time report to the President concerning activities carried on by executive agencies and offices with funds allocated under this paragraph and shall, consonant with law, exercise such direction and control with respect to those activities as he shall deem appropriate.

SEC. 10. *General Provisions.* (a) Unless inappropriate, any reference in this order to any provision of law shall be deemed to include reference thereto as amended from time to time and as affected by Reorganization Plan No. 2 of 1970 (35 F.R. 7959).

(b) Unless inappropriate, any reference in any Executive order to any Executive order which is superseded by this order, or to any Executive order provision so superseded, shall hereafter be deemed to refer to this order or to the provision of the preceding section of this order, if any, which corresponds to the superseded provision.

(c) All actions heretofore taken by the President, the Director of the Bureau of the Budget, or the Director of the Office of Management and Budget in respect of the matters affected by the provisions of the preceding sections of this order and in force at the time of the issuance of this order, including any regulations prescribed or approved by any of them in respect of such matters, shall, except as may be inconsistent with the provisions of this order, remain in effect until amended, modified, or revoked pursuant to the authority conferred by this order unless sooner terminated by operation of law.

SEC. 11. *Orders superseded.* The following are hereby superseded:

(1) Executive Order No. 10604 of April 22, 1955.

(2) Executive Order No. 11230 of June 28, 1965.

(3) Executive Order No. 11275 of March 31, 1966.

(4) Executive Order No. 11290 of July 21, 1966.

(5) Section 3 of Executive Order No. 11294 of August 4, 1966.

(6) To the extent that it is inconsistent with this order, Executive Order No. 11541 of July 1, 1970.

SEC. 12. *Taking effect.* This order shall be effective immediately except that paragraphs (1) to (13), inclusive, and paragraph (19), of section 1 hereof shall become effective ninety days after the date of this order.

CHANGE OF NAME

References to Administrator of Veterans' Affairs and to Veterans' Administration deemed to refer to Secretary of Veterans Affairs and to Department of Veterans Affairs, respectively, pursuant to section 10 of Pub. L. 100–527, set out as a Department of Veterans Affairs Act note under section 301 of Title 38, Veterans' Benefits.

EX. ORD. NO. 11690. DELEGATION OF FUNCTIONS TO EXECUTIVE DIRECTOR OF DOMESTIC COUNCIL

Ex. Ord. No. 11690, Dec. 14, 1972, 37 F.R. 26815, provided:

By virtue of the authority vested in me by the Constitution and statutes of the United States, Part II of Reorganization Plan No. 2 of 1970 [set out in 5 U.S.C. App.], and as President of the United States, it is ordered as follows:

SECTION 1. *Functions of the Executive Director of the Domestic Council.* In addition to the functions heretofore assigned, the Executive Director of the Domestic Council shall assist the President with respect to intergovernmental relations generally. In addition, he shall:

(1) serve as the coordinator for the prompt handling and solution of Federal-State-local problems brought to the attention of the President or Vice President by executive and legislative officers of State and local governments;

(2) identify and report to the President on recurring intergovernmental problems of a Federal interdepartmental and interprogram nature;

(3) explore and report to the President on ways and means of strengthening the headquarters and interagency relationships of Federal field offices as they relate to intergovernmental activities;

(4) maintain continuing liaison with intergovernmental units in Federal departments and agencies; and

(5) review procedures utilized by Federal executive agencies for affording State and local officials an opportunity to confer and comment on Federal assistance programs and other intergovernmental issues, and propose methods of strengthening such procedures.

SEC. 2. *Administrative Arrangements.* (a) All Federal departments, agencies, and interagency councils and committees having an impact on intergovernmental relations, and all Federal Executive Boards, shall extend full cooperation and assistance to the Director in carrying out his responsibilities under this order. The Director shall, upon request, assist all Federal departments and agencies with problems that may arise between them and the executive agencies or elected officials of State and local governments.

(b) The head of each Federal department and agency shall designate an appropriate official with broad general experience in his department or agency to serve, upon request of the Director, as a point of contact in carrying out Federal-State-local liaison activities under this order.

SEC. 3. *Construction.* Nothing in this order shall be construed as subjecting any department, establishment, or other instrumentality of the executive branch of the Federal Government or the head thereof, or any function vested by law in or assigned pursuant to law, to any such agency or head, to the authority of any other such agency or head or as abrogating, modifying, or restricting any such function in any manner.

SEC. 4. *Revocation.* Executive Order No. 11455 of February 14, 1969, entitled "Establishing an Office of Intergovernmental Relations", is hereby revoked.

SEC. 5. *Records, Property, Personnel, and Funds.* The records, property, personnel, and unexpended balances, available or to be made available, of appropriations, allocations, and other funds of the Office of Intergovernmental Relations are hereby transferred to the Domestic Council.

SEC. 6. *Effective Date.* This Order shall be effective thirty days after this date.

RICHARD NIXON.

ABOLITION OF DOMESTIC COUNCIL

The Domestic Council, referred to in section 5 of Ex. Ord. No. 11690, Dec. 14, 1972, 31 F.R. 26815, was abolished and its functions transferred to the President with power to delegate such functions within the Executive Office of the President pursuant to Reorg. Plan No. 1 of 1977, §§ 1, 3, 5D, 42 F.R. 56101, 91 Stat. 1633, set out preceding section 101 of this title, effective on or before Apr. 1, 1978, at such time as specified by the President. Ex. Ord. No. 12045, Mar. 27, 1978, 43 F.R. 13347, set out preceding section 101 of this title, provided that the abolition and transfer of functions of the Domestic Council be effective Mar. 26, 1978.

EXECUTIVE ORDER NO. 11713

Ex. Ord. No. 11713, Apr. 21, 1973, 38 F.R. 10069, which related to the delegation of functions to the Administrator of General Services, was revoked by section 1–404 of Ex. Ord. No. 12215, May 27, 1980, 45 F.R. 36045, set out as a note under section 3601 of Title 22, Foreign Relations and Intercourse.

EX. ORD. NO. 11732. DELEGATION OF FUNCTIONS TO SECRETARY OF HOUSING AND URBAN DEVELOPMENT

Ex. Ord. No. 11732, July 30, 1973, 38 F.R. 20429, provided:

By virtue of the authority vested in me by section 301 of title 3 of the United States Code, the Secretary of Housing and Urban Development is hereby designated and empowered to exercise, without approval, ratification, or other action by the President, the functions vested in the President by sections 305 and 301 of the National Housing Act, as amended (12 U.S.C. 1720 and 1716, respectively), relating to the authorization of the purchase of mortgages by the Government National Mortgage Association in connection with its special assistance functions and the determination that such action is in the public interest.

RICHARD NIXON.

EXECUTIVE ORDER NO. 11784

Ex. Ord. No. 11784, May 30, 1974, 39 F.R. 19443, which related to the delegation of certain authority to the Administrator of General Services to issue regulations relating to joint funding, was superseded by Ex. Ord. No. 11867, June 19, 1975, 40 F.R. 26253, formerly set out as a note under section 7103 of Title 31, Money and Finance.

EX. ORD. NO. 12001. TRANSFERRING CERTAIN BICENTENNIAL FUNCTIONS TO SECRETARY OF THE INTERIOR

Ex. Ord. No. 12001, June 29, 1977, 42 F.R. 33709, provided:

By virtue of the authority vested in me by Section 7(b) of the Act of December 11, 1973 (87 Stat. 701) [Pub. L. 93–179], hereinafter referred to as the Act, Section 202(b) of the Budget and Accounting Procedures Act of 1950 (64 Stat. 838, 31 U.S.C. 581c(b)) [31 U.S.C. 1531], and Section 301 of Title 3 of the United States Code, and as President of the United States of America it is hereby ordered as follows:

SECTION 1. The Secretary of the Interior, hereinafter referred to as the Secretary, shall, through existing National Park Service programs, provide for the continuation of appropriate commemoration of events relating to the American Revolution until December 31, 1983.

SEC. 2. The Secretary shall administer existing contracts and grants of the American Revolution Bicentennial Administration, hereinafter referred to as ARBA.

SEC. 3. In performing the functions described in Sections 1 and 2 of this Order, the Secretary may, in addition to any other available authority, exercise the following powers under the Act which are hereby transferred to him for such purposes until December 31, 1983, except as otherwise provided in subsection (b) of this Section:

(a) All powers described in Section 2(f) of the Act with respect to the expenditure of funds donated to ARBA prior to the effective date of this Order, and the expenditure of revenues received or which may be received pursuant to contracts described in Section 2 of this Order.

(b) Until December 31, 1977, all powers exercised by ARBA prior to the effective date of this Order which relate to enforcement of Section 2(i) of the Act.

(c) All powers described in Section 5(a) of the Act.

SEC. 4. All personnel, records, property and appropriations, including all funds and revenues described in Section 3(a) of this Order, as relate to the powers and functions assigned or transferred by this Order are hereby transferred to the Secretary.

SEC. 5. The Director of the Office of Management and Budget shall make such determinations and issue such orders as may be necessary or appropriate to carry out the transfers provided by this Order.

SEC. 6. Executive Order No. 11840 of February 18, 1975, is hereby revoked.

SEC. 7. This Order shall be effective June 30, 1977.

JIMMY CARTER.

EX. ORD. NO. 12152. DELEGATION OF FUNCTIONS TO DIRECTOR OF OFFICE OF MANAGEMENT AND BUDGET

Ex. Ord. No. 12152, Aug. 14, 1979, 44 F.R. 48143, provided:

By the authority vested in me as President by the Constitution and statutes of the United States of America, including Section 301 of Title 3 of the United States Code, and in order to ensure the continued delegation of certain functions which had been previously assigned but which are now vested directly in the President by virtue of H.R. 4616 [Pub. L. 96–54, Aug. 14, 1979, 93 Stat. 381] that I have signed into law today, it is hereby ordered that the functions vested in the President by Sections 305(b), 4111(b), and 4112(a) of Title 5 of the United States Code are hereby delegated to the Director of the Office of Management and Budget.

JIMMY CARTER.

EX. ORD. NO. 12396. DELEGATION OF FUNCTIONS TO SECRETARY OF DEFENSE

Ex. Ord. No. 12396, Dec. 9, 1982, 47 F.R. 55897, provided:

By the authority vested in me as President of the United States of America by Section 301 of Title 3 of the United States Code, and in order to delegate certain functions concerning the appointment, promotion, and retirement of commissioned officers of the Armed Forces, it is hereby ordered as follows:

SECTION 1. The Secretary of Defense is designated to perform, without approval, ratification, or other action by the President, the following functions vested in the President:

(a) The authority vested in the President by Sections 618(b)(1) and 628(d)(1) of Title 10 of the United States Code, to approve, modify, or disapprove the report of a selection board.

(b) The authority vested in the President by Section 629(a) of Title 10 of the United States Code, to remove the name of any officer from a promotion list to any grade below commodore or brigadier general.

(c) The authority vested in the President by Section 624(c) of Title 10 of the United States Code, to appoint officers in the grades of first lieutenant and captain in the Army, Air Force, and Marine Corps or in the grades of lieutenant (junior grade) and lieutenant in the Navy.

(d) The authority vested in the President by Section 5721(c) of Title 10 of the United States Code, to make certain temporary appointments to the grade of lieutenant commander.

(e) The authority vested in the President by Section 6323(a) of Title 10 of the United States Code, to approve the application of an officer of the Navy or the Marine Corps for retirement after the completion of more than 20 years of active service and to designate the month in which such retirements shall become effective.

(f) The authority vested in the President by Sections 3918 and 8918 of Title 10 of the United States Code, to approve the request of a regular commissioned officer of the Army or the Air Force to retire after at least 30 years of service.

(g) Nothing in this Section shall be deemed to delegate the authority vested in the President by Section 618(c) of Title 10 to remove a name from a selection board report.

SEC. 2. (a) The Secretary of Defense is designated to perform during a time of war or national emergency the following functions vested in the President, without the approval, ratification, or other action by the President.

(1) The authority vested in the President by Section 526 of Title 10 of the United States Code, to suspend the operation of any provision of Sections 523, 524 [now 12011], or 525 of Title 10 of the United States Code, relating to the authorized strength of commissioned officers.

(2) The authority vested in the President by subsections (a) and (b) of Section 603 of Title 10 of the United States Code, to make or vacate certain temporary commissioned appointments.

(3) The authority vested in the President by Section 644 [see 123] of Title 10 of the United States Code, to suspend the operation of any law relating to the promotion, involuntary retirement, or separation of commissioned officers of the Army, Navy, Air Force, or Marine Corps.

(b) The authority delegated to the Secretary of Defense by this Section may not be exercised during the time of a national emergency declared by the President, unless the exercise of any such authority is specifically directed by the President in accordance with Section 301 of the National Emergencies Act (50 U.S.C. 1631).

(c) The Secretary of Defense shall ensure that actions taken pursuant to the authority delegated by this Section are accounted for as required by Section 401 of the National Emergencies Act (50 U.S.C. 1641).

SEC. 3. The authority delegated to the Secretary of Defense by this Order may be redelegated to the Deputy Secretary of Defense, any of the Assistant Secretaries of Defense, and to any of the Secretaries of the military departments who may further subdelegate such authority to subordinates who are appointed to their office by the President with the advice and consent of the Senate.

SEC. 4. All actions taken by, for, or on behalf of the President with respect to the functions delegated by this Order, which actions would be valid if taken pursuant to this Order, are ratified.

SEC. 5. (a) Executive Order No. 10621, as amended [set out above], is further amended by revoking subsections (g), (h), (j), (k), (l), (m), and (n) of Section 1 thereof.

(b) Executive Order No. 11390, as amended [set out above], is further amended by revoking subsections 2, 3, 9, 12, and 15 of Section 1 thereof.

(c) Executive Order No. 12239 is revoked.

RONALD REAGAN.

EX. ORD. NO. 12781. DELEGATION OF FUNCTIONS AND AUTHORITIES, DEVELOPMENT OF REQUIREMENTS AND REGULATIONS, AND CORRECTION OF TITLE

Ex. Ord. No. 12781, Nov. 20, 1991, 56 F.R. 59203, provided:

By the authority vested in me as President by the Constitution and the laws of the United States of America, including section 3603 of the Financial Reports Act of 1988 (22 U.S.C. 5351 *et seq.*) [22 U.S.C. 5353], section 274A(d)(2) and (4) of the Immigration and Nationality Act ("Act"), as amended (8 U.S.C. 1324a(d)(2) and (4)), sections 4561, 6082, and 9561 of title 10 of the United States Code, the Act of June 14, 1987 [1897], ch. 2, 30 Stat. 11, 36 (16 U.S.C. 473), section 301 of title 3 of the United States Code, and in order to: (1) delegate functions concerning discussions with foreign governments to improve access by U.S. banking and financial organizations; (2) delegate authority concerning a national employment verification system; (3) delegate authority concerning the development of requirements and regulations for a uniform military ration; and (4) correct the title of the Nez Perce National Forest, it is hereby ordered as follows:

SECTION 1. *Functions Concerning Discussions with Foreign Governments to Improve Access by U.S. Banking and Financial Organizations.* The functions vested in the President by section 3603 of the Financial Reports Act of 1988 (22 U.S.C. 5353) are hereby delegated to the Secretary of the Treasury. This delegation is not in derogation of, and shall not affect, the existing authorities of the United States Trade Representative.

SEC. 2. *Authority Concerning the Employment Verification System.* The authority conferred upon the President by section 274A(d)(4) of the Act [8 U.S.C. 1324a(d)(4)], to undertake demonstration projects of different changes in the requirements of the employment verification system, is delegated to the Attorney General. Demonstration projects shall be conducted consistent with the restrictions in section 274A(d)(2) of the Act and shall not extend for a period longer than 3 years. This authority may be redelegated.

SEC. 3. *Authority, Requirements, and Regulations Concerning a Uniform Military Ration.*

(a) *Authority.* The Secretary of Defense is hereby designated and empowered to exercise, without the approval, ratification, or other action by the President, the authority conferred upon the President by section 4561(a), sections 6082(a) and (d), and section 9561(a) of title 10 of the United States Code. Under this authority the Secretary may prescribe a uniform military ration applicable to the Army, Navy, and Air Force.

(b) *Requirements.* (1) *Components and Quantities.* The components and the quantities of the uniform military ration shall reflect military member preferences and satisfy nutritional requirements. (2) *Monetary Value.* The monetary value of the uniform military ration shall be equal to the monetary value of the ration in effect on the day before the effective date of this order. (3) *Index.* The Secretary of Defense shall establish, as of the effective date of this order, an index composed of a representative market basket of items equal in value to the ration value. Subsequent to the effective date of this order, and based upon the changing prices of food components in the index, the Secretaries of the military departments shall periodically redetermine the monetary value of the ration. The Secretary of Defense shall review the index periodically, but not less than once a year, to ensure that it reflects changes in food service technology, scientific advances in nutrition, the requirements of the Armed Forces of the United States, and the food preferences of the enlisted members. Increases or decreases in the monetary value of the ration that result from changes in the composition of the food items making up the index shall not exceed 2 percent of the ration value annually.

(c) *Regulations.* Under regulations of the Secretary of Defense, the Secretary of the Army, the Secretary of the Navy, and the Secretary of the Air Force are authorized, for their respective military departments, to prescribe the issue of special allowances and such special or supplemental rations, defined by component, quantity, or monetary value, as they may consider appropriate. Executive Order No. 11339 of March 28, 1967, is hereby revoked.

SEC. 4. *Correction of Title of the Nez Perce National Forest.* Executive Order No. 854 of June 26, 1908, is hereby amended by retitling the "Nezperce National Forest" the "Nez Perce National Forest."

SEC. 5. This order shall take effect immediately.

GEORGE BUSH.

EX. ORD. NO. 13313. DELEGATION OF CERTAIN CONGRESSIONAL REPORTING FUNCTIONS

Ex. Ord. No. 13313, July 31, 2003, 68 F.R. 46073, provided:

By the authority vested in me as President by the Constitution and the laws of the United States of America, including section 301 of title 3, United States Code, it is hereby ordered as follows:

SECTION 1. The functions of the President of submitting certain recurring reports to the Congress are assigned as follows:

(a) The Secretary of State shall submit the following reports:

1. Report on Kosovo Peacekeeping, consistent with section 1213 of Public Law 106–398 [114 Stat. 1654A–327];

2. Report on Bosnia and U.S. Forces in NATO-Led Stabilization Force (SFOR), consistent with section 7(b) of Public Law 105–174 [112 Stat. 64] and section 1203(a) of Public Law 105–261 [112 Stat. 2148];

3. Report on Partnership for Peace Developments, consistent with [former] section 514 of Public Law 103–236 (22 U.S.C. 1928 note);

4. Report on U.S. Military Personnel and U.S. Civilian Contractors in Colombia, consistent with section 3204(f) of Public Law 106–246 [114 Stat. 577];

5. Report on Nuclear Nonproliferation, consistent with section 601(a) of Public Law 95–242, as amended by Public Law 103–236 (22 U.S.C. 3281(a));

6. Report on Resolution of the Cyprus Dispute, consistent with section 620C(c) of Public Law 87–195, as amended by Public Law 95–384 (22 U.S.C. 2373(c));

7. Report on Peacekeeping, consistent with section 4 of Public Law 79–264 as amended (22 U.S.C. 287b);

8. Report on Proposed Refugee Admissions, consistent with section 207(d)(1) of Public Law 96–212 (8 U.S.C. 1157(d)(1));

9. Report on Continued Compliance With the Provisions of the Jackson-Vanik Amendment, consistent with sections 402(b) and 409(b) of Public Law 93–618, as amended (19 U.S.C. 2432(b), 2439(b));

10. Report Regarding Conditions in Burma and U.S. Policy Toward Burma, consistent with section 570(d) of Public Law 104–208 [110 Stat. 3009–167];

11. Report on Tibet Negotiations, consistent with section 613(b) of Public Law 107–228 (22 U.S.C. 6901 note);

12. Report on Strategy for Meeting Security Needs of Afghanistan, consistent with section 206(c)(2) of Public Law 107–327 (22 U.S.C. 7536(c)(2));

13. Report on Proliferation of Missiles and Essential Components of Nuclear, Biological, Chemical, and Radiological Weapons, consistent with section 1308(a) of Public Law 107–228 (50 U.S.C. 2368(a));

14. Report on the National Emergency With Respect to Proliferation of Weapons of Mass Destruction, Executive Order 12938 [listed in a table under section 1701 of Title 50, War and National Defense], consistent with section 204(c) of the International Emergency Economic Powers Act, 50 U.S.C. 1703(c), and section 401(c) of the National Emergencies Act, 50 U.S.C. 1641(c);

15. Report on Adherence to and Compliance With Arms Control Agreements and Nonproliferation Agreements and Commitments, consistent with section 403 of Public Law 87–297, as amended (22 U.S.C. 2593a);

16. Report on Chemical Weapons Convention Inspections, consistent with section 309 of the Chemical Weapons Convention Implementation Act of 1998 (22 U.S.C. 6728);

17. Report on U.S. Participation in the United Nations, consistent with section 4 of Public Law 79–264, as amended (22 U.S.C. 287b); and

18. Report on Russian Proliferation to Iran and Other Countries of Proliferation Concern, consistent with section 1206 of Public Law 107–314 (22 U.S.C. 5952 note).

(b) The Secretary of the Treasury shall submit the following reports:

1. Report on the National Emergency With Respect to Libya, Executive Order 12543 [listed in a table under section 1701 of Title 50], consistent with section 401(c) of the National Emergencies Act, 50 U.S.C. 1641(c), and section 204(c) of the International Emergency Economic Powers Act, 50 U.S.C. 1703(c);

2. Report on the National Emergency With Respect to the Western Balkans, Executive Order 13219 [listed in a table under section 1701 of Title 50], consistent with section 401(c) of the National Emergencies Act, 50 U.S.C. 1641(c), and section 204(c) of the International Emergency Economic Powers Act, 50 U.S.C. 1703(c);

3. Report on the National Emergency With Respect to the Risk of Nuclear Proliferation Relating to the Disposition of Highly Enriched Uranium Extracted from Nuclear Weapons of the Government of the Russian Federation, Executive Order 13159 [listed in a table under section 1701 of Title 50], consistent with section 401(c) of the National Emergencies Act, 50 U.S.C. 1641(c), and section 204(c) of the International Emergency Economic Powers Act, 50 U.S.C. 1703(c);

4. Report on the National Emergency With Respect to Burma, Executive Order 13047 [listed in a table under section 1701 of Title 50], consistent with section 401(c) of the National Emergencies Act, 50 U.S.C. 1641(c), and section 204(c) of the International Emergency Economic Powers Act, 50 U.S.C. 1703(c);

5. Report on the National Emergency With Respect to Middle East Terrorism, Executive Order 12947 [listed in a table under section 1701 of Title 50], consistent with section 401(c) of the National Emergencies Act, 50 U.S.C. 1641(c), and section 204(c) of the International Emergency Economic Powers Act, 50 U.S.C. 1703(c);

6. Report on the National Emergency With Respect to the 1979 Iranian Emergency and Assets Blocking, Executive Order 12170 [listed in a table under section 1701 of Title 50], consistent with section 401(c) of the National Emergencies Act, 50 U.S.C. 1641(c), and section 204(c) of the International Emergency Economic Powers Act, 50 U.S.C. 1703(c);

7. Report on the National Emergency With Respect to Iranian Petroleum Resources, Executive Order 12957 [listed in a table under section 1701 of Title 50], consistent with section 401(c) of the National Emergencies Act, 50 U.S.C. 1641(c), and section 204(c) of the International Emergency Economic Powers Act, 50 U.S.C. 1703(c);

8. Report on the National Emergency With Respect to Significant Narcotics Traffickers Centered in Colombia, Executive Order 12978 [listed in a table under section 1701 of Title 50], consistent with section 401(c) of the National Emergencies Act, 50 U.S.C. 1641(c), and section 204(c) of the International Emergency Economic Powers Act, 50 U.S.C. 1703(c);

9. Report on the National Emergency With Respect to Persons Who Commit, Threaten to Commit, or Support Terrorism, Executive Order 13224 [listed in a table under section 1701 of Title 50], consistent with section 401(c) of the National Emergencies Act, 50 U.S.C. 1641(c), and section 204(c) of the International Emergency Economic Powers Act, 50 U.S.C. 1703(c);

10. Report on the National Emergency With Respect to Sierra Leone and Liberia, Executive Order 13194 [listed in a table under section 1701 of Title 50], consistent with section 401(c) of the National Emergencies Act, 50 U.S.C. 1641(c), and section 204(c) of the International Emergency Economic Powers Act, 50 U.S.C. 1703(c);

11. Report on the National Emergency With Respect to Sudan, Executive Order 13067 [listed in a table under section 1701 of Title 50], consistent with section 401(c) of the National Emergencies Act, 50 U.S.C. 1641(c), and section 204(c) of the International Emergency Economic Powers Act, 50 U.S.C. 1703(c);

12. Report on the National Emergency With Respect to Iraq, Executive Order 12722 [listed in a table under section 1701 of Title 50], consistent with section 401(c) of the National Emergencies Act, 50 U.S.C. 1641(c), and section 204(c) of the International Emergency Economic Powers Act, 50 U.S.C. 1703(c);

13. Report on the National Emergency With Respect to the Development Fund for Iraq, Executive Order 13303 [listed in a table under section 1701 of Title 50], consistent with section 401(c) of the National Emergencies Act, 50 U.S.C. 1641(c), and section 204(c) of the International Emergency Economic Powers Act, 50 U.S.C. 1703(c);

14. Classified Report on the Status of Sanctions Imposed on Significant Foreign Narcotics Traffickers, consistent with section 804(d) of Public Law 106–120 (21 U.S.C. 1903(d));

15. Report on Telecommunications Payments Made to Cuba Pursuant to Department of the Treasury Specific Licenses, consistent with section 1705(e)(6) of Public Law 102–484, as amended by Public Law 104–114 (22 U.S.C. 6004(e)(6));

16. Report on the National Emergency With Respect to Persons Undermining Democratic Processes or Institutions in Zimbabwe, Executive Order 13288 [listed in a table under section 1701 of Title 50], consistent with section 401(c) of the National Emergencies Act, 50 U.S.C. 1641(c), and section 204(c) of the International Emergency Economic Powers Act, 50 U.S.C. 1703(c); and

17. Report on International Debt Relief, consistent with section 1000(a)(5) of Public Law 106–113 [113 Stat. 1501A–313].

(c) The Secretary of Defense shall submit the following reports:

1. Report on Kosovo Benchmarks, consistent with section 1212(c) of Public Law 106–398 [114 Stat. 1654A–326]; and

2. Report on the National Emergency With Respect to Terrorist Attacks on the United States, Proclamation 7463 of September 14, 2001 [50 U.S.C. 1621 note], consistent with section 401(c) of the National Emergencies Act, 50 U.S.C. 1641(c), and section 204(c) of the International Emergency Economic Powers Act, 50 U.S.C. 1703(c).

(d) The Secretary of Commerce shall submit the Report on the National Emergency Caused by the Lapse of the Export Administration Act of 1979, Executive Order 13222 [listed in a table under section 1701 of Title 50], consistent with section 401(c) of the National Emergencies Act, 50 U.S.C. 1641(c), and section 204(c) of the International Emergency Economic Powers Act, 50 U.S.C. 1703(c).

(e) The Director of Central Intelligence shall submit the following reports:

1. Report on Foreign Economic Collection and Industrial Espionage, consistent with section 809(b) of Public Law 103–359 (50 U.S.C. App. 2170[b](b)); and

2. Reports on Commerce With, and Assistance to, Cuba from Other Foreign Countries, consistent with section 108(a) of Public Law 104–114 (22 U.S.C. 6038(a)).

(f) The Director of National Drug Control Policy shall submit the Report on Support for Plan Colombia, consistent with section 3204(e) of Public Law 106–246 [114 Stat. 576].

SEC. 2. Reports to the Congress described in certain Senate resolutions shall be submitted as follows:

(a) The Secretary of State shall submit the following reports:

1. Report on the Inter-American Convention Against Corruption, consistent with the Resolution of Advice and Consent to Ratification of the Inter-American Convention Against Corruption adopted by the Senate on July 27, 2000;

2. Report on Compliance With the Treaty on Conventional Armed Forces in Europe, consistent with Condition 5(C) of the Resolution of Advice and Consent to Ratification of the Document Agreed Among the States Parties to the Treaty on Conventional Armed Forces in Europe of November 19, 1990;

3. Report on Chemical Weapons Convention Compliance, consistent with Condition 10(C) of the Resolution of Advice and Consent to the Chemical Weapons Convention adopted by the Senate on April 24, 1997; and

4. Report on Moscow Treaty Implementation, consistent with section 2(2) of the Resolution of Advice and Consent to Ratification of the Treaty on Strategic Offensive Reductions of May 24, 2002.

(b) The Secretary of Commerce shall submit the Report on the Status of the World Intellectual Property Organization Copyright Treaty and the Performance and Phonograms Treaty, consistent with the Senate's resolution of ratification of October 21, 1998.

(c) The Secretary of Defense shall submit the Report on Moscow Treaty Implementation, consistent with section 2(1) of the Resolution of Advice and Consent to Ratification of the Treaty on Strategic Offensive Reductions of May 24, 2002.

SEC. 3. In carrying out sections 1 and 2 of this order, officers of the United States shall ensure that all actions taken by them are consistent with the President's constitutional authority to: (a) conduct the foreign affairs of the United States; (b) withhold information the disclosure of which could impair the foreign relations, the national security, the deliberative processes of the Executive, or the performance of the Executive's constitutional duties; (c) recommend for congressional consideration such measures as the President may judge necessary and expedient; and (d) supervise the unitary executive branch.

SEC. 4. Nothing in this order shall be construed to impair or otherwise affect the functions of the Director of the Office of Management and Budget relating to budget, administrative, or legislative proposals.

SEC. 5. This order is intended only to improve the internal management of the executive branch and is not intended to, and does not, create any right or benefit, substantive or procedural, enforceable at law or in equity by a party against the United States, its departments, agencies, entities, officers, employees or agents, or any other person.

GEORGE W. BUSH.

EX. ORD. NO. 13337. ISSUANCE OF PERMITS WITH RESPECT TO CERTAIN ENERGY-RELATED FACILITIES AND LAND TRANSPORTATION CROSSINGS ON THE INTERNATIONAL BOUNDARIES OF THE UNITED STATES

Ex. Ord. No. 13337, Apr. 30, 2004, 69 F.R. 25299, provided:

By the authority vested in me as President by the Constitution and the laws of the United States of America, including section 301 of title 3, United States Code, and in order to amend Executive Order 11423 of August 16, 1968, as amended [set out above], and to further the policy of my Administration as stated in Executive Order 13212 of May 18, 2001, as amended [42 U.S.C. 13201 note], to expedite reviews of permits as necessary to accelerate the completion of energy production and transmission projects, and to provide a systematic method for evaluating and permitting the construction and maintenance of certain border crossings for land transportation, including motor and rail vehicles, that do not require construction or maintenance of facilities connecting the United States with a foreign country, while maintaining safety, public health, and environmental protections, it is hereby ordered as follows:

SECTION 1. (a) Except with respect to facilities covered by Executive Order 10485 of September 3, 1953 [15 U.S.C. 717b note], and Executive Order 10530 of May 10, 1954 [set out above], the Secretary of State is hereby designated and empowered to receive all applications for Presidential permits, as referred to in Executive Order 11423, as amended, for the construction, connection, operation, or maintenance, at the borders of the United States, of facilities for the exportation or importation of petroleum, petroleum products, coal, or other fuels to or from a foreign country.

(b) Upon receipt of a completed application pursuant to paragraph (a) of this section, the Secretary of State shall:

(i) Request additional information needed from the applicant, as appropriate, before referring the application to other agencies pursuant to paragraph (b)(ii) of this section;

(ii) Refer the application and pertinent information to, and request the views of, the Secretary of Defense, the Attorney General, the Secretary of the Interior, the Secretary of Commerce, the Secretary of Transportation, the Secretary of Energy, the Secretary of Homeland Security, the Administrator of the Environmental Protection Agency, or the heads of the departments or agencies in which the relevant authorities or responsibilities of the foregoing are subsequently conferred or transferred, and, for applications concerning the border with Mexico, the United States Commissioner of the International Boundary and Water Commission; and

(iii) Refer the application and pertinent information to, and request the views of, such other Federal Government department and agency heads as the Secretary of State deems appropriate.

(c) All Federal Government officials consulted by the Secretary of State pursuant to paragraph (b)(ii) or (b)(iii) of this section shall provide their views and render such assistance as may be requested, consistent with their authority, in a timely manner, but not to exceed 90 days from the date of the request.

(d) Should any of the Federal Government officials consulted pursuant to paragraph (b)(ii) or (b)(iii) of this section request from the Department of State additional information that is necessary for them to provide their views or to render such assistance as may be required, the time elapsed between the date of that request for additional information and the date such additional information is received shall not be counted in calculating the time period prescribed in paragraph (c) of this section.

(e) The Secretary of State may also consult with such State, tribal, and local government officials and foreign governments, as the Secretary deems appropriate, with respect to each application. The Secretary shall solicit responses in a timely manner, not to exceed 90 days from the date of the request.

(f) Upon receiving the views and assistance requested pursuant to paragraphs (b) and (e) of this section, the Secretary of State shall consider, in light of any statutory or other requirements or other considerations, whether or not additional information is needed in order to evaluate the application and, as appropriate, request such information from the applicant.

(g) After consideration of the views and assistance obtained pursuant to paragraphs (b) and, as appropriate, (e) and (f) of this section and any public comments submitted pursuant to section 3(a) of this order, if the Secretary of State finds that issuance of a permit to the applicant would serve the national interest, the Secretary shall prepare a permit, in such form and with such terms and conditions as the national interest may in the Secretary's judgment require, and shall notify the officials required to be consulted under paragraph (b)(ii) of this section of the proposed determination that a permit be issued.

(h) After consideration of the views obtained pursuant to paragraphs (b) and, as appropriate, (e) and (f) of this section and any public comments provided pursuant to section 3(a) of this order, if the Secretary of State finds that issuance of a permit to the applicant would not serve the national interest, the Secretary shall notify the officials required to be consulted under paragraph (b)(ii) of this section of the proposed determination that the application be denied.

(i) The Secretary of State shall issue or deny the permit in accordance with the proposed determination unless, within 15 days after notification pursuant to paragraphs (g) or (h) of this section, an official required to be consulted under paragraph (b)(ii) of this section shall notify the Secretary of State that he or she disagrees with the Secretary's proposed determination and requests the Secretary to refer the application to the President. In the event of such a request, the Secretary of State shall consult with any such requesting official and, if necessary, shall refer the application, together with statements of the views of any official involved, to the President for consideration and a final decision.

SEC. 2. [Amended Ex. Ord. No. 11423, set out above.]

SEC. 3. (a) The Secretary of State may provide for the publication in the Federal Register of notice of receipt of applications, for the receipt of public comments on applications, and for notices related to the issuance or denial of applications.

(b) The Secretary of State is authorized to issue such further rules and regulations, and to prescribe such further procedures, including, but not limited to, those relating to the International Boundary and Water Commission, as may from time to time be deemed necessary or desirable for the exercise of the authority conferred by this order.

SEC. 4. All permits heretofore issued with respect to facilities described in section 2(a) of this order pursuant to Executive Order 11423, as amended, and in force at the time of issuance of this order, and all permits issued hereunder, shall remain in effect in accordance with their terms unless and until modified, amended, suspended, or revoked by the appropriate authority.

SEC. 5. Nothing contained in this order shall be construed to affect the authority of any department or agency of the United States Government, or to supersede or replace the requirements established under any other provision of law, or to relieve a person from any requirement to obtain authorization from any other department or agency of the United States Government in compliance with applicable laws and regulations subject to the jurisdiction of that department or agency.

SEC. 6. This order is not intended to, and does not, create any right, benefit, or trust responsibility, substantive or procedural, enforceable at law or in equity by any party against the United States, its departments, agencies, instrumentalities, or entities, its officers or employees, or any other person.

GEORGE W. BUSH.

EX. ORD. NO. 13346. DELEGATION OF CERTAIN WAIVER, DETERMINATION, CERTIFICATION, RECOMMENDATION, AND REPORTING FUNCTIONS

Ex. Ord. No. 13346, July 8, 2004, 69 F.R. 41905, provided:

By the authority vested in me as President by the Constitution and the laws of the United States of America, including section 301 of title 3, United States Code, it is hereby ordered as follows:

SECTION 1. The functions of the President in making certain waivers, determinations, certifications, recommendations, and reports to the Congress are assigned as follows:

(a) The Secretary of State is authorized to make waivers, determinations, certifications, and recommendations, and to undertake related reporting, as described in:

(i) Section 402(d)(1) of the Trade Act of 1974, as amended (19 U.S.C. 2432(d)(1)), with respect to the extension of Jackson-Vanik waivers;

(ii) Section 609 of Division A of the Omnibus Consolidated and Emergency Supplemental Appropriations Act, 1999 (Public Law 105–277) [112 Stat. 2681–112] as continued in effect by section 612 of Division B of the Consolidated Appropriations Act, 2004 (Public Law 108–199) [118 Stat. 94] with respect to cooperation related to persons missing in action and prisoners of war; and

(iii) Section 102(a)(2) of the Arms Export Control Act, as amended (22 U.S.C. 2799aa–1(a)[2]), with respect to any Presidential determination under section 102(a)(1) that is also the subject of a determination and certification by the President pursuant to section 102(a)(2).

(b) The United States Trade Representative shall submit the report relating to sub-Saharan Africa under section 106 of the African Growth and Opportunity Act (Public Law 106–200, title 1[I]) [19 U.S.C. 3705].

SEC. 2. The functions of the President in making certifications to the Congress consistent with the resolution of advice and consent to ratification of the Chemical Weapons Convention adopted by the Senate on April 24, 1997 (Resolution) are assigned as follows:

(a) The Secretary of State is authorized to make a certification consistent with section 2(7)(C)(i) of the

Resolution with respect to the effectiveness and viability of the Australia Group.

(b) The Secretary of Commerce is authorized to make a certification consistent with section 2(9) of the Resolution with respect to the interests of certain firms in the United States.

SEC. 3. [Amended Ex. Ord. No. 12163, set out as a note under section 2381 of Title 22, Foreign Relations and Intercourse.]

SEC. 4. [Amended Ex. Ord. No. 13277, set out as a note under section 3801 of Title 19, Customs Duties.]

SEC. 5. References in this order to provisions of any Act shall be deemed to include references to any provision of law that is the same or substantially the same as such provisions.

SEC. 6. In carrying out sections 1 and 2 of this order, officers of the United States shall ensure that all actions taken by them are consistent with the President's constitutional authority to: (a) conduct the foreign affairs of the United States; (b) withhold information the disclosure of which could impair the foreign relations, the national security, the deliberative processes of the Executive, or the performance of the Executive's constitutional duties; (c) recommend for congressional consideration such measures as the President may judge necessary and expedient; and (d) supervise the unitary executive branch.

SEC. 7. Nothing in this order shall be construed to impair or otherwise affect the functions of the Director of the Office of Management and Budget relating to budget, administrative, or legislative proposals.

SEC. 8. This order is intended only to improve the internal management of the executive branch and is not intended to, and does not, create any right or benefit, substantive or procedural, enforceable at law or in equity by a party against the United States, its departments, agencies, entities, officers, employees or agents, or any other person.

GEORGE W. BUSH.

EX. ORD. NO. 13358. ASSIGNMENT OF FUNCTIONS RELATING TO CERTAIN APPOINTMENTS, PROMOTIONS, AND COMMISSIONS IN THE ARMED FORCES

Ex. Ord. No. 13358, Sept. 28, 2004, 69 F.R. 58797, provided:

By the authority vested in me as President by the Constitution and the laws of the United States of America, including section 301 of title 3, United States Code, it is hereby ordered as follows:

SECTION 1. *Assignment of Functions to the Secretary of Defense.* The Secretary of Defense shall perform, except with respect to the Coast Guard during any period in which it is not operating as a service in the Navy, the functions of the President under the following provisions of title 10, United States Code:

(a) subsection 1521(a);

(b) the first sentence of subsection 12203(a);

(c) the first sentence of subsection 14111(a), except with respect to reports relating to the grades of brigadier general or above, or rear admiral (lower half) or above; and

(d) subsection 14310(a), except with respect to removals relating to a promotion list for grades of brigadier general or above, or rear admiral (lower half) or above.

SEC. 2. *Assignment of Functions to the Secretary of Homeland Security.* The Secretary of Homeland Security shall perform, with respect to the Coast Guard during any period in which it is not operating as a service in the Navy, the functions assigned to the President by the following provisions of the United States Code:

(a) subsection 1521(a) of title 10;

(b) the first sentence of subsection 12203(a) of title 10;

(c) subsection 729(g) of title 14, except with respect to approval of, or removal of a name from, a report relating to the grades of rear admiral (lower half) or above; and

(d) subsection 738(a) of title 14, except with respect to removals relating to a promotion list for grades of rear admiral (lower half) or above.

SEC. 3. *Reassignment of Functions Assigned.* The Secretary of Defense and the Secretary of Homeland Security may reassign the functions assigned to them by this order to civilian officers, within their respective departments, who hold a position for which the President makes an appointment by and with the advice and consent of the Senate, except that the Secretary of Defense and the Secretary of Homeland Security may not reassign the functions assigned by sections 1(b) and 2(b), respectively. The Secretary of Defense may not reassign the function assigned by section 1(c) of this order except to such an officer within the Office of the Secretary of Defense (as defined in section 131(b) of title 10).

SEC. 4. *General Provisions.* (a) This order shall take effect on October 1, 2004.

(b) Nothing in this order shall be construed to limit or otherwise affect the authority of the President as Commander in Chief of the Armed Forces of the United States, or under the Constitution and laws of the United States to nominate or to make or terminate appointments.

(c) This order is not intended to, and does not, create any right or benefit, substantive or procedural, enforceable at law or in equity by any party against the United States, its departments, agencies, entities, officers, employees or agents, or any other person.

GEORGE W. BUSH.

MEMORANDUM ON ASSIGNMENT OF REPORTING FUNCTIONS UNDER THE INTELLIGENCE REFORM AND TERRORISM PREVENTION ACT OF 2004

Memorandum of President of the United States, Apr. 21, 2005, 70 F.R. 48633, as amended by Memorandum of President of the United States, July 1, 2005, 70 F.R. 41341, provided:

Memorandum for the Secretary of State[,] the Secretary of Defense[,] the Director of National Intelligence[,] the Attorney General[, and] the Secretary of Homeland Security

By the authority vested in me as President by the Constitution and laws of the United States, including section 301 of title 3, United States Code:

1. The reporting functions of the President under sections 4026(a)(4)(A), 4026(c)(2), 7104(e)(4)(A), 7202(d) [now 7202(g)], 7204(c)(1)–(2), and 7120 [118 Stat. 3803] of the Intelligence Reform and Terrorism Prevention Act of 2004 (Public Law 108–458, 118 Stat. 3638) (the "Act") [8 U.S.C. 1777(g), 22 U.S.C. 2656 note, 2751 note, 7555] are hereby assigned to the Secretary of State.

The reporting function under section 7202(d) [now 7202(g)] of the Act [8 U.S.C. 1777(g)] on the Human Smuggling and Trafficking Center shall be coordinated with the Attorney General and the Secretary of Homeland Security.

Heads of departments and agencies shall, to the extent permitted by law, furnish to the Secretary of State information the Secretary requests to perform such functions, in the format and on the schedule specified by the Secretary.

2. The reporting function of the President under section 7104(i) of the Act [22 U.S.C. 7536] is hereby assigned to the Secretary of Defense.

Heads of departments and agencies shall, to the extent permitted by law, furnish to the Secretary of Defense information the Secretary requests to perform such functions, in the format and on the schedule specified by the Secretary.

3. The reporting functions under sections 1022 and 1094 of the Act [50 U.S.C. 404*o*–1, 401 note] are hereby assigned to the Director of National Intelligence.

Heads of departments and agencies shall, to the extent permitted by law, furnish to the Director of National Intelligence information the Director requests to perform such functions, in the format and on the schedule specified by the Director.

The Secretaries of State and Defense, and the Director of National Intelligence shall perform such functions in a manner consistent with the President's constitutional authority to withhold information the disclosure of which could impair foreign relations, national security, the deliberative processes of the Executive, or the performance of the Executive's constitutional duties.

Any reference in this memorandum to the provision of any Act shall be deemed to include references to any hereafter-enacted provision of law that is the same or substantially the same as such provision.

The Secretary of State is authorized and directed to publish this memorandum in the Federal Register.

GEORGE W. BUSH.

§ 302. Scope of delegation of functions

The authority conferred by this chapter shall apply to any function vested in the President by law if such law does not affirmatively prohibit delegation of the performance of such function as herein provided for, or specifically designate the officer or officers to whom it may be delegated. This chapter shall not be deemed to limit or derogate from any existing or inherent right of the President to delegate the performance of functions vested in him by law, and nothing herein shall be deemed to require express authorization in any case in which such an official would be presumed in law to have acted by authority or direction of the President.

(Added Oct. 31, 1951, ch. 655, § 10, 65 Stat. 712.)

SIMILAR PROVISIONS; REPEAL; SAVING CLAUSE

For similar provisions contained in prior law, and saving clause in connection therewith, see note preceding section 301 of this title.

§ 303. Definitions

As used in this chapter, the term "function" embraces any duty, power, responsibility, authority, or discretion vested in the President or other officer concerned, and the terms "perform" and "performance" may be construed to mean "exercise".

(Added Oct. 31, 1951, ch. 655, § 10, 65 Stat. 712.)

SIMILAR PROVISIONS; REPEAL; SAVING CLAUSE

For similar provisions contained in prior law, and saving clause in connection therewith, see note preceding section 301 of this title.

CHAPTER 5—EXTENSION OF CERTAIN RIGHTS AND PROTECTIONS TO PRESIDENTIAL OFFICES

SUBCHAPTER I—GENERAL PROVISIONS

SUBCHAPTER I—GENERAL PROVISIONS

§ 401. Definitions

(a) IN GENERAL.—Except as otherwise specifically provided in this chapter, as used in this chapter:

(1) BOARD.—The term "Board" means the Merit Systems Protection Board under chapter 12 of title 5.

(2) COVERED EMPLOYEE.—The term "covered employee" means any employee of an employing office.

(3) EMPLOYEE.—The term "employee" includes an applicant for employment and a former employee.

(4) EMPLOYING OFFICE.—The term "employing office" means—

(A) each office, agency, or other component of the Executive Office of the President;

(B) the Executive Residence at the White House; and

(C) the official residence (temporary or otherwise) of the Vice President.

(b) DEFINITIONS RELATING TO CERTAIN MATTERS.—For purposes of applying this chapter with respect to any practice or other matter—

(1) to which section 411 relates, the terms "employing office" and "covered employee" shall each be considered to have the meaning given to the term by such section;

____
[1] So in original. Does not conform to section catchline.

(2) to which section 412 relates, the term "covered employee" means a covered employee described in section 412(a)(2)(B);

(3) to which section 413 relates, the term "covered employee" excludes interns and volunteers, as described in section 413(a)(2); and

(4) to which section 416 relates, the term "covered employee" means a covered employee described in section 416(a)(2).

(Added Pub. L. 104–331, § 2(a), Oct. 26, 1996, 110 Stat. 4054.)

REGULATIONS

Section 2(b) of Pub. L. 104–331 provided that: "Appropriate measures shall be taken to ensure that—

"(1) any regulations required to implement section 411 of title 3, United States Code, shall be in effect by October 1, 1997; and

"(2) any other regulations needed to implement chapter 5 of title 3, United States Code, shall be in effect as soon as practicable, but not later than October 1, 1998."

APPLICABILITY OF FUTURE EMPLOYMENT LAWS

Section 4 of Pub. L. 104–331 provided that:

"(a) IN GENERAL.—Each provision of Federal law that is made applicable to the legislative branch under section 102 of the Congressional Accountability Act of 1995 (2 U.S.C. 1302), and that is enacted later than 12 months after the date of the enactment of this Act [Oct. 26, 1996], shall be deemed to apply with respect to 'employing offices' and 'covered employees' (within the meaning of section 401 of title 3, United States Code, as added by this Act), unless such law specifically provides otherwise and expressly cites this section.

"(b) REGULATIONS.—

"(1) IN GENERAL.—The President, or the designee of the President, shall issue regulations to implement such provision.

"(2) AGENCY REGULATIONS.—The regulations issued under paragraph (1) to implement a provision shall be the same as substantive regulations promulgated by the head of the appropriate executive agency to implement the provision, except to the extent that the President or designee may determine, for good cause shown and stated together with the regulation, that a modification of such regulations would be more effective for the implementation of the rights and protections under the section."

§ 402. Application of laws

The following laws shall apply, as prescribed by this chapter, to all employing offices (including employing offices within the meaning of section 411, to the extent prescribed therein):

(1) The Fair Labor Standards Act of 1938.

(2) Title VII of the Civil Rights Act of 1964.

(3) The Americans with Disabilities Act of 1990.

(4) The Age Discrimination in Employment Act of 1967.

(5) The Family and Medical Leave Act of 1993.

(6) The Occupational Safety and Health Act of 1970.

(7) Chapter 71 (relating to Federal service labor-management relations) of title 5.

(8) The Employee Polygraph Protection Act of 1988.

(9) The Worker Adjustment and Retraining Notification Act.

(10) The Rehabilitation Act of 1973.

(11) Chapter 43 (relating to veterans' employment and reemployment) of title 38.

(Added Pub. L. 104–331, § 2(a), Oct. 26, 1996, 110 Stat. 4054.)

REFERENCES IN TEXT

The Fair Labor Standards Act of 1938, referred to in par. (1), is act June 25, 1938, ch. 676, 52 Stat. 1060, as amended, which is classified generally to chapter 8 (§ 201 et seq.) of Title 29, Labor. For complete classification of this Act to the Code, see section 201 of Title 29 and Tables.

The Civil Rights Act of 1964, referred to in par. (2), is Pub. L. 88–352, July 2, 1964, 78 Stat. 252, as amended. Title VII of the Act is classified generally to subchapter VI (§ 2000e et seq.) of chapter 21 of Title 42, The Public Health and Welfare. For complete classification of this Act to the Code, see Short Title note set out under section 2000a of Title 42 and Tables.

The Americans with Disabilities Act of 1990, referred to in par. (3), is Pub. L. 101–336, July 26, 1990, 104 Stat. 327, as amended, which is classified principally to chapter 126 (§ 12101 et seq.) of Title 42. For complete classification of this Act to the Code, see Short Title note set out under section 12101 of Title 42 and Tables.

The Age Discrimination in Employment Act of 1967, referred to in par. (4), is Pub. L. 90–202, Dec. 15, 1967, 81 Stat. 602, as amended, which is classified generally to chapter 14 (§ 621 et seq.) of Title 29, Labor. For complete classification of this Act to the Code, see Short Title note set out under section 621 of Title 29 and Tables.

The Family and Medical Leave Act of 1993, referred to in par. (5), is Pub. L. 103–3, Feb. 5, 1993, 107 Stat. 6, as amended, which enacted sections 60m and 60n of Title 2, The Congress, sections 6381 to 6387 of Title 5, Government Organization and Employees, and chapter 28 (§ 2601 et seq.) of Title 29, amended section 2105 of Title 5, and enacted provisions set out as notes under section 2601 of Title 29. For complete classification of this Act to the Code, see Short Title note set out under section 2601 of Title 29 and Tables.

The Occupational Safety and Health Act of 1970, referred to in par. (6), is Pub. L. 91–596, Dec. 29, 1970, 84 Stat. 1590, as amended, which is classified principally to chapter 15 (§ 651 et seq.) of Title 29. For complete classification of this Act to the Code, see Short Title note set out under section 651 of Title 29 and Tables.

The Employee Polygraph Protection Act of 1988, referred to in par. (8), is Pub. L. 100–347, June 27, 1988, 102 Stat. 646, as amended, which is classified generally to chapter 22 (§ 2001 et seq.) of Title 29. For complete classification of this Act to the Code, see Short Title note set out under section 2001 of Title 29 and Tables.

The Worker Adjustment and Retraining Notification Act, referred to in par. (9), is Pub. L. 100–379, Aug. 4, 1988, 102 Stat. 890, which is classified generally to chapter 23 (§ 2101 et seq.) of Title 29. For complete classification of this Act to the Code, see Short Title note set out under section 2101 of Title 29 and Tables.

The Rehabilitation Act of 1973, referred to in par. (10), is Pub. L. 93–112, Sept. 26, 1973, 87 Stat. 355, as amended, which is classified generally to chapter 16 (§ 701 et seq.) of Title 29. For complete classification of this Act to the Code, see Short Title note set out under section 701 of Title 29 and Tables.

SUBCHAPTER II—EXTENSION OF RIGHTS AND PROTECTIONS

PART A—EMPLOYMENT DISCRIMINATION, FAMILY AND MEDICAL LEAVE, FAIR LABOR STANDARDS, EMPLOYEE POLYGRAPH PROTECTION, WORKER ADJUSTMENT AND RETRAINING, EMPLOYMENT AND REEMPLOYMENT OF VETERANS, AND INTIMIDATION

§ 411. Rights and protections under title VII of the Civil Rights Act of 1964, the Age Discrimination in Employment Act of 1967, the Rehabilitation Act of 1973, and title I of the Americans with Disabilities Act of 1990

(a) DISCRIMINATORY PRACTICES PROHIBITED.— All personnel actions affecting covered employees shall be made free from any discrimination based on—

(1) race, color, religion, sex, or national origin, within the meaning of section 703 of the Civil Rights Act of 1964;

(2) age, within the meaning of section 15 of the Age Discrimination in Employment Act of 1967; or

(3) disability, within the meaning of section 501 of the Rehabilitation Act of 1973 and sections 102 through 104 of the Americans with Disabilities Act of 1990.

(b) REMEDY.—

(1) CIVIL RIGHTS.—The remedy for a violation of subsection (a)(1) shall be—

(A) such damages as would be appropriate if awarded under section 706(g) of the Civil Rights Act of 1964; and

(B) such compensatory damages as would be appropriate if awarded under section 1977 of the Revised Statutes, or as would be appropriate if awarded under sections 1977A(a)(1), 1977A(b)(2), and, irrespective of the size of the employing office, 1977A(b)(3)(D) of the Revised Statutes.

(2) AGE DISCRIMINATION.—The remedy for a violation of subsection (a)(2) shall be—

(A) such damages as would be appropriate if awarded under section 15(c) of the Age Discrimination in Employment Act of 1967; and

(B) such liquidated damages as would be appropriate if awarded under section 7(b) of such Act.

In addition, the waiver provisions of section 7(f) of such Act shall apply to covered employees.

(3) DISABILITIES DISCRIMINATION.—The remedy for a violation of subsection (a)(3) shall be—

(A) such damages as would be appropriate if awarded under section 505(a)(1) of the Rehabilitation Act of 1973 or section 107(a) of the Americans with Disabilities Act of 1990; and

(B) such compensatory damages as would be appropriate if awarded under sections 1977A(a)(2), 1977A(a)(3), 1977A(b)(2), and, irrespective of the size of the employing office, 1977A(b)(3)(D) of the Revised Statutes.

(c) DEFINITIONS.—Except as otherwise specifically provided in this section, as used in this section:

(1) COVERED EMPLOYEE.—The term "covered employee" means any employee of a unit of the executive branch, including the Executive Office of the President, whether appointed by the President or by any other appointing authority in the executive branch, who is not otherwise entitled to bring an action under any of the statutes referred to in subsection (a), but does not include any individual—

(A) whose appointment is made by and with the advice and consent of the Senate;

(B) who is appointed to an advisory committee, as defined in section 3(2) of the Federal Advisory Committee Act; or

(C) who is a member of the uniformed services.

(2) EMPLOYING OFFICE.—The term "employing office", with respect to a covered employee, means the office, agency, or other entity in which the covered employee is employed (or sought employment or was employed in the case of an applicant or former employee, respectively).

(d) REGULATIONS TO IMPLEMENT SECTION.—

(1) IN GENERAL.—The President, or the designee of the President, shall issue regulations to implement paragraphs (1) and (3) of subsection (a) and paragraphs (1) and (3) of subsection (b).

(2) AGENCY REGULATIONS.—The regulations issued under paragraph (1) shall be the same as substantive regulations promulgated by the appropriate officer of an executive agency to implement the statutory provisions referred to in paragraphs (1) and (3) of subsection (a) and paragraphs (1) and (3) of subsection (b)—

(A) except to the extent that the President or designee may determine, for good cause shown and stated together with the regulation, that a modification of such regulations would be more effective for the implementation of the rights and protections under this section; and

(B) except that the President or designee may, at the discretion of the President or designee, issue regulations to implement a provision of section 717 of the Civil Rights Act of 1964 or section 501 of the Rehabilitation Act of 1973 that applies to employees in the executive branch of the Federal Government in lieu of an analogous statutory provision referred to in paragraph (1) or (3) of subsection (a) or paragraph (1) or (3) of subsection (b), if the issuance of such regulations—

(i) would be equally effective for the implementation of the rights and protections under this section; and

(ii) would promote uniformity in the application of Federal law to employees in the executive branch of the Federal Government.

(e) APPLICABILITY.—Subsections (a) through (c), and section 417 (to the extent that it relates to any matter under this section), shall apply with respect to violations occurring on or after the effective date of this chapter.

(f) EFFECTIVE DATE.—This section shall take effect on October 1, 1997.

(Added Pub. L. 104–331, §2(a), Oct. 26, 1996, 110 Stat. 4055.)

Sections 703, 706, and 717 of the Civil Rights Act of 1964, referred to in subsecs. (a)(1), (b)(1)(A), and (d)(2)(B), are classified to sections 2000e–2, 2000e–5, and 2000e–16, respectively, of Title 42, The Public Health and Welfare.

Sections 7 and 15 of the Age Discrimination in Employment Act of 1967, referred to in subsecs. (a)(1) and (b)(2), are classified to sections 626 and 633a, respectively, of Title 29, Labor.

Sections 501 and 505 of the Rehabilitation Act of 1973, referred to in subsecs. (a)(3), (b)(3)(A), and (d)(2)(B), are classified to sections 791 and 794a, respectively, of Title 29.

Sections 102 to 104 and 107 of the Americans with Disabilities Act of 1990, referred to in subsecs. (a)(3) and (b)(3)(A), are classified to sections 12112 to 12114 and 12117, respectively, of Title 42, The Public Health and Welfare.

Sections 1977 and 1977A of the Revised Statutes, referred to in subsec. (b)(1)(B), (3)(B), are classified to sections 1981 and 1981a, respectively, of Title 42.

Section 3(2) of the Federal Advisory Committee Act, referred to in subsec. (c)(1)(B), is section 3(2) of Pub. L. 92–463, which is set out in the Appendix to Title 5, Government Organization and Employees.

The effective date of this chapter, referred to in subsec. (e), is Oct. 1, 1997, unless otherwise provided, see section 471 of this title.

Subsec. (d) of this section effective Oct. 26, 1996, see section 471(b) of this title.

For provisions requiring that appropriate measures be taken to ensure that any regulations required to implement this section be in effect by Oct. 1, 1997, see section 2(b)(1) of Pub. L. 104–331, set out as a note under section 401 of this title.

§412. Rights and protections under the Family and Medical Leave Act of 1993

(a) FAMILY AND MEDICAL LEAVE RIGHTS AND PROTECTIONS PROVIDED.—

(1) IN GENERAL.—The rights and protections established by sections 101 through 105 of the Family and Medical Leave Act of 1993 shall apply to covered employees.

(2) DEFINITIONS.—For purposes of the application described in paragraph (1)—

(A) the term "employer" as used in the Family and Medical Leave Act of 1993 means any employing office; and

(B) the term "eligible employee" as used in the Family and Medical Leave Act of 1993 means a covered employee who has been employed in any employing office for 12 months and for at least 1,250 hours of employment during the previous 12 months.

(b) REMEDY.—The remedy for a violation of subsection (a) shall be such remedy, including liquidated damages, as would be appropriate if awarded under paragraph (1) of section 107(a) of the Family and Medical Leave Act of 1993.

(c) REGULATIONS TO IMPLEMENT SECTION.—

(1) IN GENERAL.—The President, or the designee of the President, shall issue regulations to implement this section.

(2) AGENCY REGULATIONS.—The regulations issued under paragraph (1) shall be the same as substantive regulations promulgated by the Secretary of Labor to implement the statutory provisions referred to in subsections (a) and (b)—

(A) except to the extent that the President or designee may determine, for good cause shown and stated together with the regulation, that a modification of such regulations would be more effective for the implementation of the rights and protections under this section; and

(B) except that the President or designee may, at the discretion of the President or designee, issue regulations to implement a provision of subchapter V of chapter 63 of title 5, United States Code, that applies to employees in the executive branch of the Federal Government in lieu of an analogous statutory provision referred to in subsection (a) or (b), if the issuance of such regulations—

(i) would be equally effective for the implementation of the rights and protections under this section; and

(ii) would promote uniformity in the application of Federal law to employees in the executive branch of the Federal Government.

(d) EFFECTIVE DATE.—Subsections (a) and (b) shall take effect on the earlier of—

(1) the effective date of regulations issued under subsection (c); or

(2) October 1, 1998.

(Added Pub. L. 104–331, § 2(a), Oct. 26, 1996, 110 Stat. 4057.)

The Family and Medical Leave Act of 1993, referred to in subsecs. (a) and (b), is Pub. L. 103–3, Feb. 5, 1993, 107 Stat. 6, as amended, which enacted sections 60m and 60n of Title 2, The Congress, sections 6381 to 6387 of Title 5, Government Organization and Employees, and chapter 28 (§ 2601 et seq.) of Title 29, Labor, amended section 2105 of Title 5, and enacted provisions set out as notes under section 2601 of Title 29. Sections 101 to 105 and 107 of the Act are classified to sections 2611 to 2615 and 2617, respectively, of Title 29. For complete classification of this Act to the Code, see Short Title note set out under section 2601 of Title 29 and Tables.

EFFECTIVE DATE

Subsec. (c) of this section effective Oct. 26, 1996, see section 471(b) of this title.

§ 413. Rights and protections under the Fair Labor Standards Act of 1938

(a) FAIR LABOR STANDARDS.—

(1) IN GENERAL.—The rights and protections established by subsections (a)(1) and (d) of section 6, section 7, and section 12(c) of the Fair Labor Standards Act of 1938 shall apply to covered employees.

(2) INTERNS AND VOLUNTEERS.—For the purposes of this section, the term "covered employee" does not include an intern or a volunteer as defined in regulations under subsection (c).

(3) COMPENSATORY TIME.—Except as provided in regulations under subsection (c)(3), covered employees may not receive compensatory time in lieu of overtime compensation.

(b) REMEDY.—The remedy for a violation of subsection (a) shall be such damages, including liquidated damages, as would be appropriate if awarded under section 16(b) of the Fair Labor Standards Act of 1938.

(c) REGULATIONS TO IMPLEMENT SECTION.—

(1) IN GENERAL.—The President, or the designee of the President, shall issue regulations to implement this section.

(2) AGENCY REGULATIONS.—Except as provided in paragraph (3), the regulations issued under paragraph (1) shall be the same as substantive regulations promulgated by the Secretary of Labor to implement the statutory provisions referred to in subsections (a) and (b) except to the extent that the President or designee may determine, for good cause shown and stated together with the regulation, that a modification of such regulations would be more effective for the implementation of the rights and protections under this section.

(3) IRREGULAR WORK SCHEDULES.—The President or designee shall issue regulations for covered employees whose work schedules directly depend on the schedule of the President or the Vice President that shall be comparable to the provisions in the Fair Labor Standards Act of 1938 that apply to employees who have irregular work schedules.

(d) EFFECTIVE DATE.—Subsections (a) and (b) shall take effect on the earlier of—

(1) the effective date of regulations issued under subsection (c); or

(2) October 1, 1998.

(Added Pub. L. 104–331, § 2(a), Oct. 26, 1996, 110 Stat. 4058.)

The Fair Labor Standards Act of 1938, referred to in subsecs. (a)(1), (b), and (c)(3), is act June 25, 1938, ch. 676, 52 Stat. 1060, as amended, which is classified generally to chapter 8 (§ 201 et seq.) of Title 29, Labor. Sections 6, 7, 12, and 16 of the Act are classified to sections 206, 207, 212, and 216, respectively, of Title 29. For complete classification of this Act to the Code, see section 201 of Title 29 and Tables.

EFFECTIVE DATE

Subsec. (c) of this section effective Oct. 26, 1996, see section 471(b) of this title.

§ 414. Rights and protections under the Employee Polygraph Protection Act of 1988

(a) POLYGRAPH PRACTICES PROHIBITED.—No employing office may require a covered employee to take a lie detector test where such a test would be prohibited if required by an employer under paragraph (1), (2), or (3) of section 3 of the Employee Polygraph Protection Act of 1988. In addition, the waiver provisions of section 6(d) of such Act shall apply to covered employees.

(b) REMEDY.—The remedy for a violation of subsection (a) shall be such damages as would be appropriate if awarded under section 6(c)(1) of the Employee Polygraph Protection Act of 1988.

(c) REGULATIONS TO IMPLEMENT SECTION.—

(1) IN GENERAL.—The President, or the designee of the President, shall issue regulations to implement this section.

(2) AGENCY REGULATIONS.—The regulations issued under paragraph (1) shall be the same as substantive regulations promulgated by the Secretary of Labor to implement the statutory provisions referred to in subsections (a) and (b) except to the extent that the President

or designee may determine, for good cause shown and stated together with the regulation, that a modification of such regulations would be more effective for the implementation of the rights and protections under this section.

(d) EFFECTIVE DATE.—Subsections (a) and (b) shall take effect on the earlier of—

(1) the effective date of regulations issued under subsection (c); or

(2) October 1, 1998.

(Added Pub. L. 104–331, § 2(a), Oct. 26, 1996, 110 Stat. 4058.)

REFERENCES IN TEXT

Sections 3 and 6 of the Employee Polygraph Protection Act of 1988, referred to in subsecs. (a) and (b), are classified to sections 2002 and 2005, respectively, of Title 29, Labor.

EFFECTIVE DATE

Subsec. (c) of this section effective Oct. 26, 1996, see section 471(b) of this title.

§ 415. Rights and protections under the Worker Adjustment and Retraining Notification Act

(a) WORKER ADJUSTMENT AND RETRAINING NOTIFICATION RIGHTS.—

(1) IN GENERAL.—Except as provided in paragraph (2), no employing office shall be closed or mass layoff ordered within the meaning of section 3 of the Worker Adjustment and Retraining Notification Act until the end of a 60-day period after the employing office serves written notice of such prospective closing or layoff to representatives of covered employees or, if there are no representatives, to covered employees.

(2) EXCEPTION.—

(A) IN GENERAL.—In the event that a President (hereinafter in this paragraph referred to as the "previous President") is not elected to a successive term in office as a result of the election of a new President—

(i) no notice or waiting period shall be required under paragraph (1) with respect to the separation of any individual described in subparagraph (B), if such separation occurs pursuant to a closure or mass layoff ordered after the term of the new President commences; and

(ii) if any individual is separated from service, or begins a period of leave under the Family and Medical Leave Act of 1993, before such term commences, nothing in this chapter shall require reinstatement or restoration to employment of the individual after such term commences.

(B) DESCRIPTION OF INDIVIDUALS.—An individual described in this subparagraph is any covered employee serving pursuant to an appointment made during—

(i) the term of office of the previous President; or

(ii) any term, earlier than the term referred to in clause (i), during which such previous President served as President or Vice President.

(b) REMEDY.—The remedy for a violation of subsection (a) shall be such damages as would be

appropriate if awarded under paragraphs (1), (2), and (4) of section 5(a) of the Worker Adjustment and Retraining Notification Act.

(c) REGULATIONS TO IMPLEMENT SECTION.—

(1) IN GENERAL.—The President, or the designee of the President, shall issue regulations to implement this section.

(2) AGENCY REGULATIONS.—The regulations issued under paragraph (1) shall be the same as substantive regulations promulgated by the Secretary of Labor to implement the statutory provisions referred to in subsections (a) and (b) except to the extent that the President or designee may determine, for good cause shown and stated together with the regulation, that a modification of such regulations would be more effective for the implementation of the rights and protections under this section.

(d) EFFECTIVE DATE.—Subsections (a) and (b) shall take effect on the earlier of—

(1) the effective date of regulations issued under subsection (c); or

(2) October 1, 1998.

(Added Pub. L. 104–331, § 2(a), Oct. 26, 1996, 110 Stat. 4059.)

REFERENCES IN TEXT

Sections 3 and 5 of the Worker Adjustment and Retraining Notification Act, referred to in subsecs. (a)(1) and (b), are classified to sections 2102 and 2104, respectively, of Title 29, Labor.

The Family and Medical Leave Act of 1993, referred to in subsec. (a)(2)(A)(ii), is Pub. L. 103–3, Feb. 5, 1993, 107 Stat. 6, as amended, which enacted sections 60m and 60n of Title 2, The Congress, sections 6381 to 6387 of Title 5, Government Organization and Employees, and chapter 28 (§ 2601 et seq.) of Title 29, amended section 2105 of Title 5, and enacted provisions set out as notes under section 2601 of Title 29. For complete classification of this Act to the Code, see Short Title note set out under section 2601 of Title 29 and Tables.

EFFECTIVE DATE

Subsec. (c) of this section effective Oct. 26, 1996, see section 471(b) of this title.

§ 416. Rights and protections relating to veterans' employment and reemployment

(a) EMPLOYMENT AND REEMPLOYMENT RIGHTS OF MEMBERS OF THE UNIFORMED SERVICES.—

(1) IN GENERAL.—It shall be unlawful for an employing office to—

(A) discriminate, within the meaning of subsections (a) and (b) of section 4311 of title 38, against an eligible employee;

(B) deny to an eligible employee reemployment rights within the meaning of sections 4312 and 4313 of title 38; or

(C) deny to an eligible employee benefits within the meaning of sections 4316, 4317, and 4318 of title 38.

(2) DEFINITION.—For purposes of this section, the term "eligible employee" means a covered employee performing service in the uniformed services, within the meaning of section 4303(13) of title 38, whose service has not been terminated upon the occurrence of any of the events enumerated in section 4304 of such title.

(b) REMEDY.—The remedy for a violation of subsection (a) shall be such damages as would be appropriate if awarded under section 4323(d) of title 38.

(c) REGULATIONS TO IMPLEMENT SECTION.—

(1) IN GENERAL.—The President, or the designee of the President, shall issue regulations to implement this section.

(2) AGENCY REGULATIONS.—The regulations issued under paragraph (1) shall be the same as substantive regulations promulgated by the Secretary of Labor to implement the statutory provisions referred to in subsections (a) and (b)—

(A) except to the extent that the President or designee may determine, for good cause shown and stated together with the regulation, that a modification of such regulations would be more effective for the implementation of the rights and protections under this section; and

(B) except that the President or designee may, at the discretion of the President or designee, issue regulations to implement a provision of section 4314 or 4324 of title 38, United States Code, that applies to employees in the executive branch of the Federal Government in lieu of an analogous statutory provision referred to in subsection (a) or (b), if the issuance of such regulations—

(i) would be equally effective for the implementation of the rights and protections under this section; and

(ii) would promote uniformity in the application of Federal law to employees in the executive branch of the Federal Government.

(d) EFFECTIVE DATE.—Subsections (a) and (b) shall take effect on the earlier of—

(1) the effective date of regulations issued under subsection (c); or

(2) October 1, 1998.

(Added Pub. L. 104–331, § 2(a), Oct. 26, 1996, 110 Stat. 4060; amended Pub. L. 111–275, title VII, § 703(c), Oct. 13, 2010, 124 Stat. 2888.)

AMENDMENTS

2010—Subsec. (b). Pub. L. 111–275 substituted "under section 4323(d) of title 38" for "under paragraphs (1) and (2)(A) of section 4323(c) of title 38".

EFFECTIVE DATE

Subsec. (c) of this section effective Oct. 26, 1996, see section 471(b) of this title.

§ 417. Prohibition of intimidation or reprisal

(a) IN GENERAL.—It shall be unlawful for an employing office to intimidate, take reprisal against, or otherwise discriminate against, any covered employee because the covered employee has opposed any practice made unlawful by this chapter, or because the covered employee has initiated proceedings, made a charge, or testified, assisted, or participated in any manner in a hearing or other proceeding under this chapter.

(b) REMEDY.—A violation of subsection (a) may be remedied by any legal remedy available to redress the practice opposed by the covered employee or other violation of law as to which the covered employee initiated proceedings, made a charge, or engaged in other conduct protected under subsection (a).

(Added Pub. L. 104–331, § 2(a), Oct. 26, 1996, 110 Stat. 4061.)

PART B—PUBLIC ACCESS PROVISIONS UNDER THE AMERICANS WITH DISABILITIES ACT OF 1990

§ 421. Rights and protections under the Americans with Disabilities Act of 1990

(a) RIGHTS AND PROTECTIONS.—The rights and protections against discrimination in the provision of public services and accommodations established by sections 201, 202, and 204, and sections 302, 303, and 309, of the Americans with Disabilities Act of 1990 shall apply, to the extent that public services, programs, or activities are provided, with respect to the White House and its appurtenant grounds and gardens, the Dwight D. Eisenhower Executive Office Building, the New Executive Office Buildings, and any other facility to the extent that offices are provided for employees of the Executive Office of the President.

(b) REMEDY.—The remedy for a violation of subsection (a) shall be such remedy as would be appropriate if awarded under section 203 or 308 of the Americans with Disabilities Act of 1990, as the case may be, except that, with respect to any claim of employment discrimination, the exclusive remedy shall be under section 411 of this title. A remedy under the preceding sentence shall be enforced in accordance with applicable provisions of such section 203 or 308, as the case may be.

(c) DEFINITION.—For purposes of the application under this section of the Americans with Disabilities Act of 1990, the term "public entity" as used in such Act, means, to the extent that public services, programs, or activities are provided, the White House and its appurtenant grounds and gardens, the Dwight D. Eisenhower Executive Office Building, the New Executive Office Buildings, and any other facility to the extent that offices are provided for employees of the Executive Office of the President.

(d) REGULATIONS TO IMPLEMENT SECTION.—

(1) IN GENERAL.—The President, or the designee of the President, shall issue regulations to implement this section.

(2) AGENCY REGULATIONS.—The regulations issued under paragraph (1) shall be the same as substantive regulations promulgated by the appropriate officer of an executive agency to implement the statutory provisions referred to in subsections (a) and (b)—

(A) except to the extent that the President or designee may determine, for good cause shown and stated together with the regulation, that a modification of such regulations would be more effective for the implementation of the rights and protections under this section; and

(B) except that the President or designee may, at the discretion of the President or designee, issue regulations to implement a provision of section 1, 2, 3, or 6 of the Act entitled "An Act to insure that certain buildings financed with Federal funds are so designed and constructed as to be accessible to the physically handicapped", approved August 12, 1968 (commonly known as the "Architectural Barriers Act of 1968") or section

501 of the Rehabilitation Act of 1973 that applies to agencies of the executive branch of the Federal Government in lieu of an analogous statutory provision referred to in subsection (a) or (b), if the issuance of such regulations—

(i) would be equally effective for the implementation of the rights and protections under this section; and

(ii) would promote uniformity in the application of Federal law to agencies of the executive branch of the Federal Government.

(e) EFFECTIVE DATE.—Subsections (a), (b), and (c) shall take effect on the earlier of—

(1) the effective date of regulations issued under subsection (d); or

(2) October 1, 1998.

(Added Pub. L. 104–331, §2(a), Oct. 26, 1996, 110 Stat. 4061; amended Pub. L. 106–92, §2, Nov. 9, 1999, 113 Stat. 1309.)

REFERENCES IN TEXT

The Americans with Disabilities Act of 1990, referred to in subsecs. (a) to (c), is Pub. L. 101–336, July 26, 1990, 104 Stat. 327, as amended, which is classified principally to chapter 126 (§12101 et seq.) of Title 42, The Public Health and Welfare. Sections 201 to 204, 302, 303, 308, and 309 of the Act are classified to sections 12131 to 12134, 12182, 12183, 12188, and 12189, respectively, of Title 42. For complete classification of this Act to the Code, see Short Title note set out under section 12101 of Title 42 and Tables.

Sections 1, 2, 3, and 6 of the Act of August 12, 1968, commonly known as the Architectural Barriers Act of 1968, referred to in subsec. (d)(2)(B), are classified to sections 4151 to 4153 and 4156, respectively, of Title 42.

Section 501 of the Rehabilitation Act of 1973, referred to in subsec. (d)(2)(B), is classified to section 791 of Title 29, Labor.

AMENDMENTS

1999—Subsecs. (a), (c). Pub. L. 106–92 substituted "Dwight D. Eisenhower Executive Office Building" for "Old Executive Office Building".

EFFECTIVE DATE

Subsec. (d) of this section effective Oct. 26, 1996, see section 471(b) of this title.

PART C—OCCUPATIONAL SAFETY AND HEALTH ACT OF 1970

§ 425. Rights and protections under the Occupational Safety and Health Act of 1970; procedures for remedy of violations

(a) OCCUPATIONAL SAFETY AND HEALTH PROTECTIONS.—

(1) IN GENERAL.—Each employing office and each covered employee shall comply with the provisions of section 5 of the Occupational Safety and Health Act of 1970.

(2) DEFINITIONS.—For purposes of the application under this section of the Occupational Safety and Health Act of 1970—

(A) the term "employer" as used in such Act means an employing office; and

(B) the term "employee" as used in such Act means a covered employee.

(b) REMEDY.—The remedy for a violation of subsection (a) shall be an order to correct the violation, including such order as would be appropriate if issued under section 13(a) of the Occupational Safety and Health Act of 1970.

(c) PROCEDURES.—

(1) REQUESTS FOR INSPECTIONS.—Upon written request of any employing office or covered employee, the Secretary of Labor shall have the authority to inspect and investigate places of employment under the jurisdiction of employing offices in accordance with subsections (a), (d), (e), and (f) of section 8 of the Occupational Safety and Health Act of 1970.

(2) CITATIONS, NOTICES, AND NOTIFICATIONS.—The Secretary of Labor shall have the authority, in accordance with sections 9 and 10 of the Occupational Safety and Health Act of 1970, to issue—

(A) a citation or notice to any employing office responsible for correcting a violation of subsection (a); or

(B) a notification to any employing office that the Secretary of Labor believes has failed to correct a violation for which a citation has been issued within the period permitted for its correction.

(3) HEARINGS AND REVIEW.—If after issuing a citation or notification, the Secretary of Labor determines that a violation has not been corrected—

(A) the citation and notification shall be deemed a final order (within the meaning of section 10(b) of the Occupational Safety and Health Act of 1970) if the employer fails to notify the Secretary of Labor within 15 days (excluding Saturdays, Sundays, and Federal holidays) after receipt of the notice that the employer intends to contest the citation or notification; or

(B) opportunity for a hearing before the Occupational Safety and Health Review Commission shall be afforded in accordance with section 10(c) of the Occupational Safety and Health Act of 1970, if the employer gives timely notice to the Secretary that he intends to contest the citation or notification.

(4) VARIANCE PROCEDURES.—An employing office may request from the Secretary of Labor an order granting a variance from a standard made applicable by this section, in accordance with sections 6(b)(6) and 6(d) of the Occupational Safety and Health Act of 1970.

(5) JUDICIAL REVIEW.—Any person or employing office aggrieved by a final decision of the Occupational Safety and Health Review Commission under paragraph (3) or the Secretary of Labor under paragraph (4) may file a petition for review with the United States Court of Appeals for the Federal Circuit under section 1296 of title 28.

(6) COMPLIANCE DATE.—If new appropriated funds are necessary to correct a violation of subsection (a) for which a citation is issued, or to comply with an order requiring correction of such a violation, correction or compliance shall take place as soon as possible, but not later than the end of the fiscal year following the fiscal year in which the citation is issued or the order requiring correction becomes final and not subject to further review.

(d) REGULATIONS TO IMPLEMENT SECTION.—

(1) IN GENERAL.—The President, or the designee of the President, shall issue regulations to implement this section.

(2) AGENCY REGULATIONS.—The regulations issued under paragraph (1) shall be the same as substantive regulations promulgated by the Secretary of Labor to implement the statutory provisions referred to in subsections (a) and (b)—

(A) except to the extent that the President or designee may determine, for good cause shown and stated together with the regulation, that a modification of such regulations would be more effective for the implementation of the rights and protections under this section; and

(B) except that the President or designee may, at the discretion of the President or designee, issue regulations to implement a provision of section 19 of the Occupational Safety and Health Act of 1970 that applies to agencies or employees of the executive branch of the Federal Government in lieu of an analogous statutory provision referred to in subsection (a) or (b), if the issuance of such regulations—

(i) would be equally effective for the implementation of the rights and protections under this section; and

(ii) would promote uniformity in the application of Federal law to employees in the executive branch of the Federal Government.

(3) EMPLOYING OFFICE RESPONSIBLE FOR CORRECTION.—The regulations issued under paragraph (1) shall include a method of identifying, for purposes of this section and for different categories of violations of subsection (a), the employing office responsible for correction of a particular violation.

(e) EFFECTIVE DATE.—Subsections (a) through (c) shall take effect on the earlier of—

(1) the effective date of regulations issued under subsection (d); or

(2) October 1, 1998.

(Added Pub. L. 104–331, § 2(a), Oct. 26, 1996, 110 Stat. 4062.)

REFERENCES IN TEXT

The Occupational Safety and Health Act of 1970, referred to in subsecs. (a) to (c)(4) and (d)(2)(B), is Pub. L. 91–596, Dec. 29, 1970, 84 Stat. 1590, as amended, which is classified principally to chapter 15 (§ 651 et seq.) of Title 29, Labor. Sections 5, 6, 8 to 10, 13, and 19 of the Act are classified to sections 654, 655, 657 to 659, 662, and 668, respectively, of Title 29. For complete classification of this Act to the Code, see Short Title note set out under section 651 of Title 29 and Tables.

EFFECTIVE DATE

Subsec. (d) of this section effective Oct. 26, 1996, see section 471(b) of this title.

PART D—LABOR-MANAGEMENT RELATIONS

§ 431. Application of chapter 71 of title 5, relating to Federal service labor-management relations; procedures for remedy of violations

(a) LABOR-MANAGEMENT RIGHTS.—Subject to subsection (d), chapter 71 of title 5 shall apply to employing offices and to covered employees and representatives of those employees, except that covered employees shall not have a right to reinstatement pursuant to section 7118(a)(7)(C) or 7123 of title 5.

(b) DEFINITION.—For purposes of the application under this section of chapter 71 of title 5, the term "agency" as used in such chapter means an employing office.

(c) REGULATIONS TO IMPLEMENT SECTION.—

(1) IN GENERAL.—The Federal Labor Relations Authority shall issue regulations to implement this section.

(2) AGENCY REGULATIONS.—Except as provided in subsection (d), the regulations issued under paragraph (1) shall be the same as substantive regulations promulgated by the Authority to implement the statutory provisions referred to in subsection (a), except—

(A) to the extent the Authority may determine, for good cause shown and stated together with the regulation, that a modification of such regulations would be more effective for the implementation of the rights and protections under this section; or

(B) as the Authority may determine that a modification of such regulations is necessary to avoid a conflict of interest or appearance of a conflict of interest.

(d) SPECIFIC REGULATIONS REGARDING APPLICATIONS TO CERTAIN EMPLOYING OFFICES.—

(1) REGULATIONS REQUIRED.—The Authority shall issue regulations on the manner and the extent to which the requirements and exemptions of chapter 71 of title 5 should apply to covered employees who are employed in the offices listed in paragraph (2). The regulations shall, to the greatest extent practicable, be consistent with the provisions and purposes of chapter 71 of title 5 and of this chapter, and shall be the same as the substantive regulations issued by the Authority under such chapter, except—

(A) to the extent the Authority may determine, for good cause shown and stated together with the regulation, that a modification of such regulations would be more effective for the implementation of the rights and protections under this section; and

(B) that the Authority shall exclude from coverage under this section any covered employees who are employed in offices listed in paragraph (2) if the Authority determines that such exclusion is required because of—

(i) a conflict of interest or appearance of a conflict of interest; or

(ii) the President's or Vice President's constitutional responsibilities.

(2) OFFICES REFERRED TO.—The offices referred to in paragraph (1) include—

(A) the White House Office;

(B) the Executive Residence at the White House;

(C) the Office of the Vice President;

(D) the Office of Policy Development;

(E) the Council of Economic Advisers;

(F) the National Security Council;

(G) the Office of Management and Budget; and

(H) the Office of National Drug Control Policy.

(e) EFFECTIVE DATE.—
(1) IN GENERAL.—Except as provided in paragraph (2), subsections (a) and (b) shall take effect on the earlier of—
(A) the effective date of regulations issued under subsection (c); or
(B) October 1, 1998.

(2) CERTAIN EMPLOYING OFFICES.—Subsections (a) and (b) shall take effect, with respect to employing offices, and employees of employing offices, referred to in subsection (d)(2), on the earlier of—
(A) the effective date of regulations issued under subsection (d); or
(B) October 1, 1998.

(Added Pub. L. 104–331, §2(a), Oct. 26, 1996, 110 Stat. 4064.)

EFFECTIVE DATE

Subsecs. (c) and (d) of this section effective Oct. 26, 1996, see section 471(b) of this title.

PART E—GENERAL

§ 435. Generally applicable remedies and limitations

(a) ATTORNEY'S FEES.—If a covered employee, with respect to any claim under this chapter, or a qualified person with a disability, with respect to any claim under section 421, is a prevailing party in any proceeding under section 453(1), the administrative agency may award attorney's fees, expert fees, and any other costs as would be appropriate if awarded under section 706(k) of the Civil Rights Act of 1964.
(b) INTEREST.—In any proceeding under section 453(1), the same interest to compensate for delay in payment shall be made available as would be appropriate if awarded under section 717(d) of the Civil Rights Act of 1964.
(c) CIVIL PENALTIES AND PUNITIVE DAMAGES.—Except as otherwise provided in this chapter, no civil penalty or punitive damages may be awarded with respect to any claim under this chapter.
(d) EXCLUSIVE PROCEDURE.—
(1) IN GENERAL.—Except as provided in paragraph (2), no person may commence an administrative or judicial proceeding to seek a remedy for the rights and protections afforded by this chapter except as provided in this chapter and in sections 1296 and 1346(g) and chapter 179 of title 28.
(2) VETERANS.—A covered employee under section 416 may also utilize any provisions of chapter 43 of title 38 that are applicable to that employee.

(e) SCOPE OF REMEDY.—Only a covered employee who has undertaken and completed the procedures described in section 452 may be granted a remedy under part A of this subchapter.
(f) CONSTRUCTION.—
(1) DEFINITIONS AND EXEMPTIONS.—Except where inconsistent with definitions and exemptions provided in this chapter, the definitions and exemptions in the laws made applicable by this chapter shall apply under this chapter.
(2) SIZE LIMITATIONS.—Notwithstanding paragraph (1), provisions in the laws made applicable under this chapter (other than paragraphs (2) and (3) of section 2(a) of the Worker Adjustment and Retraining Notification Act) determining coverage based on size, whether expressed in terms of numbers of employees, amount of business transacted, or other measure, shall not apply in determining coverage under this chapter.

(g) POLITICAL AFFILIATION.—It shall not be a violation of any provision of this chapter to consider, or make any employment decision based on, the party affiliation, or political compatibility with the employing office, of an employee who is a covered employee.

(Added Pub. L. 104–331, §2(a), Oct. 26, 1996, 110 Stat. 4066.)

REFERENCES IN TEXT

Sections 706 and 717 of the Civil Rights Act of 1964, referred to in subsecs. (a) and (b), are classified to sections 2000e–5 and 2000e–16, respectively, of Title 42, The Public Health and Welfare.
Section 2 of the Worker Adjustment and Retraining Notification Act, referred to in subsec. (f)(2), is classified to section 2101 of Title 29, Labor.

SUBCHAPTER III—ADMINISTRATIVE AND JUDICIAL DISPUTE RESOLUTION PROCEDURES

§ 451. Procedure for consideration of alleged violations

The procedure for consideration of alleged violations of part A of subchapter II consists of—
(1) counseling and mediation as provided in section 452; and
(2) election, as provided in section 453, of either—
(A) an administrative proceeding as provided in section 453(1) and judicial review as provided in section 1296 of title 28; or
(B) a civil action in a district court of the United States as provided in section 1346(g) of title 28.

(Added Pub. L. 104–331, §2(a), Oct. 26, 1996, 110 Stat. 4067.)

§ 452. Counseling and mediation

(a) IN GENERAL.—The President, or the designee of the President, shall by regulation establish procedures substantially similar to those under sections 402 and 403 of the Congressional Accountability Act of 1995 for the counseling and mediation of alleged violations of a law made applicable under part A of subchapter II.
(b) EXHAUSTION REQUIREMENT.—A covered employee who has not exhausted counseling and mediation under subsection (a) shall be ineligible to make any election under section 453 or otherwise pursue any further form of relief under this subchapter.

(Added Pub. L. 104–331, §2(a), Oct. 26, 1996, 110 Stat. 4067.)

REFERENCES IN TEXT

Sections 402 and 403 of the Congressional Accountability Act of 1995, referred to in subsec. (a), are classified to sections 1402 and 1403, respectively, of Title 2, The Congress.

EFFECTIVE DATE

Section effective Oct. 1, 1997, except that subsec. (a) of this section effective Oct. 26, 1996, see section 471 of this title.

§ 453. Election of proceeding

Not later than 90 days after a covered employee receives notice of the end of the period of mediation, but no sooner than 30 days after receipt of such notification, such covered employee may either—

(1) file a complaint with the appropriate agency, as determined under section 454; or

(2) file a civil action under section 1346(g) of title 28.

(Added Pub. L. 104–331, § 2(a), Oct. 26, 1996, 110 Stat. 4067.)

§ 454. Appropriate agencies

(a) IN GENERAL.—Except as provided in subsection (b), the appropriate agency under this section with respect to an alleged violation of part A of subchapter II shall be the Board. The complaint in an action involving such an alleged violation shall be processed under the procedures specified by the President, or the designee of the President, in such regulations as the President or designee may issue.

(b) EXCEPTIONS.—

(1) DISCRIMINATION.—For purposes of any action arising under section 411 (or any action alleging intimidation, reprisal, or discrimination under section 417 relating to any practice made unlawful under section 411), the appropriate agency shall be the Equal Employment Opportunity Commission, and the complaint in any such action shall be processed under the same administrative procedures as any such complaint filed by any employee in the executive branch of the Federal Government (other than a covered employee).

(2) MIXED CASES.—In the case of any covered employee (within the meaning of section 411) who has been affected by an action which an employee of an executive agency may appeal to the Board and who alleges that a basis for the action was discrimination prohibited by section 411 (or any action alleging intimidation, reprisal, or discrimination under section 417 relating to any practice made unlawful under section 411), the initial appropriate agency shall be the Board, and such matter shall thereafter be processed in accordance with section 7702(a)–(d) (disregarding paragraph (2) of such subsection (a)) and (f) of title 5.

(3) JUDICIAL REVIEW.—Notwithstanding any other provision of law (including any provision of law referenced in paragraph (1) or (2)), judicial review of any administrative decision under this subsection shall be by appeal to the United States Court of Appeals for the Federal Circuit under section 1296 of title 28.

(Added Pub. L. 104–331, § 2(a), Oct. 26, 1996, 110 Stat. 4067.)

EFFECTIVE DATE

Section effective Oct. 1, 1997, except that subsec. (a) of this section effective Oct. 26, 1996, see section 471 of this title.

§ 455. Effect of failure to issue regulations

In any proceeding under section 453(1), if the President, or the designee of the President, has not issued a regulation on a matter for which this chapter requires a regulation to be issued, the administrative agency shall apply, to the extent necessary and appropriate, the most relevant substantive executive agency regulation promulgated to implement the statutory provision at issue in the proceeding.

(Added Pub. L. 104–331, § 2(a), Oct. 26, 1996, 110 Stat. 4068.)

§ 456. Confidentiality

(a) COUNSELING.—All counseling under section 452 shall be strictly confidential, except that, with the consent of the covered employee, the employing office may be notified.

(b) MEDIATION.—All mediation under section 452 shall be strictly confidential.

(Added Pub. L. 104–331, § 2(a), Oct. 26, 1996, 110 Stat. 4068.)

SUBCHAPTER IV—EFFECTIVE DATE

§ 471. Effective date

(a) IN GENERAL.—Except as otherwise provided in this chapter, this chapter shall take effect on October 1, 1997.

(b) REGULATIONS.—Sections 411(d), 412(c), 413(c), 414(c), 415(c), 416(c), 421(d), 425(d), 431(c), 431(d), 452(a), and 454(a) shall take effect on the date of enactment of this Act.[1]

(Added Pub. L. 104–331, § 2(a), Oct. 26, 1996, 110 Stat. 4068.)

REFERENCES IN TEXT

The date of enactment of this Act, referred to in subsec. (b), probably means the date of enactment of Pub. L. 104–331, which enacted this chapter and was approved Oct. 26, 1996.

---

[1] See References in Text note below.

www.ingramcontent.com/pod-product-compliance
Lightning Source LLC
Chambersburg PA
CBHW060807260726
48660CB00002B/825